FAITH AND REASON:

FAITH AND REASON

THE CONFLICT OVER THE RATIONALISM OF MAIMONIDES

By

JOSEPH SARACHEK

HERMON PRESS
NEW YORK

First edition: New York, 1935
Reprinted: HERMON PRESS, New York, 1970
LC 77-136766
SBN 0-087203-024-5

PREFACE

The present study is the first attempt which has been made to give in connected form a history of the anti-Maimonidean controversy. So great was the impact made by Maimonides on medieval Judaism that people divided themselves into admirers and enemies of his rationalism. The story of the conflict is important both for history and for theology. It sheds considerable light on the war between faith and reason among Jews. It is a chapter also in the clash between the conservative and progressive forces in Judaism.

These pages enrich our knowledge of the medieval mind and constitute a fascinating episode in the history of rationalism.

I have had the pleasure and benefit of frequent consultation with Prof. Richard Gottheil of Columbia University in whose Seminar these chapters were read and who was always ready to advise me on these studies; Prof. Alexander Marx of the Jewish Theological Seminary who gave many hours to read the thesis and improved it substantially by his suggestions and corrections; Prof. Salo W. Baron of Columbia University who read large parts of the book and greatly assisted me; Prof. Chaim Tchernowitz of the Jewish Institute of Religion who saw the work in its early stages and suggested the scope and the technique of the treatment. To all of these scholars and teachers I tender my sincerest thanks.

I take this means of acknowledging my gratitude to Prof. John B. Schamus, Chairman of the Department of

Speech, Evander Childs High School, and formerly of
the Fordham University Graduate School, for his assistance in preparing the copy for publication.

JOSEPH SARACHEK,

New York.

June, 1935.

CONTENTS

Philosophic Allegorization
Rational Typology
The Urim and Thummim and the
Astrolabe
Rationalizing the Precepts
Other Heresies
Rationalizing Talmudic Legends

ABBREVIATIONS

M G W J	Monatsschrift fur Geschichte und Wissenschaft des Judenthums
Ginze	Ginze Nistarot
Min. Ken.	Minhat Kenaot
Kobetz	Kobetz Teshubot ha Rambam
Malmad	Malmad ha Talmidim
R E J	Revue des Etudes Juives
J Q R	Jewish Quarterly Review
Kitab	Kitab al Rasail
W Z J T	Wissenschaftliche Zeitschrift fur judische Theologie

Chapter I

INTRODUCTION

Moses Maimonides was born in Cordova, Spain, 1135, and died in Cairo, Egypt, 1204. His philosophic writings, the *Guide for the Perplexed*, and the *Book of Knowledge*, provoked a violent controversy in the 13th century which continued to show its influence somewhat less vigorously among the Jews in later times. To the student of history its important features are the parts played by eminent men, the social and economic background of the communities involved, and the measures taken by the opposing parties against one another. Incidentally, the contemporary literature on the subject reveals many interesting sides of medieval communal life. The fundamental motives behind the conflicts, however, were philosophical and the student of Judaism or of religion in general enters a new world of doctrinal dissension.

Like wars and other upheavals that suddenly burst upon a country, though induced by remote causes, the Maimonean conflict had both an immediate cause and a deeper underlying one. The spark igniting the fire was the theology of Maimonides, though a chain of circumstances made the time ripe for such conflict. Historians have generally agreed in naming the 13th century the most eventful period of the Middle Ages. It was the apex of medieval intellectualism, and it saw radical changes in the civil, social and ecclesiastical organization of the European countries. It is at times of such unusual activity that the seeds of heterodoxy easily

1

take root; hence the sprouting of numerous heresies. There can be no doubt that the spread of heretical tendencies in the Christian world had a bearing upon the denunciation of the Jewish philosophic movement.

The restless temper of the day frightened certain rabbis who feared that the purity of Jewish thought would be sullied by foreign and novel influences, and the future of Judaism imperilled. For philosophy was in the air and the sciences were being cultivated assiduously; universities teemed with excitement over the popularity of Aristotle. Judaism might be crowded out in the eager pursuit of the arts and sciences. The more secularism encroached upon the field of traditional Judaism (*Kabbala,* used by the unphilosophic orthodox as the opposite of *Hokma,* philosophy), the keener grew the feeling in certain circles that a sharp cleavage between the two must be preserved. It was claimed that the spread of philosophy among the Jews laid waste their religious life. People relinquished their phylacteries and prayer books. The study of sacred writings was neglected. Faith in God was shaken. From this a general laxity in the ethical conduct of individuals and of the community was feared. Antipathy toward Judaism developed, which was traced by strict traditionalists directly to the infiltration of Greek culture into the sacred precincts of Jewish homes and schools. This situation contributed to the outburst of hostility toward a man who embodied the finest learning of his times.

1. *The Anti-Philosophic Movement in the Middle Ages*
The Conflict in Islam

In each of the three dominant religions, anti-philosophic sentiment reached a point where drastic action was

taken to check philosophic study. The anti-Maimonist
agitation corresponded in principle, if not in fact, to the
general intolerance toward any progressive thought. In
Islam the clash between reason and revelation, striking
possibly before it did in Judaism, was caused by the difficulty of squaring the principle of God's unity with the
many attributes which Scripture ascribes to Him; by the
seeming contradiction between man's free-will and God's
foreknowledge; by the problem of an eternal God cre-
ating this world in time.[1]

Maimonides borrowed much of his speculative material
from two Arabic philosophers, Alfarabi (d. 950) and
Avicenna (d. 1037). The Arabic intellectualist movement was checked by Algazali (d. 1111), who offset his knowledge of philosophy with a deep distrust for
it and a zeal for the refinement of religious life. He
opposed all sects that aimed to reconcile reason and
revelation. He wrote a polemical work, *The Destruction of Philosophy,* criticizing the rational thought of his
time, and assailing philosophy for its direct or implied
denial of creation, divine attributes, omniscience, nature
of the spheres, the soul, miracles, corporeal resurrection,
and physical retribution in the hereafter.[2]

The anti-Aristotelian trend was given impetus by this
orthodox theologian. If it is true that the anti-Maimonists were not influenced by the anti-Aristotelian propaganda of the Church, they certainly could not escape the

[1] J. Oberman, *Der philosophische u. religiose Subjectivismus Ghazalis,*
1921, p. 6.
[2] Munk, *Melanges de philosophie juive et arabe,* 1859, pp. 378, 375;
Malter, *Die Abhandlung des Abu Hamid al-Gazzali Antworten auf
Fragen die an ihm gerichtet worden,* 1894; *Mozne Zedek* ed. by J.
Goldenthal; *The Destruction of Philosophy* was written against the
Aristotelian harmonizers, Alfarabi and Avicenna, whom Maimonides
cites.

effect of Algazali's teaching. The contacts between Islamic and Jewish culture were quite close. Algazali, looked to as the staff of life by the conservatives, was perhaps even more widely read than Averroes, the mainstay of the rationalists. They were the two pole-stars which, although not of the Jewish firmament, beckoned the Jews to follow their direction. There is an affinity of thought between Averroes and Maimonides, and the events of their lives run parallel in many respects. They lived almost within the same period; both were born in Cordova and spent a good part of their lives in Northern Africa. Both held official positions as judges. Averroes (born 1126) was very popular with the Caliphs, but on account of his philosophical turn of mind he was suspected of heresy; his books were burned, and he himself exiled. The influence of Averroes on Jews appears clear from the fact that all his works have survived in Hebrew, or in Latin versions based on the Hebrew. Averroes' reply to Algazali's *The Destruction of Philosophy,* called *Destruction of Destruction,* became the text book of the rationalists. Averroes finds the sanctions for free intellectual exercise in the Koran itself. Religion and reason agree; the former embraces the truths of revelation, the latter the truths of the human mind.[3] Since truth cannot contradict truth, both reason and religion must by nature be in accord. The Koran is capable of a double meaning, the literal for the multitude and the interpretative for the scholar. Scholarly works should not be circulated among the ignorant and esoteric knowledge should not be imparted to them. The two chief

[3] Averroes wrote *On the Harmony of Religion with Philosophy;* Maimonides mentions a "Book of Harmony" that he had written or planned to write, (*Moreh Nebukim,* Wilna, ed., p. 6). He may have incorporated it into his Guide.

doctrines of Averroism which Jewish philosophers were suspected of having taken over and for which they were often attacked, were the eternity of the world and the existence of one universal reason or soul.

The Conflict in the Church

The 13th century was above everything else the age of intellectual expansion. The capture of Constantinople by the Crusaders in 1204 (the year of Maimonides' death) brought before the world the full and original works of Aristotle. Constantinople had been the storehouse of classical learning in the early Middle Ages. Up to Maimonides' day, scholars had to depend on the Arabic versions of only a part of Aristotle's writings. With the circulation of all his works, learning took a great stride forward. The large universities, among them Montpellier, the seat of the anti-Maimonist conflict, and Paris fought for the right of education with the monasteries, and gradually superseded them. Montpellier at this time was a stronghold of Christian orthodoxy; both the Dominicans and the Franciscans maintained theological schools there. Here, too, ancient learning and rational philosophy, especially that of Aristotle, were cultivated at the expense of reverence for the canonical literature. The Albigensian heretics who were astir in Languedoc and Provence, laid their rejection of hell and their denial of resurrection to the fact that only the soul can inherit eternal bliss.[4] Maimonides was accused by his people of holding similar views. Other heretical sects that spread over Europe were antinomistic; they rejected the authority of the church and tradition. The Cathari denied miracles and explained

[4] F. J. F. Jackson, *An Introduction to the History of Christianity*, p. 209.

away the wonders of the Bible. The extent of Christian
heresy in Southern France tells its tale in the Crusade
directed by Pope Innocent III for many years against
the Albigensians. He called Simon de Montfort and an
army of North French soldiers to suppress the southern
heretics. One of the cities that suffered heavily was
Beziers, which supported the Maimonist position in the
conflict.[5]

Antagonism of the Church toward Aristotle is revealed in the interdict issued by a synod in Paris in
1210, against the public or private reading of the books
of Aristotle on natural philosophy, as well as commentaries on them. A year before, the University of Paris
banned all Arabic writings.[6] In 1215, the statutes drawn
up for the University of Paris by the papal legate of Innocent III forbade the reading of the *Physics* and *Metaphysics* while allowing the *Ethics*.[7] The harmful influence of Aristotle is voiced by Roger Bacon in a complaint
against the ignorance of the learned Greek's translators,
who know neither the language from which, nor into
which, they translate.[8] The Italian poet Petrarch tells
how scholars of Venice and Padua fell away from religion in consequence of their admiration for Aristotle. In
1225 the *De Divisione Naturae* by Scotus Erigena was
condemned and burned as heretical by Pope Honorius
III. Pope Gregory IX renewed the ban against the use of
Aristotle's writings in the University of Paris in 1231,
until "they shall have been examined and purged of all

[5] *Ginze Nistarot*, IV (1878) pp. 12, 15.
[6] Steinschneider: *Jewish Literature*, 1857, p. 84 note 4.
[7] Tilley: *Medieval France*, 1922, p. 226; J. Guttmann, *Die Scholastik
des 13 Jahrhundert in ihren Beziehungen zum Judenthum u. zur judischen Literatur*, 1902, p. 8.
[8] Hallam: *State of Europe in the Middle Ages*, IV, p. 389.

heresy."[9] The same year the Pope began a permanent inquisition against heretics, ordering them to be delivered to the secular arm for execution when condemned to death. In all the cities of Southern France courts of heresy were instituted under the control of Dominicans and Franciscans. In Spain an inquisition was set up in the Kingdom of Aragon in 1232. Into this general picture we are to set the story of the opposition among certain orthodox Jews to Maimonides' rationalism.

The Conflict in Judaism

The seed of the conflict which we are studying lies in the Talmud. The sages were aware of the duality of human thought: the self-reliant, inquiring disposition, as opposed to that which completely submits to the revealed word of God. Even the irreligious are spoken of. The fear of the scholars is shown by the enactment of prohibitions against the study of philosophy and the Greek language, and by other measures intended to safeguard Israel from heretical influences. When the Talmudists talk with bated breath of "external writings" they probably mean philosophic books as well as apocryphal or agnostic literature.[10] Their warnings against the free study of the history of creation (Genesis, I) and the chariot vision (Ezekiel, I) restricting it only to certain qualified people were made with a purpose. While some teachers were steeped in this higher lore, as for

[9] Ben Abraham in *ha-Goren,* 1898, p. 51, says it is possible that Solomon ben Abraham was not aware of the Church's action.

[10] *Sanhedrin,* 100b; Graetz, *Gnosticism und Judenthum,* 1846; see Hamburger, *Real Encyclopedia,* II, pp. 66-70, 255-277; Sefarim Hizonim included 1.) Books written in Biblical period but forbidden because they contradict revealed Law, 2.) books written after Biblical period and hence excluded, 3.) Apocalyptic works, 4.) uninspired writings, or general literature, and 5.) anti-Jewish writings by Christians, gnostics, Sadducees and Hellenists.

instance, Akiba, upon whom it had no anti-religious effect; others were led away from Judaism by it. Hence the protest and precautions of the rabbis. When speaking of *maase bereshith,* the story of the world's creation, the Talmud probably refers to the debatable question of creation from nothing or from primary matter. Greek philosophy, in which some Talmudic teachers were absorbed, taught that the world was formed out of some elementary substance. The chariot vision relates to the character and rule of God and His angels. When they allude to the *Pardes,* (paradise) they speak figuratively of the blissful life in the hereafter, in the millennium. Certain critical opinions found in the Talmud such as that Job never existed, that the vision of the resurrection in Ezekiel is a metaphor, or that Israel has no Messiah, reveal diversity of views and perhaps some broader outside influence. Yet they are not to be taken as heretical. They may merely show us the sages in the stage of evolving a definite conception of these problems.

There are other proofs that some of the Talmudists had decided predilections for secular learning. We meet with scholars who are engrossed in the science of astronomy, mathematics and medicine, as well as in alien literature and philosophy. The renowned Geonim, Saadia, Hai, and many others gleaned considerable knowledge from the speculative systems of their day and used it in their expositions of Judaism. The Spanish authorities either exalted exclusive study of the Bible and the Talmud and condemned philosophy, or sought to blend the two.

It is fair to suppose that the church's war against philosophy and heretics and the setting up of the Inquisition may be correlated in Jewish life with the antagonism between traditionalists and intellectualists.[11] If these clashes in church and synagogue are not connected as cause and effect, they are at any rate analogous movements. The seeds of an alleged heresy were blowing in all directions.

In a wider sense, struggles like the Maimonean controversy have been fought on other battlefields of thought, under other names and in almost every century. In this instance, as in others, men sought to clothe revelation with even greater reliability than they found in reason. It was a conflict between self-assertion and a desire to assimilate the culture of the day on the one hand, and complete subjugation to the Law (Torah) on the other. The anti-Maimonists were actuated by implicit faith, which held their loyalty above reason. It was this proposition that the Maimonists challenged, for they believed that when reason apparently contradicts faith we must seek to bring the two into harmony.

2. *Opposition to Maimonides an Anti-Philosophic Movement*

Neither Maimonides nor his ardent champions who appeared a generation after his passing professed to be the founders of a new system of theology. Whatever they taught seemed to them perfectly normal and no departure from orthodoxy. They had behind them a brilliant history of philosophy nurtured by Isaac Israeli,[12]

[11] Some slight parallel to medieval orthodox opposition toward Maimonidean philosophy may be found in the Scopes Trial in Tennessee in 1925 and the proscription of evolutionary studies in certain southern states of the United States.

[12] *Kobetz Teshubot Rambam*, Leipzig, 1859, II, p. 28d. In a letter to Samuel ibn Tibbon, Maimonides gives his opinion on several Greek and Arabic philosophers, but of his own faith he mentions only Isaac Israeli and Joseph ibn Zaddik. He ridicules Israeli, but expresses his respect for ibn Zaddik.

Saadia ben Joseph, Solomon ibn Gabirol, Joseph ibn
Zaddik, Judah Halevi, Moses and Abraham ibn Ezra,
and Abraham ibn Daud, to mention only the better
known. It was the anti-Maimonists who formed the aggressive party and who raised the cry of heresy. While
most anti-Maimonists were ready to admit that Maimonides' secular learning did not impair his piety nor
his position as a rabbinic authority, they regarded it as a
potential source of danger. For his intellectualism gave
birth to a new theology, and in the hands of men of less
learning and piety it could wreck faith.

But why did the clash occur over Maimonides? Other
renowned theologians of the Middle Ages had borrowed
from Greek philosophy, notably Abraham ibn Daud. The
answer is that it was not until the 13th century that the
real conflicts over heresy in Christendom were fought,
and then the general mood of ferreting out and punish-
ing heresy was transferred to the Jewish field. Maimonides, more than any other Jewish thinker, became
infatuated with Aristotle's philosophy, convinced that
Judaism although based on truths revealed by God to
Moses and the prophets, need not oppose philosophy.
Then again, Maimonides' widespread reputation as a religious authority gained through his *Mishneh Torah,* the
Commentary to the Mishna, and his *Responsa* lured his
many readers to study his metaphysics. To those who believed that the Torah contained all the knowledge necessary for mankind, explorations into the learning of other
people and other languages was an affront to the God
of Israel and His revealed Law. That a leader of Maimonides' standing looked with favor upon alien, un-
Jewish philosophies afforded dangerous example for

those less qualified to pursue his speculative course. Maimonides himself anticipated that the ignorant would object to the Guide because it dared to expose their absurd views. Here we see his intellectual honesty and courageous personality.[13] He regarded philosophy as a rightful pursuit for the Jews of his day. It had flourished formerly in Israel as a native product.[14] Already Abraham had established the belief in creation by philosophical research.[15] Maimonides identified respectively the Talmudic terms, Maase Bereshith (the story of Creation) and Maase Mercabah (the vision of the chariot), with natural science and metaphysics.[16] Philosophy had dwindled away with the dispersion, but the trend of the times made the revival of this forgotten culture urgent.

It is especially worth noting that Maimonides had built up a wall, separating select, intelligent individuals from the masses (hamon). His entire thought-system was opposed to the traditional ideas of the multitude. This invidious distinction he inherited from Aristotle and from the latter's Arabic popularizers. The people at large, being mentally inferior, can never gain the spiritual satisfactions of the scholars, while mere religious study, piety, and excessive prayer will not satisfy the mentally alert. This position he takes not only toward the masses, but toward their spiritual but unphilosophic teachers. He had little regard for the preachers

---

[13] H. Wolfson: Maimonides and Judah Halevi, J. Q. R. II, (1911-1912), pp. 297 seq.

[14] This view goes back to the Greek authors Aristobulus and Philo; see, *Guide*, I, 71, 11; *Kuzari*, II, 66; also Malter J. Q. R. N. S., I, (1910-1911), p. 167 and note 29. Graetz, *History*, (Hebrew IV, p. 57, for further references). P. Heinlich, *Griechische Philosophie und Altes Testament*, 1913, pp. 6-9, treats this point.

[15] *Guide*, II, 13.

[16] Ibid., beginning of Introduction.

who stressed the literal meaning of scriptures and of the rabbinic legends.

The great master himself was against the indiscriminate study of metaphysics and natural science by the common people, on the ground of the Talmudic injunction that the chapter on creation must not be expounded in the presence of two.[17] Such study is an unfit and indigestible pabulum for the immature and is certain to be fatal to their religious convictions and ideals. He finds that the early philosophers of other races likewise treated of the *principia rerum* in a reserved and metaphorical manner.

Maimonides sets down several conditions for the study of secular subjects, such as the mastery of Jewish learning and of the preliminary studies and mental fitness to pursue the higher range of knowledge. At the same time he offers five reasons why instruction in metaphysics cannot be given indiscriminately to the young.[18] The subject is so abstruse that the average person is not qualified to undertake it. Man's intelligence at first exists only *in potentia*; it matures as he grows older. Metaphysics needs a well-disciplined mind and the knowledge of some preliminary sciences such as logic and mathematics. The student must be morally and physically fit. He must be free from care and the burdens of life. He also notes that even honey, the sweetest food, may sicken one if eaten to excess. So the pursuit of knowledge should be limited to a person's ability to absorb it. The opponents of philosophy constantly appeal

[17] Ibid., I, 17.
[18] Ibid., I, 34. The order of studies according to Maimonides is: 1.) Logic, 2.) arithmetic, geometry, astronomy; 3.) Natural Sciences; 4.) Metaphysics.

to these restrictions set by Maimonides as witness against him. Actually all these cautions were flung to the winds, for it is difficult to set up a censorship over a book, and when once the Guide began to circulate, it became available to everybody.

Maimonides sought to systematize his legal works and his theology. This was a practice of the scholastics and Aristotle would have done the same thing. Maimonides consistently applied system, which is really the scientific method, to medicine, metaphysics and jurisprudence. And this was one of the facts that aroused opposition to his summation of the Talmud and kindred literature. In other words, the Code had the defect of its virtues. The oral law had been regarded as of divine authority and it was therefore considered nothing short of arrogance for Maimonides to have omitted the sources, the discussions and names of the sages of the Talmud from his Code. "Were it possible," he says "to condense the entire Talmud into one chapter, I certainly would not use two chapters."[19] Sound systematization requires discrimination. Conservative leaders did not discern any fine shades of religious opinion. Hair-splitting in discussing legal matters, their minds shut out the nice points of the doctrines. To take one example, Maimonides grades eleven kinds of prophetic experience. To his opponents, prophecy was a divine communication, a spiritual reality which it was not necessary to analyze.

[19] *Kobetz,* II, p. 10b.

PART I

THE FIRST CONFLICT

Opposition in His Life-Time

Chapter II

THE TEACHINGS FOR WHICH HE WAS ATTACKED

Maimonides' philosophy created a sensational problem for the people of his day and succeeding ages. The *Guide for the Perplexed* ushered in a new epoch of Jewish history. It substituted an untraditional meaning for the literalness of scripture; it not only infused the Bible with philosophy, but held out to the Jew a new conception of God. Its profound effect upon the Jews appears from the two Hebrew translations during the author's lifetime. That it also gripped the attention of the Christian world is shown by the Latin translation, made perhaps within a decade after his death.[1] Although Maimonides retained the old nomenclature of Judaism, he seems to have understood the terms very differently. God, soul, God-given Torah, world to come, miracle, prophecy, angels and other terms meant one thing to the untutored Jew and another to Maimonides. The people, at large, led by orthodox teachers, materialized the objects of belief, like God, soul and the world to come. They could not understand immateriality. For them God had concreteness, and He could be represented as something spatial and having form. They believed the same about the soul. The mystics went further than the orthodox in this materialization. Maimonides, on the con-

---

[1] Guttmann, *Die Scholastik*, p. 22.

14

trary, reduced these objects of belief, to intellectual existence, retaining their spiritual significance. Reason, not sensation, can understand or experience them.

The two books by Maimonides which roused the ire of the traditionalists, were the *Book of Knowledge*, the first book of the Code, completed *circa* 1180, and the *Guide for the Perplexed*, *circa* 1195. His first treatise, *On Apostasy*, was written in 1160. In 1168, he completed his *Commentary on the Mishna*, and in 1192 he penned his polemical *Essay on Resurrection*. Besides, he wrote to the Jews of Yemen on the Messianic advent, on astrology to Montpellier, and numerous legal responses, theological articles and letters.[2]

The chief points on which the great sage was severely attacked were his reliance on philosophy, his transcendental conception of God, his rational attitude toward the Torah, his spiritual view of eschatological doctrines and his rejection of superstitions. Altogether there were twenty-five distinct charges:

1. Maimonides was one of the few Jewish teachers who took the extreme step of studying philosophy for its own sake and of seeking consistently to bring Jewish tradition into accord with it. Not even the methods of certain philosophic Geonim satisfied him because the Kalam was not scientific enough; it took too much for granted. Secular studies were not unique in the days before Maimonides. The Geonim no doubt were familiar with these, but metaphysical inquiry and the use Maimonides made of it was new.

2. He even incorporated philosophy into his Code. This, to the anti-Maimonists, wrongly emphasized the

2 These are published in the *Kobetz*.

theoretical side of Judaism instead of the practical. Hence it vitiated the great work.

3. He rated the advantages gained from intellectual exercise above those of pious living and religious study of the Talmud.[3] He denounced those scholars whose literalism led them to embrace erroneous theological ideas of intellectual astigmatism. It would be a waste of time to try to convince them by argument. Their learning is traditional, not scientific.[4]

4. He attempted to reveal the mysteries of the creation and of the chariot, which the Talmud expressly prohibited.[5]

5. He gave Israel an Aristotelian conception of God, and endeavored to prove His existence from the eternal circular motion of the sphere.[6] To the pious Israelite no proofs were necessary. His existence is as axiomatic as that two plus two are four, or that the sun gives light.

6. Under the influence of Aristotle's idea of God, Maimonides made a doctrine of God's incorporeality and termed the disbeliever in this doctrine a heretic.[7] Ignoring the literalism of scripture, he states that there is no excuse for upholding the view of corporeality. The literal view is inbred in the people from early youth, hence their difficulty in receiving the broader conception. The doctrine of incorporeality, as that of God's existence and unity, must not wait for logical demonstration before it can be popularly accepted. It must be taught to everybody, young and old, man and woman. Other teachings, however, such as relate to attributes, prophecy, provi-

[3] *Guide*, III, 51.
[4] Essay on Resurrection, *Kobetz*, II, p. 8a.
[5] *Guide*, II, 30; III, 1 and following chapters.
[6] *Guide*, I, 70, last sentence.
[7] *Comm. Mishna Sanhedrin*, X, Principle 3.

dence, and free will, comprise the "secrets of the law," and their study is restricted to qualified persons. This view of Maimonides was not welcome in his day nor among his opponents of later centuries because the Bible speaks of God corporeally and one should have the right to believe in Him in that manner. Further, Judaism centers around three or four all-embracing principles and within certain limits, freedom is allowed the individual to take them in his own way.

7. In denying to God attributes which Scripture clearly ascribes to Him, Maimonides acted on the ground that they negate His incorporeality and unity. Even such essential properties as existence, life, power, wisdom and will cannot according to his theory be referred to God.[8]

8. God is separate from the universe and is not in any contact with it whatsoever.[9] Maimonides, of course, believed as a philosopher that this transcendental being was the only true reality. But the orthodox could not conceive of such a God as being real, as capable of receiving the worship of people; of knowing what occurred on earth, or meting out punishment or reward.

9. After defining the nature of God, Maimonides devotes considerable effort to the question of the world's origin. The first line of Scripture states that the world was created; tradition always declared it meant a creation from nothing. Maimonides loudly professes this view. But he provoked the people by saying that he would have rejected the Jewish teaching of creation if

[8] *Guide*, I, 55; D. Kaufmann, *Geschichte der Attributenlehre in der judischen Religionsphilosophie des Mittelalters von Saadja bis Maimuni*, 1877.
[9] Ibid., I, 72.

Aristotle had successfully proved the theory of the world's eternity. His refusal to accept the Mutakallimun proof of divine existence, is based on the fact that creation is a debatable problem; for, says Maimonides, if the philosophic view of eternity be correct, the existence of God becomes uncertain.[10] Some scholars saw in the regard he paid to the Aristotelian view, a certain insincerity or equivocation on the Jewish idea of creation.

10. Maimonides raised doubt among some people as to his view on miracles. He contended as a good Aristotelian that the laws of nature are supreme and immutable and that even God cannot interpose Himself in the cosmos to alter their course. As for the miracles he escaped the difficulty by assuming that when God formed the world, He predetermined what changes in nature should happen. The traditionalists, however, maintained that God in His wisdom can freely alter nature when occasion demands.[11]

11. His theory of Providence was open to attack, for he made its action depend upon a person's intellectual association with the active reason.[12] The more philosophic a person, the more divine protection he enjoys. The orthodox resented this as a blow against the Torah in which the pious, honest and humble life is held to be desired above all else and deserving of the highest reward.

12. The authority of the Bible suffered most from Maimonides' reliance on philosophy. For every philoso-

[10] Ibid., I, 71; 25 end. Judah Alfakar criticized Maimonides for his tolerance toward the pagan view of eternity, *Kobetz*, III, p. 1b; William of Auvergne also reproves Jews for this heretical doctrine and for other heresies traceable to their rationalism, Guttmann, *Die Scholastik*, p. 24.

[11] *Guide*, II, 35; *Kobetz*, II, p. 11 cd.

[12] *Guide*, III, 17.

pher is a rationalist and Maimonides rationalized the Bible from two motives: First, he had another criterion of truth besides revelation, and second, he wanted to make the Bible agree with the formulated Greek philosophy. He taught as a first step that Scripture must not be taken literally, and criticized preachers who think that wisdom consists in knowing the meaning of words.[13] The dilemma of choosing the alternatives of literalism or the metaphorical method confronts only the person who combines traditional and universal knowledge. The simple person need not concern himself with rationalistic exegesis.

He treats the Torah as ordinary legislation, *nimus medini,* and thus seemed to belittle its supernatural purpose and origin.[14] By stressing certain practical ends of the Torah such as bodily health, social justice, inculcation of correct opinion, he traveled a long way from the traditional concept that the Torah was a mystic bond between God and Israel.

13. His interpretation of the Sinaitic revelation met criticism on the ground that he believed (a) that the people did not reach the prophetic level which would fit them for the reception of the ten commandments; (b) that they heard only a voice; Moses alone heard articulate commands; (c) that the voice did not emanate directly from God, but was an instrument created for the purpose.[15] Maimonides held that Moses heard articulate physical speech coming from a Voice, and did not believe that a sort of communion of Moses' spirit and the

13 *Comm. Mishna Sanhedrin,* X.
14 Letter of Maimonides to Hasdai ha Levi of Alexandria, *Kobetz,* II, p. 23d.
15 *Guide,* II, 33.

Divine Mind took place. Maimonides asserted "if indeed Scripture did not teach that Moses heard a voice speaking to him, I would accept the latter interpretation."[16]

14. The traditionalists were troubled by his ambiguous explanation of the term prophecy, which made it mean one thing in the case of Moses and an altogether inferior experience in the case of the prophets.[17] Connected with this was his view that prophecy was a natural faculty, and depended for the greater part upon a person's developed powers rather than upon the arbitrary selection of God. Maimonides was inclined also to minimize the importance of the wonder-working of the prophets.

15. He denied that angels were corporeal beings, regarding them as identical with the intelligences of Aristotle[18]. This view was a severe blow to the prevalent angelology in mystical and traditional circles.

16. He taught that all Scriptural stories in which angels appear or speak are dreams or visions. Hence, the stories of the angels connected with Abraham, Jacob, and Balaam were not actual occurrences. In the minds of many this view affects the authenticity of Biblical history.[19]

17. Maimonides' conception of the soul was different from that of the traditionalists. According to him, the soul present in man at birth is only a faculty which vanishes at death. The real, immortal soul is the intellect,

---

[16] *Kobetz,* II, p. 23d.
[17] *Comm. Mishna Sanhedrin,* X, 1; *Code,* Hilkot Yesode ha Torah, VII, 6; *Guide,* II, 35.
[18] *Guide,* II, 6, 42.
[19] Ibid.

which becomes united through knowledge with the active universal intellect.[20]

18. His quest for the meaning of the precepts was intellectual and he affirmed that every precept has a reason. He applied a sort of comparative research method in explaining such precepts as the sacrificial cult, the wearing of wool and linen clothes, the planting of mixed species, the wearing of disguised clothes, and the use of incense.[21] His view that certain foods are prohibited simply because of their unwholesomeness turned the orthodox against him. The opposition to Maimonides for assigning reasons to the precepts emanated from two classes of people: (a) those who objected on principle, because they accepted a Talmudic view that the laws are the arbitrary wishes of an absolute and wise God and we must not speculate on their reason, (b) those who, like Nahmanides and the mystics, were displeased with the historical or social reasons which Maimonides offered.

19. He taught that permanent life in the world to come would be spiritual, not physical. The *summum bonum* which he depicts is attainable by enlightened people of every religion and there is nothing peculiarly Jewish in it. His conception of the after-life was not considered personal enough.[22]

20. In the *Commentary* and the *Mishneh Torah*, he treated the resurrection very meagerly in contrast with the importance he attached to immortality. This fact gave rise to the belief that Maimonides denied the awakening of the dead. In his *Essay on Resurrection*

[20] *Eight Chapters*, ch. 1; *Hilkot Yesode ha Torah,* IV, 9; *Teshubah,* VIII, 3; *Guide,* I, 41.

[21] *Guide,* III, 29, 32, 45.

[22] *Comm. Sanhedrin,* X; *Hilkot Teshubah,* VIII, 2; *Kobetz,* II, p. 24a.

and in a letter to Hasdai ha Levi, he reaffirms his belief in the doctrine on the assumption that this created world is subject to the divine will.[23] In other words, if God created the world, He could also revive the dead. He had as a young man inserted the doctrine in his creed. Despite all these professions the doubt has remained even to this day as to whether Maimonides believed in it whole-heartedly or not.

21. He held that the Midrash and Aggadot were not intended to be taken literally, but were to teach a moral or embellish the text of the Bible.[24] The question became extremely important because Jews were forced to take a definite stand toward the authority of the aggada on account of their polemical disputations, their rationalism, or simply as preachers desiring to expound the oral law.

22. He departed from the customary thought of the people in denouncing astrology.[25]

23. He denied the existence of demons and spirits.[26]

24. He formulated a creed having debatable philosophic principles, and laying unconventional stress on certain selected beliefs.[27] The establishment of a creed was not Jewish; it bore rather a Mohammedan flavor. People raised the question, did Maimonides write a maximum or minimum creed?

25. His book of laws, the *Mishneh Torah*, upset the scholars. Regardless of the merits of the code, consid-

---

[23] The omission of the resurrection doctrine from the *Guide* is explained by the fact that it is not philosophically demonstrable.

[24] *Guide*, II, 43; *Hilkot Melakim*, XII, 12.

[25] *Hilkot Akkum*, XI; *Kobetz*, II, pp. 24c-26; *Israelitische Annalen*, 1839, p. 276. The scholastics took the same position because of their concern about free will and human responsibility.

[26] *Guide*, III, 46.

[27] *Comm. Sanhedrin*, X, 13 Principles.

ered by all to be a work of genius, it had serious shortcomings for which the author was not forgiven. Among
these were that (a) he did not include the sources of
the laws nor the names of Talmudic authors whose opinions he cited; (b) he omitted the dissenting opinions of
Talmudic and later teachers; (c) he established the law
as beyond appeal and (d) he aspired that his work
should supplant the Talmud.

The points we have enumerated show the drift of Jewish rationalism away from obscure thinking and ignorance toward an oriented viewpoint, away from formative
beginnings to dogmatic formulation, away from literalism
to greater spirituality and intellectualism. Putting aside
the question whether his critics were justified in their
doctrinal attacks upon Maimonides, it is certain
that the blame for the religious laxity of the age could
not be placed upon him. In principle and in fact, the
rationalism of Maimonides or even of the more extreme
of his school did not harm their every-day religious life.
Whatever irreligiousness might be complained of was
due to a number of liberalizing forces, of which Aristotelian philosophy was only one of the effects.

It must be made clear that his rationalization did not
arise from skepticism or agnosticism, as some may believe, but resulted from the acceptance of Aristotelian
philosophy with Platonic elements which differed from
other Greek philosophy by its idealistic and monotheistic
strain. That the idealism of Aristotle was far apart from
the supernaturalism of Scripture goes without saying.
Hence, the dualism that faced Maimonides and his attempt to reconcile the two. What the anti-Maimonists protested against was not only the bad fruits of

the reconciliation, but the very presence of the dualism. Most of them could see no place for Greek philosophy in the Jewish mind and school. They preferred to avoid trouble by excluding it.

Despite Maimonides' heroic labors to bring Aristotelianism into Judaism, and the cultivation of this philosophy by many followers, most of whom were certainly orthodox, Aristotelianism never became part and parcel of Judaism. Maimonides' rationalism survived as long as the stimulus of Peripateticism was present. Maimonides of course was within his rights in honoring the value and profundity of Greek philosophy. Despite all that has been said against him, he did not capitulate to philosophy, but Judaized it.

The fact of the matter is that Maimonides did not follow Aristotle blindly. Occasionally he admits that Aristotle's knowledge was not perfect, and on several fundamental teachings he disagrees with him. One should never forget that Maimonides following the two Arab Neo-Platonsits, Alfarabi and Avicenna, who influenced him most, was a good deal of a Neo-Platonist. Thus he believes contrary to Aristotle in: (1) The creation of the world. (2) The creation of the spheres and intellects which Aristotle held were co-eternal with the primal cause. (3) The view that God's knowledge and providence extended to sublunary affairs and to the individuals of the human species. (4) The superiority of prophecy over philosophy, which Maimonides admits even though he was a metaphysician of a high order.[28]

Then, too, the positive religious side of Maimonides' thinking appears in the importance he places upon creed

---

[28] *Kobetz*, II, p. 24d; The Christian scholastics differed with Aristotle on these very points; *Die Scholastik*, p. 86.

and ritual. The code itself shows that like the best of the scholastics he balanced his intellectualism with faith.[29] His thirteen articles of Judaism are well known.[30] He tabulated the 613 precepts in his *Book of Precepts*. He also takes pains to enumerate among others, the following misbeliefs of Jews in his day:[31] that there is no God and ruler; that there is more than one God; that God is corporeal; that a world of matter co-existed with God from eternity; that heavenly bodies are to be worshiped as intercessories; that there is no prophecy and communication of knowledge from God to man; that Moses was no prophet; that God does not know the acts of man; the denial, even in the slightest degree, of the divine promulgation of the Law; the denial of the oral law; the denial that precepts and ordinances of the Bible are immutable.

In view of all this, it certainly would be wrong to charge Maimonides with free thought or skepticism. The most that can be said of him is that he openly subjected Jewish beliefs to analysis, and brought to the task whatever light he could from common-sense and science. We shall see on what grounds his re-interpretations of his inherited beliefs were alleged to constitute negations of Judaism.

That the controversy, fought so bitterly, did not lead to a new sect is remarkable. Maimonides himself in his life-

[29] See *Kobetz*, II, pp. 23c and 28d where he puts prophecy above philosophy. On a contradiction in his attitude toward religion and philosophy, as appears from the letter to Jonathan Hakohen, *Kobetz*, I, p. 12c and the *Guide*, II, 51, see Zion (Hebrew periodical) 1840, p. 25.

[30] Introduction to his *Comm. Mishna Sanhedrin*; see J. Holzer, *Zur Geschichte der Dogmenlehre* in *der judischen Religiose philosophie des Mittelalters*, 1901.

[31] *Hilkot Teshubah*, III, 7-8.

time was neither discredited nor proscribed. Even in the heat of the quarrel, he retained the universal admiration of the people as a legal and religious authority. They resented only his laying stress upon philosophy and certain theological ideas. The fact that nothing worse resulted from the agitation shows that the forces of cohesion and solidarity were stronger than those which might have torn Judaism apart. The Maimonist, or philosophic party was composed for the most part of Talmudists of the highest order. Hence, it was not a case of secession from the fold, but rather of supplementing Jewish knowledge with the new philosophy.

A nascent force that in a few years was destined to check the irresistible march of secularism in Jewish life was the cabala (mysticism). To it belonged men like Nahmanides, and later on Shem Tob ben Shem Tob and Jehiel of Pisa. Whereas the liberal party made scientific investigation of primary importance, the mystics stressed the good and ecstatic pious life. For metaphysics they substituted a unique theosophy.

Chapter III

OPPOSITION TO THE TECHNIQUE OF THE CODE AND THE BOOK OF KNOWLEDGE

Although the actual conflict did not occur until a quarter of a century after Maimonides' death, he could hear its threats and rumblings during his life. His brilliant Code became the chief source of friction and the first evidence of this appeared soon after its circulation. The Code aroused many religious leaders against it because its novel methodology, its simple categorical statements and the organization of its material were unlike the dialectic method of the Talmud and its cultivators. Furthermore, his assumption of authority in codifying the laws and in regarding his Code as final and as superseding all earlier works of a similar character was irritating. Opposition to the codification of rabbinic law was not new. The Geonim had fought against it on the ground that the legal digests would put Talmudic study in the background.[1]

For the same reason some anti-Maimonists feared that the Code might drive out the study of the Talmud. The practical utility of the Code was not appreciated by many scholars because of its brevity, and the omission of Talmudic sources and later authorities. The Code challenged the prestige of the judges and interfered with the authority of the Geonim in the East. The theology of the first book was objectionable *per se* and some scholars voiced their disapproval of its affirmations in clear

[1] See Ginzberg, *Geonica,* I, 1909, pp. 117-119, for the letter of Joseph ibn Migash against the Pesak Halaka.

language. So that despite Maimonides' defense, the Code
was not popular everywhere. It met with enthusiastic
admiration but also with violent antagonism in Provence,
Spain, Egypt and in the Orient.

In Cairo where he lived, it was received with hostility.
Moved by jealousy, people refused to consult the book.
Maimonides calmly declined to enter into any dispute
with his detractors. He faced even his most deadly foes
with the utmost tolerance.

Very pointed criticism of the Code came from the chief
judge of Alexandria, Phineas ben Meshullam, who hailed
from Provence, and whom, no doubt, the philosopher
knew well. Maimonides answered Phineas' complaint
in a lengthy letter which is our source for information
of the judge's objections. He had charged that the omission of the names of Talmudic sages whose opinions are
cited is contrary to Jewish practice; it is disrespectful to
their memory and may ultimately lead to the disappear-
ance of their names.[2] The failure to refer to the Talmudic sources made it difficult for students to learn the
logic behind his summarized decisions; finally, Phineas
repeats the accusation that Maimonides had dreams of
making the Code supplant the Talmud.

Opposition at Bagdad

A more forceful opposition confronted Maimonides in
Bagdad, where at this time, as many as 40,000 Jews lived
securely and boasted of 28 synagogues and many noted
scholars.[3] Saadia, Sherira and Hai had presided over

[2] *Kobetz*, I, pp. 25-27. In the preface to the *Eight Chapters*, Maimonides says he purposely omits the names of his authorities in order
to simplify his work. On the similar practice of Christian legal com-
pilers, see Hallam, *Literature of Europe*, I, pp. 81-87.

[3] The *Itinerary of Benjamin of Tudela*, ed. Adler, p. 63, Ch. 15;
Petahiah of Regensberg, *Travels*, Eisenstadt, *Otzar Massot*, Ch. 4, p. 49.

her colleges and spread her inspiring influence over the entire Jewish world. The city had several Talmudic colleges, the highest of which, the "Yeshivat Gaon Jacob" had been presided over by Samuel ben Ali for about thirty years (1164 to 1193-94). After steadily declining for 150 years, this Bagdad Yeshiva received a new lease of life under Samuel ben Ali, who regarded himself as the successor of the Babylonian Geonim.[4] The head of the Damascus College received his authority from him. Samuel's spiritual influence extended to Egypt and even to Europe.[5]

His personal as well as his public life was striking in character. His daughter has been immortalized in the songs of the poet, Eleazar ben Jacob, for her beauty and learning. Concealed from the gaze of the students, she instructed them in the Talmud.[6] The traveler, Petahiah, describes the power and learning of the Bagdad Gaon as supreme throughout the Orient. It is particularly mentioned that the Gaon discussed astronomy and other sciences with his disciples.[7] In spite of this interest in general learning, it is improbable that his accomplishments rivalled those of Maimonides. His sumptuous palace and pompous living contrast sharply with the humility and simplicity of the Fostat scholar.

To Bagdad flocked eager students from Egyptian cities to catch the genius of the historic schools of Sura and Pumbadita. We can thus understand why Samuel was determined to preserve his prestige against the encroach-

[4] *Tarbiz*, I, 1930, p. 103. Acc. to Poznanski, *Die Babylonischen Gaonen*, 1914, p. 36, Samuel ben Ali was still living in 1220; Samuel's correspondence was published for the first time by Asaf.

[5] *Tarbiz*, pp. 110-11; Mann, *Texts and Studies in Jewish History*, 1931, Vol. I, p. 214.

[6] *Die Babylonischen Gaonen*, p. 55.

[7] Ibid., Anhang, III, nos. 6, 10, also p. 25.

ments of his rival, the Egyptian leader. He was concerned primarily about preserving the tradition that the college of Bagdad must exercise religious and legal authority over all Jewry, and the wide fame enjoyed by Maimonides no doubt wounded his pride.

Samuel ben Ali began his correspondence with the sage probably in 1189 when he questioned the latter's decision permitting travel on the river on the Sabbath. The Bagdad authority addressed the philosopher with becoming homage, as "master of majestic wisdom and of various kinds of philosophies, and of wonderful benevolence; his writings are well known and spread in the lands; we do not cease to praise them."[8] He reminds Maimonides that he defended his statement on resurrection in the Book of Knowledge, when the Jews of Yemen sought his opinion on it.

Another Bagdad opponent of Maimonides was Samuel's associate, Zechariah ben Berakael, second in control of the "Gaon Jacob" College.[9] His superior, Samuel, extols him for his personal virtues and superb learning. Zechariah criticized the decisions in Maimonides' Code and allowed personal feelings and bias to prejudice him. Maimonides deals freely with him, and refers sarcastically to his arrogance. "He thinks he is the only one of his generation who has arrived at the goal. He is an ignoramus who imagines he is learned.[10] Mai-

[8] Petahiah of Regensburg, *Travels*, Ch. 4.

[9] Mann, Hazofeh, VI, pp. 110, 220, thinks that Zechariah hailed from Egypt and came to Bagdad to study. According to Asaf, Tarbiz, I, p. 109, Zechariah came from Aleppo. Asaf surmises that Zechariah succeeded Samuel to presidency of the College. He identifies Azariah, son-in-law of Samuel, in Eleazar ben Jacob's poems, with Zechariah. Cf. Mann, *Texts and Studies*, pp. 237-242.

[10] *Kobetz*, II, p. 31b. The Hebrew text is difficult to understand because of poor translation from the Arabic. The sources for the relations between Maimonides and Zechariah are entirely inadequate.

monides declares that all of the issues raised by Zechariah refer to points in which he had followed certain
reliable and recognized authorities. Even if he were
the original author of the laws in the Code, he would
not claim finality for them. He is not infallible, on the
contrary, he stands ready to modify any statement that
may be found inaccurate in any of his books. It appears
that the critic Zechariah wrote Maimonides a letter of
apology.

The hostility of the Gaon Samuel ben Ali infected
another disciple, Daniel ben Saadia, one of the foremost
scholars of Damascus. The latter strenuously disputed
the decisions of Maimonides in the Code as well as his
formulation of the precepts in fourteen classes. He did
not challenge his theology except as regards the belief
in demons.[11] Daniel's queries on the *Mishneh Torah*
and *Sefer ha Mizwot* were sent to Abraham, son of the
philosopher, to Fostat on Adar 1, 1213, when he was but
twenty-seven years of age.[12] Daniel praises father and
son profusely and acknowledges the debt of all Jewry to
the stupendous legal works of the master. However,
certain decisions annoy him and he summons "the anoint-
ed prince" to remove doubt from the people. Abraham
replied in the same year. He speaks sarcastically of
Daniel's learning, and charges him with the base motive
of disparaging the works of the codifier in order to wean
the people away from his authority. The Mishneh Torah,
he avers, has been attacked by "lions," eminent scholars,
who failed to destroy it; how much less will the little
foxes be able to harm it.

[11] *Kobetz*, III, p. 16d.
[12] *Maase Nissim*, Paris, 1867, p. 104; *Birkat Abraham*, ed. Goldberg,
Lyck, 1860.

In a fine rhetorical manner, Abraham Maimoni pictures a vision in which his father seeks vindication. He avows that God will surely make Daniel answer at the Judgment for the aspersion cast upon his illustrious father. He tells him sharply that his language may be very complimentary, excessively so, but that cannot serve as a cloak for defaming the foremost religious authority, since the close of the Talmud. If he, Abraham, were the injured party, he would forgive, but he cannot overlook the indignity heaped upon his father's memory.

Many years after this bitter exchange of letters, Daniel composed a commentary on Ecclesiastes in which he again vehemently set upon the philosopher. Joseph Ibn Aknin, who informed Maimonides' son of these new attacks, and other friends, advised that Daniel be excommunicated. With the delicacy and sensitiveness which characterized his father, Abraham declined to do this, because he regarded himself as a litigant in the case. Furthermore, Daniel did not controvert the essential doctrines proposed by Maimonides, but the lesser teachings. Abraham concedes, too, that public policy was against the suggested action. Daniel's exemplary life and his skilful preaching exert a splendid spiritual influence upon the Jews of the Orient. This tolerant attitude of Abraham did not satisfy the local partisans of Maimonides. Possibly they saw that the unjustified criticism was more harmful than the distant Abraham could imagine. Accordingly, they turned to the exilarch David of Mosul whom they persuaded to put Daniel under the ban.[13] Daniel eventually gave up his anti-Maimonism. In the presence of a Jewish court he prostrated himself, re-

[13] *Kobetz*, ibid.

tracted all of his derogatory opinions and was duly absolved. Shortly thereafter, he died of grief, in Damascus.

Maimonides Defends His Code

In answering the complaints against the Code, Maimonides feels constrained to refer to its originality and magnitude. As a systematic presentation of the legal contents of the written and oral law, it has no parallel since the Mishna of Judah the Prince. His precursors made only a partial collection of the laws. If unqualified persons read the Code and stumble he cannot be held liable, for no author can choose his readers.[14] The omission of names and sources is necessary for the type of book he intended to write. Maimonides says there are two ways of writing a book, either as a compilation or as a commentary. The Mishna is an example of the first kind, with any number of views given anonymously. The best example of the commentary is the Talmud with its pros and cons. His intention being to compile a law book, he was concerned with decisions, and not with their authors.[15] The addition of the scholar's name to a decision does not add strength. In the Mishna, the law of an anonymous sage is often preferred to that of the one quoted. Another motive that prompted him to omit the names of the Talmudists was the fear that disbelievers and Karaites would charge that a certain Jewish belief or practice voiced an individual opinion and was not approved by the nation at large.

To justify his claim that he did not intend to displace the Talmud, Maimonides certifies that he himself con-

[14] See *Kobetz*, I, p. 12c for Maimonides' praise of his Code in the letter to the Lunel rabbi, Jonathan ha Cohen.
[15] Ibid., I, pp. 25c-d; see Blau, Das Gesetzbuch Maim., historisch betrachtet, in Guttmann, Moses ben Maimon, II, pp. 331-358.

tinues to study the Talmud and the work of Alfasi with
his learned circle. "Did I command or did it ever enter
my mind to burn all the books that were made before the
Code? I explicitly stated in the beginning of my Code
that I compiled it only for those who were unqualified
to descend into the depths of the Talmud and who would
not understand from it the matter of forbidden and permitted things."[16] He did not intend to capitalize the
fame that might result from this achievement. He was
only anxious to provide a condensed form of rabbinic
law.

Whatever inadequacy may characterize the Code
should not be laid at his door because its contents are
not his own, but are garnered from the *Babylonian* and
Jerusalem Talmud, Tosefta, Sifra and *Sifre*. Geonic cita-
tions and views are quoted as such. His personal opinions are introduced by the phrase, "It appears to me,"
or similar language.

The confusion complained of by his Alexandrian critic
because he cannot locate the Talmudic sources of the
text is quite natural. Some chapters, declared Maimonides, include laws taken from ten, or even more places
in the Talmud. If this is a defect, it is the defect of a
virtue, because his unique object was to gather together
all pertinent information scattered throughout rabbinic
literature on any one question. In proof of this, Maimonides tells of finding himself in a quandary in tracing
the Talmudic origin of a certain law. Some judge had
requested the source of a law of homicide treated in
Nezikin; Maimonides guessed twice and was wrong.
After a while, he recalled having taken the law from the
tractate Yebamot; Maimonides expressed his regret over

[16] Letter to Phineas, *Kobetz,* I, p. 25c.

this defect in the book, and promised to supplement the Code with a source-book.[17]

He predicts that the Code will arouse envy and that it will be severely judged by ignorant people and by beginners in Talmudic study, especially because of the inclusion of his theological opinions. "And if there be no one but you, (Ibn Aknin) who prizes the Code, it will satisfy me," he states. The book had been favorably received by French scholars and by those of other lands where it was eagerly sought. He feels certain that in the future when rivalry and jealousy have disappeared, the Code will be sought by all Israel and other books will be discarded.[18]

Maimonides is not surprised at the attacks made upon him in Bagdad. The whole thing springs from envy, because many scholars availed themselves of the Code and took their opinions from it. It thus challenged the prestige and the authority of the flourishing Geonim. The people generally look to the head of the academy as chief arbiter and judge. The latter can continue to wield supremacy over the multitude only by suppressing the Code.

Maimonides was kept informed by several admirers of the vehement agitation against him in Bagdad. Chief among these was Joseph ibn Aknin, famous disciple of the philosopher, who survived him many years. Joseph, born in the province of Fez, Africa, was about thirty when he became a pupil of Maimonides at Fostat, i. e.,

---

[17] It is interesting to know that Matathias Strasshun in his addition to Katzenellenbogen's *Netibot Olam*, Wilna, 1858, p. 136, locates the passage in Hilkot Rozeah, V, hal, 2, the source of which is found in Baraita *Yebamot*, 120b, and also in *Gittin* 70b, where Maimonides looked and didn't find it.

[18] *Kobetz*, II, p. 30d.

old Cairo. Being for many years childless, (his son Abraham was born to him when he had reached the age of 51), Maimonides loved Joseph as his own son, and even alludes to him as such. Like his master, Joseph studied mathematics, astronomy and medicine, as well as the Talmud. Maimonides taught him the first two subjects. It has been surmised that his family had been converted to Mohammedanism during the religious persecutions and that Joseph returned to Judaism.[19]

For some reason, Joseph left Egypt and established himself at Aleppo in 1187, as physician and religious teacher. He served as physician to the son of Saladin. The vizier of the sultan, Alkifti, has left an interesting account of the relations he had with this versatile Jew.[20] The latter traveled to Irak and India, and returned to Aleppo where his reputation grew. The praises bestowed upon him by Maimonides, his son Abraham, and the rhapsodies of the poet Alharizi concerning him, indicate the weighty influence he enjoyed. Like other scholars of his day, Ibn Aknin was beset by the agony of doubt. He portrays his own perplexity by an allegory. He had become wedded to Maimonides' beautiful daughter, philosophy, but she had become faithless to him, even while standing under the canopy, and was won over by other loves. He holds Maimonides, the parent, responsible for his disillusion, and appeals to him to restore his love, faith.[21] In the same style, Maimonides declares that his daughter, the bride, namely, his philosophic system, is blameless; he, Joseph, is guilty of abusing

[19] Munk, *Notice sur Joseph ben Jehouda*, p. 36; *Tahkemoni*, p. 446; p. 361, ihn Aknin is said to have settled in Aleppo about thirty years before Alharizi visited there in 1217, which gives the date 1187.
[20] Munk, *Notice*, pp. 16-17.
[21] *Kobetz*, II, p. 29a.

her; he neither understands nor appreciates her wonderful qualities. He urges his pupil not to seek the incomprehensible. He may be unfit for the quest. One ought to know the practical, but not necessarily the speculative. It is wrong to suppose that philosophy must be pursued at every cost.

Maimonides cautions him not to forsake Scripture, but to devote energy and time to it. To aid him in the mastery of both religious and universal learning, he composed the Guide, and as the sage completed each part, he sent it to ibn Aknin in Aleppo. He further advises him not to waste time on the subtleties and commentaries of the Talmud, but to study the decisions of Alfasi in connection with the Code. Ibn Aknin visited Bagdad several times and had opportunity to observe the hostility toward his master. He planned to establish a rabbinical school there, in order to offset this ill-will; Maimonides permitted him to carry out his plans.[22] This scholar bequeathed to us a beautiful poem on the controversy, in which he likens the Guide to the manna of the desert. This second Moses has sustained the people by offering them his spiritual pabulum. He has taken the blind and led them on their dark way. His writings contain treasures that the mind's eye alone can see.[23]

Another adherent in Bagdad who challenged the opposition of the local Gaon, Samuel ben Ali, was Joseph ibn Gabir. It appears from a letter sent after 1190 by Maimonides to ibn Gabir, that the latter asked for a translation of the Code into Arabic, so that he might be sufficiently conversant with his views to defend them against

[22] Ibid., p. 31c.
[23] *Moreh Makom ha Moreh*, Kobetz al Yad (Mekize Nirdamin Soc.) 1885, p. 6, no. 27.

"certain Bagdad people who attack parts of the Code."[24]
He also sought the truth about resurrection, immortality
and ritual laws.

Maimonides received two letters directly from Samuel
ben Ali which widened the breach between them. Besides, Joseph ibn Aknin had sent the Gaon's essay on
resurrection to the Fostat sage in 1191, in order to prove
the Gaon's lack of enlightenment. In reply, Maimonides
severely censures Samuel ben Ali, not so much as an
individual, but as a representative of a class of vindictive
and erring religionists.[25] He is nothing but a chattering
preacher. His views are unsound and inane. It were
better if he occupied himself with the customary ritual
questions rather than with philosophy. He belongs to
that office-holding type that will "sacrifice all modesty
when their positions are involved." Maimonides advises
ibn Aknin to avoid the Gaon altogether. "May God deliver you from one who is great and important to himself and to the people, but who possesses no excellence,
no real greatness or importance. But I would counsel
you to honor any one who is humble in his own eyes and
those of others. However, do not feel grieved that he
spoke and wrote against me and be not surprised as
when you ask where is the justice and religion of such
a man? People like him and even his greater predecessors, regard the Alpha and Omega of religion as con-
sisting of observances, and their chief fear is transgression of the precepts as is the case with ordinary people.
They do not realize the necessity of ethical conduct as do
true philosophers and men of spiritual insight."

[24] *Kobetz,* II, p. 15a; ref. may be to Samuel ben Ali. Ibn Gabir is
mentioned in Maimonides' letter to Joseph ibn Aknin as having written
him many letters.
[25] Ibid., II, p. 31d.

Having relieved his hurt feelings in this manner, Maimonides showed the broadness of his character by harboring no malice against his Bagdad opponents, nor does he allow himself to be drawn into any quarrel. If he had been personally present when these attacks were made, he says, he either would have kept his peace, or replied with humility. For he regards the enemies' misconception of the truth as more reprehensible than any personal insult to him. He seeks no victory over his enemies because the preservation of his honor and character is more important to him than a verbal victory over his detractors. He advises Joseph ibn Aknin and Joseph ibn Gabir to take the same attitude and to refrain from strife. He pardons even his most undistinguished disciple who may want to shine by assailing him. Jewish ethics inculcate in us mercy to our foes. Besides, his forgiving nature, age and the trials of life have bowed his spirit.

Confusion Over Maimonides' Views on Resurrection

The real bone of contention between Samuel ben Ali and Maimonides was the eschatological doctrine.[26] The statement which aroused suspicion that the philosopher denied resurrection, was made in the section on Repentance (Hilkoth Teshubah) VII, 2: i. e., in the world to come there is no body or materiality; only, the souls of the righteous become like the ministering angels. This implies immortality and not physical quickening of the dead. Another statement in the Code to the effect that "the Messiah will not have to perform signs and

[26] See Sarachek, *The Doctrine of the Messiah*, pp. 153-157. Shem Tob ben Shem Tob in *Sefer Emunot* mentions Samuel ben Ali with Abraham ben David of Posquieres, Meir ben Todros and Samson of Sens as attacking Maimonides on resurrection.

wonders or revive the dead" (in order to demonstrate his supremacy) led to the deduction that resurrection will not occur, since it certainly has been placed in the Messianic era. Maimonides explains that the Messiah will not perform any miracles, but that God himself will. Furthermore, the sage placed the goal of future life in the world to come, minimizing the importance of the great miracle. Again, since Maimonides regarded the spirit as the true reality and essence, and retribution as spiritual only, the resurrected body will be unnecessary. Added to all this was the damaging fact that by his metaphorical method he explained away the resurrection stories in Holy Writ.

Maimonides had stirred up a hornet's nest. Disgruntled voices were heard from all parts of the known world, from the Orient as well as from Spain and France. In Damascus a scholar openly rejected resurrection, and in answer to the protests of his associates he referred to Maimonides as teaching that the *summum bonum* is in the world to come, and not in the resurrected life.[27] The Jews of Yemen whose political status had been improved by Maimonides, and who adored him, also sought a correct opinion of the doctrine. Their letter, reaching him in 1188, asked whether he taught that the body will be completely destroyed, that retribution applies only to the soul, and that the resurrection passages in the Bible must be taken figuratively. Possibly out of courtesy, the Yemenite Jews also sought light on the subject from Samuel ben Ali.

Maimonides' opinion of Samuel ben Ali's views on resurrection is not very complimentary. He ranks them

[27] *Kobetz*, II, p. 8d.

on a par with women's tales. His Bagdad critic pretends to be familiar with philosophic views on the subject, but in reality he repeats the discredited Mutakallemun ideas. Among other things, Samuel does not even have a clear idea of what the term soul means. He mistakenly argues that philosophers dispute the belief in immortality. "I do not know," says Maimonides, "if in his philosophy, soul and reason are one; or whether the soul will survive and the reason become extinct ...... Perhaps he upholds the Mutakallemun notion that reason is an accident, and hence destructible."[28] It would be more becoming to this Gaon to content himself with collecting traditional viewpoints and narratives which indicate that resurrection is clearly taught in Scripture, rather than to philosophize about it.

A fragment of a manuscript written by a pro-Maimonist against Samuel ben Ali states that the Code does not gainsay resurrection; it does tell of the bliss and survival of the soul that will occur in the post-resurrection era.[29] The author of this fragment, however, upholds the literal truthfulness of the materialistic legends about a throne of God, of the Leviathan and the banquet.

What did the sage really believe concerning resurrection? He indignantly refutes the slanderous charge that he rejected resurrection, the return of the soul to the body.[30] "The accuser is either a wicked and crafty person who makes false deductions from my views, or an ignoramus who confuses the two concepts, the world to come and resurrection." He excuses those who fumble

[28] Ibid., p. 9a.
[29] *Die babylonischen Gaonen*, p. 26.
[30] Essay on Resurrection, *Kobetz*, II, p. 22a b

with the doctrine, however, as being incompetent to occupy themselves with such abstruse problems.

Maimonides admits that many of the resurrection passages in the Bible are figurative or rhetorical.[31]   The story in Ezekiel of the dry bones that spring into life, concerning which even the Talmud presents dissenting opinions falls into this class. The meaning of another group of passages, as those in Isaiah, is doubtful. A third group, of which Daniel 12:2, 13 is an example, should be taken literally to teach the fact of re-existence.

The failure of the Pentateuch to inculcate resurrection is explained by the sage in the following manner: As the miracle was to be enacted in the distant future, it was necessarry to implant in Israel a firm belief in the possibility of miracles, before the resurrection could be promised. This the Pentateuch does, by spreading ideas of God's omnipotence and the creation of the world out of nothing. These teachings were instilled in the people by way of miracles that occurred in their early history. The people's established belief in the supernatural, and their deep-seated trust in God qualified them to accept the doctrine of resurrection expounded by the prophets, at a later time.

Moreover, this doctrine is bound up with the idea of reward and punishment for good and evil. If resurrection had been taught in the Mosaic law, it is doubtful whether fear of punishment, or anticipation of reward would have any effect on the people, since it was not to occur until the remote future. The fact is that the promises and threats in the Torah were for the immediate present. Hence, formal promulgation of the belief was delayed until a much later period.

31 *Job* 14:14; 7:9 *Isaiah* 39:18; *II Sam.* 14:14; *Psalms* 88:11; 78:39.

Having considered a number of Bible verses that seem to deny corporeal life after death, Maimonides concludes that they must be taken as allegories, and that whatever might be said against the natural possibility of the resurrection, supernaturally it is possible.

Maimonides draws a distinction between the Messianic state and the future world, and assigns resurrection to the former period. It will occur soon after the Messiah has appeared, and will constitute the first great act of redemption. The last verse of Malachi, which speaks of God sending Elijah before the great and terrible day is a veiled reference to resurrection. Elijah was not translated alive to any celestial region. He actually died in the flesh. His promised return at the redemption is complete proof that the reawakening depends upon the Messiah, for Elijah will precede and prepare the way for the redeemer. This assumption does not conflict with an opinion, elsewhere stated, that the Messiah will not perform miracles. In reality, the opinion implies that the Messiah will not need to perform resurrection or any supernatural deeds to prove his genuineness. His identity will be quickly established by the course of historic events, and by his self-revelatory nature.

The sequence of the eschatological eras, according to Maimonides is: (1) At death the soul enters the world to come (world of souls). (2) At the proper time resurrection, or the recombination of body and soul, will occur. (3) The Messianic era will begin and the resurrected will live during this period. (4) The Messiah and the entire generation will die. (5) The lasting world to come, in which the soul only will survive eternally, will be inaugurated. This is the period of immortality.

All who are revived then in the Messianic era will die after a long and consecrated life. The souls of the righteous will then pass into a future world where, upon reaching the stage of spiritual completeness, they will abide forever. The immortal soul is not the physical but the rational soul. There will be no further need of the body, because the new world will be of a spiritual, not a mechanical order. It will be populated by soul-beings whose exclusive delight will be intellectual and eternal association with God. This is the banquet of the legend, and will constitute the reward for which the pious have waited. God, the secret, will be known; God, the perfect One, will be imitated; God, the brilliant, will illumine all space. "I will not enlarge," says the sage, "on all that is stated figuratively concerning final bliss. Verily, the purport of this chapter is to inform you that this bliss will be obtained by every upright person in the measure that he deserves. There is no divergence on this matter among the opinions (of the writer), the philosophers, or the devotees of the Torah."[32]

The great master laughs out of court the common-sense argument that it is difficult to conceive of a being that has no bodily existence, and that therefore individual personality in the future world must be corporeal. The practical purpose of the human anatomy, of its internal and external organs, is to preserve the human species. In the future world, however, life will be endless and will render unnecessary the presence of any physical frame. The opposing view, that denizens of the future world will be physical, is a concession to the popular prejudice and fallacy that actual existence must

[32] See "Chapters on Bliss", *Kobetz*, II, pp. 32-34. Their ascription to Maimonides is doubted.

be corporeal. In reality, intellect separated from body is more real than body. The corporeal is subject to change, even extinction, but not so the spiritual.

Maimonides condemns as childish the counter-arguments of those who point to Moses and Elijah in order to prove that the highest spiritual status can be enjoyed in a corporeal frame. The instances are not adequate because Moses and Elijah lapsed into the higher state for intervals only. Before and after, they were merely a part of the physical life about them. But there is a wide gap between an occasional spiritual exaltation in this world, and the continuous, glorified existence in the world to come.

Yet, Maimonides has no quarrel with those who persistently maintain that corporeality is essential to existence in so far as human survival is concerned. They are safe theologically so long as they do not extend their theory to apply corporeality to God, which would be heresy. He admits, too, that his view of disembodied soul-existence has given rise to misunderstanding. It has misled people into believing that if there is no bodily existence in the world to come, there need be no resurrection. But this does not deter him from espousing his view. He would rather be right alone than wrong with a thousand.

Paradise, according to Maimonides, is an actual, fertile spot, rich in streams and delectable fruits. Consequently, it is strange that he considers Gehinnom not a locality, but a mere figurative term to describe the affliction of doomed souls. The definite nature of the punishment has not been made known. He cites rabbinic views that the heat of the sun will burn the wicked or that a strange heat in their bodies will consume them.[32a]

Maimonides does not pry into the detailed setting of the world to come; for the reason that though Scripture foretells the marvels and glories of the Messianic state, it is silent about the new world. No one's subtle insight can penetrate the world beyond. Language and reason are adequate to picture the finite possibilities of earthly felicity, but the infinite possibilities of a world re-made transcend the widest stretches of human imagination. Bodily senses cannot guess the delights that make up the ideal spiritual world.[33]

Maimonides answers the attack made upon him for elaborating the importance of the world to come while contrarily dismissing the subject of resurrection with a paltry reference.[34] He explains his preference for the former subject by arguing that although the world to come is a mysterious, transcendental realm and is inhabited by the immortal souls yet it can be proven to exist. He therefore offers such proofs to establish its existence and to describe it. Resurrection, however, is a miracle, which demands only the exercise of *faith* for acceptance. One who accepts the doctrine of creation will also accept this one. Thus, there is no need to elaborate on it.

[32a] Aboda Zara, 3b, Nedarim, 8b.
[33] *Hilkot Teshubah*, VIII, p. 6.
[34] *Kobetz*, II, p. 10b. Immortality and Resurrection are contrasted, the former as a fact of nature, the latter as a miracle. The important part played by these beliefs in Jewish life appears clearly from this controversy. It bears out the contention of Prof. Kaplan in his *Judaism as a Civilizaion* that the idea of other worldliness united the Jews everywhere by offering them compensation in the beyond for their present misfortune.

Chapter IV

AGITATION OF MEIR ABULAFIA OF TOLEDO

His Argument

The criticism of Samuel ben Ali was followed by the sharp agitation of Meir ben Todros Abulafia of Toledo. He was born of an aristocratic family in Burgos about 1180, the year that saw the publication of the monumental code, the Mishneh Torah. He began his polemical activities about 1200, and as late as 1235 figured in the violent struggle over the banning of the Guide. From all indications, he ranked high as a rabbinic scholar, and possibly he occupied the position of Nasi over the Toledo community. He wrote a commentary on certain Talmudic tractates as well as a book on the Masora.[1] Alharizi enumerates him among the distinguished scholars of Toledo.[2]

Meir Abulafia was the son-in-law of the Nasi, Abraham ben Alfakar, and this relationship may account for Judah Alfakar's support of the anti-Maimonist cause in the conflict of 1232.[3]

Unlike that of many other anti-Maimonists, the agitation of Meir was characterized by great persistence as well as intolerance. He was angered chiefly by the

[1] *Kitab Alrasail*, Paris, 1871, Introduction (Notes) p. 15. His published works are *Yad Ramah* on the Talmud and *Sefer Masoret u seyag l'Torah*. His legal responses are found in *Or Zadikim* (Salonica; 1799).

[2] *Tahkemoni*, p. 350. The prominent Maimonist and translator, Abraham ben Samuel ibn Hasdai, is eloquent in his praises of Meir, and Isaac ben Jacob de Lattes describes him as one who composed great and wonderful books on the Midrash and Torah. *Kobetz*, III, p. 7c. *Shaare Zion*, p. 38; Meiri in his *Magen Abot*, London, 1909, p. 14.

[3] *Kitab*, p. 32 and Introd. (Notes) p. 16.

47

other-worldly views given in the *Mishneh Torah*. He
understood the codifier to deny corporeal resurrection
and material existence in the world to come. Maimonides, he contended, had wrongly inferred from a statement in *Berakot* 17a about there being no eating, or
physical activities in the world to come, that there will
be no body, or corporeality in that remote era. Meir
concluded then that the philosopher believed in the immortality of the soul and not in a resurrected life. Such
teaching tainted the entire Code.[4] It seems that one of
the common Christian heresies was the denial of orthodox tenets concerning the after-life.[5] It is worth noting
that although Meir vehemently combats Maimonides on
this doctrine, he omits any mention of the other debatable
questions over which later anti-Maimonists were aroused,
namely the incorporeality of God, the rationalization of
miracles and precepts, and the right of philosophic
study. This omission may be explained by the fact that
the Guide did not begin to circulate until 1205 (Ibn Tibbon translated it into Hebrew two weeks before Maimonides died), and it was only then, with the rise of
the rationalist expositors, that the scope and method of
the Maimonidean theological system threw the traditionalists into panic.[6] When Meir wrote his attack upon the Mishneh Torah's statement of resurrection
he was ignorant of the *Essay on Resurrection*, which

[4] Ibid., p. 14, veiled suggestion that the book should be called Mes-
haneh Torah (altering the Torah).

[5] The Fourth Lateran Council, (1215) reiterated the doctrine of
corporeal resurrection in order to combat the heresy that resurrection
meant the rise of soul from death of sin to a life of grace. Greek
thought, too, favored immortality.

[6] Meir ben Todros nowhere in his correspondence to Proverce and
France mentions the Guide. See the interesting article by H. Brody,
Elegy of R. Meir Halevy on Maimonides, Tarbiz, VI, 1935, pp. 1-9.

7 4 - 5 3

reached him later; and when he saw this exposition of the doctrine he gave up his opposition.[7] However, there can be no doubt that Meir Abulafia suspected the new direction taken by Maimonides' theology. He realized that the dogma of resurrection involved the question of the literal *versus* the metaphorical interpretation of Scripture and of Talmudic legends.

Toledo, where Meir lived, obviously did not share his anti-Maimonidean ideas, and the critic could not persuade its rabbis to issue a manifesto against the philosopher's unorthodox conception of life in the hereafter. Therefore, he sought a favorable opinion from the scholars of the distinguished center of learning, Lunel, in 1203-1204.[8]

Sympathy for Maimonides in Provence

Meir Abulafia was quite young, not over twenty-five years of age, when he wrote to the aged Aaron ben Meshullam, of Lunel. This city, which harbored so able a champion of Maimonides, had contributed much to the study of philosophy and to the rationalist trend of Maimonides. The traveler, Benjamin of Tudela, visited it in 1166 and describes it as a town of about three hundred Jews, a city of scholars who studied day and night. Students from other communities were provided with shelter, food and clothes.[9] It was superfluous to praise it; if God were to endow it with more wisdom, it would be like adding brilliance to the sun, or a drop of water to the

[7] Graetz, *History*, (Hebrew) V, p. 39. Meir ben Todros discusses the doctrine very fully in his *Yad Ramah* on *Sanhedrin*, Ch. X.

[8] *Kitab*, p. 13; according to Brull, the correspondence began in 1202 and ended in 1206, for the Tosafist Samson speaks of Maimonides as dead, *Kitab*, p. 131. In letter to Nahmani (*Kobetz*, III, p. 6d) Meir refers to this agitation as having occurred thirty years ago.

[9] *Itinerary of Benjamin of Tudela*, p. 4.

ocean, or palm trees to Jericho, the city of palms. Here
lived Meshullam, a lover of science, and with him his
five sons, all of whom wielded a powerful influence in
the religious life of the period. One son, called the
Nazir, became the father of the spreading Cabala. Joseph ben Meshullam was the grandfather of Abba Mari
ben Moses, the chief anti-philosophic agitator of the 14th
century. Aaron ben Meshullam, whose devastating replies to the attacks of the Toledo anti-Maimonist, Meir
ben Todros, we will now treat, was the fourth of the five
noted sons.[10] It is possible that Aaron succeeded his
father as head of the Lunel rabbis. Certain it is that
he was an outstanding scholar.

Meir sought also the aid of Lunel's chief authority,
Jonathan ben David Hakohen, but Jonathan, although a
disciple of Abraham ben David, was an ardent admirer
of the philosopher. The association between Jonathan
ben David and Maimonides appears from the latter's
answers about 1197 to Jonathan's questions on the Code.
It was, too, at Jonathan's request that Maimonides sent
the Guide to Lunel, where it was translated by Samuel
ibn Tibbon. In the set of questions addressed to Maimonides, Jonathan showers praise on him for uniquely
merging the Hebraic and secular cultures. The intellect
is his brother, the Talmud, his father.[11] He bestows high
praise on the Guide. Maimonides' reply is interesting
as it shows his concern for his work. He states that he
sent the third part of the Guide to Lunel in Arabic. He
would fain gratify their wish to translate the Guide into

[10] R E J, IV, pp. 192-207; *Temim Deim*, No. 6. He wrote Halakik
works, and is cited as an authority by his nephew, Meshullam ben
Moses, in the *Sefer ha-hashlamah*; Judah ibn Tibbon in his ethical will
tells his son Samuel to seek the advice of Aaron.

[11] *Kobetz*, I, p. 6b.

Hebrew, but he lacks time. He therefore advises them that he authorizes their townman, Samuel ibn Tibbon, to translate it. In like manner, Maimonides informs Jonathan, that he spent ten successive years on the compilation of his Code, and great men like him will realize what he has done.[12]

Meir's Letters to Lunel

Despite the esteem in which the Lunel congregation held Maimonides, Meir dared to suggest to its leaders that they take action against the spread of Maimonides' subversive teachings.[13] He takes them to task for regarding the Code as an oracle of truth and enlightenment. However deserving Maimonides may be of honors, no one is so great as to be above rebuke when he is in the wrong.

Meir disclaims any malicious motive. Only the dominant purpose of preserving a fundamental Hebrew dogma motivates him. He claims that the complacency of the leaders in the face of such loss of faith increases heresy by leaps and bounds. "Let the leaders assert their belief in resurrection, and the multitudes will unhesitatingly follow their way." Aaron ben Meshullam, whom he addressed as "the staff of understanding is called upon, like the high priest of old, to guard the sanctuary of Israel."[14]

The arguments of Meir Abulafia are found in Samuel ben Ali and others, with a new nuance. He rejects the theory of Maimonides that death will overtake the resurrected life, after which, the soul only will survive. "I

---

[12] Ibid., p. 12c.
[13] *Kitab*, pp. 8, 15.
[14] The Cohen (Aaron ben Meshullam) and Levi (Meir ben Todros) must defend the Torah.

would rather stay dead than be resurrected to die a second time," says Meir. He contends that the resurrected person will live forever in the World to Come, which will ensue immediately upon the destruction of the present mundane sphere.[15]

The stock argument that the eschatological teachings are not clearly defined in Holy Writ and must therefore remain mysteries beyond anyone's categorical formulation, is met with the answer that we likewise are ignorant of the duration of the Messianic era and the intervals between this era, the Resurrection and the World to Come. Still, belief in these remote periods is required of every Jew.

The whole controversy of Meir ben Todros turns around the following four propositions: (1) that the Bible and Talmud teach corporeal resurrection; (2) that it will occur in the World to Come, thus making the combined body and soul the final form of human survival; (3) that divine retribution will be made in the World to Come, making necessary the presence of body and soul; (4) that death will be abolished in the World to Come.[16] Biblical passages which negate these principles can be satisfactorily explained. For instance, Job 7:9, "As the cloud passes by, so he who descends into the grave will not come up," is the despairing cry of one who is overwhelmed with extreme grief and sorrow. The fact that the Talmudic dictum reads, "In the World to Come there

[15] *Kitab*, p. 54. For the views of Medieval authorities on Ressurection, see Sarachek, *Doctrine of the Messiah*.

[16] Ibid., pp. 59-62. (a) Gen. 13:15; 26:3; 28:13; Deut. 1:3; 11:21; 32:29. (b) I Sam. 2:6; Isaiah 26:19; 42:11; Ezek. 37:10; Hos. 6:2. (c) Ps. 72:16; 104:30; 50:4, 5; 68:23; Dan. 12:2; 13:13. See *Yad Ramah* on Sanhedrin, Ch. X.

is no eating, etc.," indicates that the body will exist, but that its physical functions will be held in abeyance.[17]

The miracle is destined to occur on a large scale in the World to Come. A small or partial resurrection will take place in the Messianic era and some of the Biblical passages that point to the first resurrection do not conflict with the Amora Samuel's familiar statement that the Messianic era will not differ from the present world, save that Israel will be free from foreign domination.[18] For Samuel did not intend to bar miracles that may be divinely ordained for the advent. He meant to exclude any changes in the normal operations of the universe. Resurrection can occur in the future, as it did in the past in the case of the son of the Shunamite and the vision of Ezekiel, and in the stories told in the Talmud.[18a] Meir argues strongly against applying the term resurrection to the soul's immortal state.[19] The impression spread that the philosophers, Maimonides among them, taught immortality instead of resurrection.

The question of the literal *versus* the metaphorical interpretation of the eschatological statements draws the following pointed query from Meir: "Is there a mandatory order that one must interpret sacred statements other than in a literal way?[20] He is fully mindful of conflicting opinions concerning the hereafter, but in all cases the traditional conception of the doctrines must be favored. The belief in resurrection especially, cannot be turned into a metaphor in view of the number of dicta that teach it. He concedes, however, the right of con-

[17] *Kitab*, p. 53.
[18] *Sanh*, 90a, 91b, 92a; *Rosh Hashonah*, 16b.
[18a] *Megilla* 7b, and *Aboda Zara* 10b.
[19] *Kitab*, p. 64.
[20] Ibid., p. 53.

struing symbolically the food that the sages state will be eaten in the World to Come. Food symbolizes the enjoyment of the Divine Glory (Shekina) by the righteous. Although the risen dead will live on in their bodies it will be a glorified, transfigured existence and not a sensuous one.

It is worth noting that Meir here defends a doctrine in the form that it was taught by orthodox Christians; while Maimonides taught the philosophic or heretical view.

Aaron's Reply

Meir's request to the Lunel scholars struck them like a thunderbolt. They were amazed at its drastic, destructive character. Of course the request was turned down by Aaron, who eloquently vindicated the Maimonidean conception. Meir is lashed again and again in vitriolic manner for his insolence in assailing the philosopher. The Lunel scholar exposes the unpleasant traits in the character of Meir, especially the lack of respect for his father, Todros Abulafia of Burgos.[21] Aaron describes him as a midget (nephil) in a family of giants (anakim). He is most unlike his parent and teachers in the homage which they pay to learned men. Aaron feels certain that if Meir had consulted his father he would have been deterred from this shameful step. If he were not a son of Todros, prince and rabbi, and son-in-law of the Nasi, Abraham Alfakar, whose fame spread throughout the

---

[21] *Tahkemoni*, Ch. 46; *Sefer Yuhasin*, p. 100. It seems that after Meir attained a distinguished rank in Toledo he declined to visit his father. Perhaps the basis for this story is that the father stood up in his presence as a Nasi and Meir did not want him to humble himself before him.

Jewish world, Aaron would order him to visit Maimonides and confess his wrong.[22]

Aaron suspects the Spanish scholar of malice. What Meir sorely needs, he says, is humility, the true adornment of a learned man; without humility, learning is dangerous. "How dare you, an immature stripling, voice an opinion on the foremost Jew of our day, one who traces his ancestry through an unbroken line of scholars to Hillel and Judah the Prince?" "How could you say of Maimonides, he betrays and nullifies the covenant of God and blasts the hopes of man in resurrection? This is nothing less than slander."

In Jobian rhetoric he describes the formidable learning of Maimonides who is a firmly rooted tree in fertile soil, whereas his Spanish critic is a sapling in the desert. "You have tasted the honey of philosophy at the end of the staff and your eyes have become enlightened to venture to come this far. If you are as thorough as he is in Talmud, in metaphysics and in astronomy, why then do you not put a bridle on your mouth? He raised his hand and stretched forth his mighty staff on the ocean of the Talmud so that Israel might pass through dry shod. He drew out his people from the sea of ignorance and gave them a Torah...... From the time of Rabina and Ashi none appeared like Moses, and his achievements are greater than those of R. Hiyya."[23]

Aaron stoutly denies that Maimonides disbelieved in corporeal resurrection, for in the Book of Knowledge he states explicitly that one who rejects resurrection is a heretic. However, the revived corporeal life is tempo-

[22] *Kitab,* pp. 32, 33. The hostility shown here toward Meir is probably due to the heat of the conflict and because of Meir's severe tone toward his correspondents.
[23] Ibid,. p. 30.

rary. Death will overtake it in the Messianic era and
human personality will survive only as a soul in the
World to Come. Aaron claims the support of Saadia and
Hai for this Maimonean view.[24] He answers Meir's ridicule of a second death, by pointing to the dead restored
to life in Ezekiel's vision, and their second natural de-
mise. To laugh at a second death is to impugn the authenticity of that event. He counsels his correspondent
to become clear in his own mind whether Maimonides'
assertion of a non-physical existence refers to the resurrection era or to the subsequent World to Come. These
two stages must be marked off by an interim. Maimonides held that the body and soul life will be lived in the
first era. After the renewal of the world, existence will
be spiritual only.

The Lunel Maimonist goes a step further by stating
that no intelligent person can construe the eschatological
passages in their literal sense.[25] We are forced to do
this when confronted by the glaring discrepancy in the
Talmudic views, one telling of a feast on the Leviathan,
and the other stating that there will be no eating in the
hereafter. The mystery in these passages shrouds many
other pertinent questions of the hereafter.

Lastly, Aaron pays tribute to the Mishneh Torah. It
deserves to be called the Ephod. It is the ark of God,
enclosing the two tables of testimony, the breastplate of
Judgment, and the Urim and Tummim. The equal of
Maimonides has not appeared in the East or the West.
The celebrities who preceded have not dimmed his luster.
Of all the books of the Geonim, his Code ranks the high-
est, and since the close of the Talmud no book like it

[24] Ibid., p. 36.
[25] Ibid., p. 37.

has been written. The heart of its author is as deep as the heart of the great ocean. If the Spanish critic has discovered any errors, he should endeavor to explain them and spare Maimonides. He should blame his own ignorance for not understanding the Code and not set himself up as a consummate scholar and final arbiter.

Meir Writes to Northern France

Having been unsuccessful with the Lunel scholars, Meir ben Todros next turned, in 1204-1205, to the orthodox rabbis of Northern France.[26] Among the authorities to whom he addressed himself are Solomon ben Judah, the leading scholar of Dreux, the Tosafist Isaac ben Abraham, head of the school in Dampierre, and his brother, Samson ben Abraham of Sens, Samson of Corbeil, David of Chateau-Thierry, Abraham of Toul, Eleazar ben Aaron of Bourgogne. He pleads for impartiality in judging the great as well as the small, and appeals to the French not to remain indifferent, but to take up the cudgels against the destroyers of Judaism. Meir tells them that his protests to Lunel have been in vain, and that Aaron ben Meshullam seemed bent on vindicating the philosopher by fair means or foul. Instead of attacking Maimonides they attacked him. The rejection of resurrection is more to be deprecated since it strikes down other related dogmas, the redemption of Israel, the Messianic advent, the restoration of the tribes, the vengeance upon Israel's foes, the Day of Judgment and retribution. Such disbelief deprives the religious life of its incentive. "What benefit is there to the body that has adhered to the divine word? The world will laugh at Israel, because the wicked and undeserving will go unpunished."

[26] Ibid., p. 4.

The Tosafist Samson Attacks Maimonides

The result of Meir's letter was quite favorable, for one
of the outstanding Northern rabbis, the Tosafist Samson
ben Abraham who succeeded his teacher, the Tosafist
Isaac in 1190 as head of the school in Sens, entered into
a correspondence with the Toledo critic and sided with
him on the doctrine of resurrection.[27] Otherwise he
speaks of Maimonides with respect. In contrast to his
mild manner in ritualistic discussions, Samson ben Abraham opposes Maimonides on the point at issue with a
good deal of animus. Not being familiar with philosophic
literature, he is amazed at the attitude of the Lunel
scholars. It is with trepidation that he approaches the
combat between the two great lions, Meir ben Todros
and Aaron ben Meshullam, whose knowledge and acumen
are formidable. Of Maimonides he says, "I do not come
to refute the great lion (Maimonides) after his death....
We have heard his repute. To him were revealed the
gates of understanding. Nevertheless, (I give my views)
because it is Torah and we are duty bound to study it."[28]

He illustrates the present controversy with the vision
of the combat in Daniel 8:4-7. The ram that pushed in
every direction is Maimonides; the he-goat that smote
the ram is Meir ben Todros; the two horns that were
broken are Maimonides and his aid, Aaron ben Meshullam. "And none could deliver the ram out of his
hand," signifies the French rabbis, who upheld corporeal
life in the World to Come.

[27] This letter was delivered by Abraham ben Nathan ha Yarhi, author
of *Sefer ha-Manhig;* he was a pupil of the Raved and shared the anti-
Maimonist views; cf. Higger, Yarhi's Comm. on Kallah Rabbati, J Q R,
XXIV (1934), pp. 331-348.

[28] Samson refers to Maimonides' death in *Kitab,* p. 131. Samson
rejected Maimonides decisions in the Code on the questions raised by
Meir ben Todros.

Like Meir ben Todros, he did not entertain the view
of a second death. The body that is revived in the Messianic era will continue until endless time, without
performing any natural functions.

Samson accuses the codifier of misquoting the familiar
passage in Berakot 17a which probably resulted from
different readings in the Talmuds they used. After stating that there will be no eating nor drinking in the World
to Come, it ends with the verse, "They saw God and did
eat and drink." Samson contends that the mention of the
verse proves the presence of the body in the Great Beyond. He holds, however, that the body will be sustained
by the Divine Glory and not by food. Samson cites the
corroborating views of Saadia Gaon on the physical character of the resurrected life.[29]

He opposes the figurative method of the Maimonists,
and is amazed at the readiness with which Aaron ben
Meshullam ignores the literal import of agadic statements. He cites a relevant remark in the Talmud
that the sages used metaphorical language in three places
only. This clearly forecloses the construing of all other
passages in any save a literal way. In this, Samson follows Rashi who became the standard for Biblical and
Midrashic exegesis among the anti-Maimonists.

The contradiction involved in the statements that there
is no eating or drinking in the World to Come, and that
God will make a feast of the Leviathan for the righteous
in the World to Come, does not force us to look for a
metaphorical explanation. Wherever corporeal delight
is promised it must refer to the Messianic era. As for
the use of the term the World to Come it is sometimes

[29] Ibid., pp. 136, 137; compare *Emunot v Deot*, Bialystok, p. 172;
Jonathan cited Saadia to prove the contrary.

used interchangeably with Messianic era because the
latter is in a way, a renewal of the world.[30]

The first suggestion of a ban against Maimonides appears in the warning of Samson to the Spanish anti-
Maimonist, "Let no one spend his labors on these sealed
books." Samson took a decided stand against the *Mishneh Torah.* A thorough Talmudist of his stamp could
have no use for it. He actually forbade anyone to use
it because the laws are given without the names of the
Talmudic authors. There is also an advantage in studying both sides of the question, and the entire discussion
as found in the Mishna, the Talmud, Sifra, Sifre and
Tosefta.[31]

In the year 1211, Samson joined many English and
French rabbis who sailed for Palestine when the op-
pression of Pope Innocent III, 1198-1216, made life intolerable. Samson died in Acco. According to later authorities, he is said to have continued his fight
against Maimonides in Palestine in a polemic with Caleb,
a Maimonist, but of this only the bare fact is known.[32]
Abraham Maimoni states that Samson did not visit him
in Cairo on his way to Palestine as did the other rabbis,
and that he never learned the real grounds of this scholar's opposition. It was several years after Samson's
death, that he learned of his hostility, and then he found
it difficult to believe. It is possible, too, that Samson's
avoidance of Cairo was due to his following another
route, and not to enmity. At any rate, Abraham denied
the charge, made by an unnamed opponent, that he
anathematized Samson.

[30] *Kitab,* p. 135.
[31] Ibid., pp. 131, 132.
[32] *Sefer Yuhasin,* p. 218b; *Kobetz,* III, p. 16c. Since Abraham Maimoni wrote in 1235, Samson must have died a long time before.

Failure of Meir Abulafia's Agitation

On the whole, it appears that despite his protests the Toledo anti-Maimonist did not succeed in arousing Jewry against the Fostat sage. In considering the apathy of the Lunel scholars, it should be borne in mind that Provence shared the wider culture of Mohammedan Spain and accordingly regarded Maimonides with high favor. Furthermore, the Guide with its new ideas had not yet become popularly known. The failure of the first assaults on the Code, no doubt, led Meir ben Todros to give up any idea of attacking the Guide.

Provence, which became the theatre of the Maimonidean controversy, was vitally affected by the personal influence of Maimonides. This is evident from the friendly scholarly contacts he had with the Provencal congregations and teachers. They bear testimony to the intellectual status of Provencal Jewry and to the esteem in which the master was held. Maimonides praised the congregation of Lunel very highly in a letter written to it some time after 1190.[33] He alludes to his sending them the third part of the Guide. He also mentions Jonathan ha-Kohen and Samuel ibn Tibbon, to both of whom he had written fully. Lunel and the cities in Provence are described as the only spiritual centers of refuge. Everywhere else in the East and also in the West Jewish spiritual life is dying. He summons the Lunel Jewry to carry on his spiritual and intellectual endeavors.

Sheshet ha Nasi of Saragossa Defends Maimonides

Meir's propaganda against Maimonides in Lunel was also opposed by his own countryman, the Nasi Sheshet (1131-1210) famous physician and scholar of Spain.[34]

[33] *Kobetz*, II, pp. 44a, b.
[34] Marx, J Q R, April, 1935, pp. 406-428.

In a letter to Lunel, he defended the philosophic conception that the soul only will live eternally in the World to Come. Like the Provencal Maimonists, Sheshet thought little of Meir Abulafia and berated him as a stripling, a fool, a psychopath for his audacity in suspecting the orthodoxy of Maimonides. He himself idolized Maimonides as a man of God, the preeminent philosopher, whose learning was recognized by the Gentile world. After indulging in these personalities, Sheshet takes up the issues raised by the critic. First as to resurrection. Sheshet appears to reject the doctrine of resurrection, at any rate the traditional form of it, a corporeal second life. He has no proofs from Bible, Talmud, reason or nature to offer for its possibility. If one is to believe it, it must be only by the exercise of faith. Sheshet does propose and defend the philosophic view of immortality, that at death, the soul survives forever. The liberation of the intellectual soul *ha nefesh ha maskellet* from the body at death and its survival is resurrection. The wicked soul endures forever in suffering; the good soul in angelic bliss. He is proud to acclaim this as the view of the philosophers and theologians. He regards the rabbinic concept of a bodily resurrection and survival into the World to Come, with the notions of a material Paradise and Hell as an accommodation to ignorant people. Sheshet records his discussion with Arabic scholars who conceded that the orthodox ideas on these matters were intended for the ignorant people who would not understand happiness and existence in an ideal, spiritual sense.[35]

Sheshet defends his stand and gives reasons why he cannot support some of the traditional arguments in favor

[35] Ibid., p. 425.

of corporeal resurrection. The divine promises to the patriarchs that they and their descendants will inherit Palestine which Meir, speaking for the resurrectionists, had taken eschatologically were understood by Sheshet to refer to the historical conquest and possession of the holy land.[36] Another Scriptural proof, based on the revival of the dead in Ezekiel, is taken as an allegory of the restoration of Israel. The anti-Maimonists contended that the resurrected person will live corporeally but without food, sensuous or sex activities. It will be a transfigured, glorified existence. This they claimed is possible, and they cited the cases of Moses and Elijah who according to the stories abstained from food and sensual pleasure for a certain length of time. Sheshet finds no analogy in the case of these two persons and the life awaited in the future. Moses and Elijah lived only temporarily without eating; furthermore Moses had an angelic nature and no comparison can be made with him. As for Elijah he frequently sought after food and one meal had sufficed him for his fast of many days.[37]

Sheshet refutes the whole contention of Meir that God can change the natural, physical laws of life and sustain the body without food. This contention is untenable philosophically as a change in natural law involves a change in the mind and will of God, and this is contrary to our concept of the Divine Unity. Sheshet admits the miracles of the past, but only because they were temporary, not permanent changes and were called forth by certain emergencies. For that matter argues Sheshet the most important laws like fasting on the Day

[36] Ibid., p. 418.
[37] Ibid., p. 419.

of Atonement may be violated under certain conditions, but that is quite different from abrogating a law.

Lastly, our Maimonist cannot see how resurrection can be possible. At death the body decomposes; in the course of centuries or thousands of years it is annihilated. Where, then, is the body that is to be revived? If the Almighty will rebuild a new body, the one purpose of resurrection will be defeated which is to offer retribution to the same body that lived.[38]

Sheshet gives us interesting testimony as to the way Maimonides' legal work was received. Jealousy was aroused in Andalusia (Southern Spain), he charges, when the Mishneh Torah first appeared there. "I heard one of the judges, whose name I do not care to mention, murmur, 'What does he (Maimonides) know that we do not know. Since he offers no proofs for his views from the Talmudic sages, who is bound to listen to him? It is much better to study the laws of Talmud; what have we to do with his books.' "[39]

Sheshet states that before the Code reached Spain the people had great difficulty in mastering the Talmud's legal science. A certain judge, for instance, decided questions on his own authority. No one could dispute with him because everyone was ignorant of the laws. "When they saw the fourteen books of the Code, and all who knew Hebrew had studied it and appreciated the harmonious arrangement of the precepts and the didactic and philosophic contents of the Book of Knowledge, their eyes were opened; they wrote each one a separate copy; they praised it, old and young, and all learned persons

[38] Ibid., p. 426. See Sarachek, *The Doctrine of the Messiah*, pp. 44-47 for Saadia's views; also pp. 221-224 for Albo's statement.

[39] Graetz, *History* (Hebrew), Vol. V, Hadashim gam Yeshenim, p. 10; Marx, J Q R, p. 427.

assembled to study its laws and opinions." The present opposition to the Code, avers Sheshet, is also animated by jealous motives.

This Maimonist wrote a few trenchant lines against Meir ben Todros, who in speeding his poisoned arrows against Maimonides, condemns himself as a rebellious son.[40] Sheshet Hanasi notes the paradox between his name (Meir, light) and his sinister activity.

"My friends have asked me, why designate
As light, him who walketh in darkness?
I replied, our sages have called
The night, light — it is a paradox."

The Spanish poet, Judah Alharizi, born in 1165, who translated the Guide, as well as part of the Commentary on the Mishna into Hebrew, praises Maimonides, and finds that the omission from the Code of "the names of the expounders, the sermons, comments, legends, and supplements which confuse one's thoughts," to be a decided good.[41] The poet refers to the struggle which developed after the master's death, "when bold and foolish men attacked him" in Spain, France, Palestine, and Bagdad.

[40] *Moreh Makom ha-Moreh*, pp. 3, 4; no. 11; *Kobetz*, III, p. 7.
[41] *Tahkemoni*, p. 352.

Chapter V

CRITICISM OF ABRAHAM BEN DAVID
OF POSQUIERES

The earliest systematic opposition against Maimonides came from the foremost Provencal legalist, Abraham ben David of Posquieres, (1125-1199) whose disputes cover the entire Code, its legal as well as its theological parts. His object had been to defend the Geonim against Alfasi, Zerahia Gerondi and Maimonides, the three who did not yield to them with unquestioning submission. Abraham ben David's jealousy of Zerahia, upon whom he heaped violent epithets began in their student days.[1] Toward Alfasi he was critical, but respectful. Among the critics of Maimonides Abraham ben David is the oldest and most comprehensive who tore apart the Code. His hostile treatment of this work especially of the theology in the first part, the Book of Knowledge, opened the religious controversy over the codifier which did not take on a definite form until the appearance of the Guide. The halo of authority and popular homage that enwrapped him was manifested by the fact, that contrary to the law Cohanim (priests) dug his grave as a tribute of reverence.

Among his outstanding disciples were Meir ben Isaac of Carcassone, mentioned by Maimonides in his letter to Samuel ibn Tibbon, Jonathan ben David hakohen of Lunel, who as we saw did not share the anti-Maimonist views of his master. It is worth noting also that Jona-

[1] See Marx, R. Abraham ben David et R. Zerahyah ha Levi in R E J, LIX, (1910), pp. 200-224. Gross, *Gallia Judaica*, 1897, p. 449, also Gross, *Abraham ben David aus Posquieres*, 1873.

than's twenty-four queries sent to the codifier are in part the same as the laws criticized by ben David, due no doubt to the association of the two men in Lunel. These queries were answered by Maimonides at about 1197. Another exponent of Maimonides' theology who corresponded with Abraham ben David was Aaron ben Meshullam. It was he who voiced the amicable feelings of the Lunel scholars toward Maimonides in the dispute with Meir Abulafia.

Abraham ben David made his strictures after 1193 or 1194. Maimonides did not know of them although he knew their author and had a high opinion of him. Not only in halaka, but ideologically, Abraham ben David opposed the sage of Fostat. The latter startled his generation by his new ideas and methods in theology, Biblical interpretation and the use of philosophy. Although secular and philosophic learning was beginning to permeate Provencal Jewry in the second half of the 12th century, Abraham ben David represented the strict rabbinic party. He took for his model, his father-in-law, Abraham ben Isaac who frowned upon all secularism, rather than Meshullam ben Isaac of Lunel, pioneer in scientific and profane learning. His intimate association with Judah ibn Tibbon, translator of the Kuzari and the Emunot ve Deot into Hebrew (1167 and 1186 respectively), and champion of philosophic Judaism, left him unmoved. We can therefore understand the epithets, "pious" and "holy" applied to him. He lived within the small compass of the halaka. Some even thought to make him out a mystic.

He did not interest himself in secular learning except to defy it.[2] The Bible and Talmud comprise his only

[2] *Temim Deim,* Warsaw, 1879, No. 238.

source of knowledge. It is characteristic that he finds
nothing in the chapters on astronomy in the Code to
criticize because, as he says, "he knows nothing about
it." He feels that all philosophy is detrimental to Judaism. It certainly is wasteful of time and effort in many
ways. He finds that Maimonides comes back to revelation after attempts at speculating on some of the doctrines. "Why," he asks, create problems and doubts in
people's minds?" Still, he was forced to admit the value
of the compilation.[3]

The Provencal Talmudist was among the first to air
his views on the objectionable methods of the Code.[4] He
protested against the innovation of omitting the Talmudic and Geonic sources of the decisions. "He aimed
to improve, but made no improvement; for he abandoned
the path of all authors who preceded him; they supported their contention by quoting authority. Moreover,
there are matters concerning which the Geonim disagree.
This author comes and selects the opinion of one in
preference to another; why should I rely upon his choice,
when the opinion does not please me, or when the dissenting party is unknown to me, and is probably not
competent to take issue on a question. This is nothing
but sheer arrogance."

He disputes Maimonides' extreme view that one is a
heretic if he relies on the literalism of the Bible and
Talmudic legends for proof that God is corporeal.[5] It
was perhaps this statement that provoked the French
rabbis of the next century to denounce the Book of
Knowledge and the Guide. Abraham ben David claims

[3] *Kelayim*, VI, 2.
[4] Introduction to the Code.
[5] *Teshubah*, III, 7.

that greater scholars than Maimonides had entertained the corporeal conception and under no circumstances can one be called heretic on that ground.

The mental gulf between Maimonides and his critic appears in the former's view that the patriarch, Abraham, first conceived of God at the age of forty in the full natural maturity of his intellect, while the latter holds that through a supernatural act, he recognized God at the age of three.

On the mooted question of the world to come, and its allegorization by the codifier, the critic declares "it were better if he (Maimonides) were silent.[6] He also opportunely disputes with the sage on the question of resurrection. He believes it will be corporeal and that life in the hereafter will be physical. These bodies, however will be as strong and durable as those of angels. The crowns to be worn by the righteous will be real ones. He inclines to construe the Messianic stories literally rather than metaphorically as does Maimonides. Contrary to Maimonides' teaching of the indestructibility of the universe to which he was led by the philosophic notion of the eternal reign of natural law, the Provencal Talmudist affirms that it will be destroyed. This was the orthodox and mystical view.

He rejects the philosopher's explanation of the difficulty of squaring God's foreknowledge with man's free will and responsibility.[7] The problem is this: God's knowledge of man's actions leaves him no freedom; therefore, man cannot be held accountable for his actions. Maimonides insists on human free-will, as for God's foreknowledge we must confess our incapacity

[6] Ibid., VIII, 4; VIII, 2; VIII, 8.
[7] Ibid., V, 5.

to understand it. The critic offers what he thinks is more
of a solution to the problem. Man's actions are determined by the stars. His reason can free him from their
control. God knows beforehand the course and influence
of the stars, but man's margin of freedom consists in the
effort of his own reason to change the star's power over
him. The power of man then is the unknown factor.
God knows the future actions of the human race, but not
of individuals.

Maimonides says that man cannot fathom the knowledge of God. This, in the opinion of Abraham ben David,
is proof of the weakness of philosophy. Although the
sage sets out to demonstrate the metaphysical principles
of Judaism, he is forced to return to mere faith, as witness his quotations, "For no man shall see me and live,"
and "For My thoughts are not your thoughts, and your
ways are not My ways." This being so, why not rest content with faith and reject philosophic investigations entirely. The effect of philosophy is only to arouse doubt
and disbelief.

The Provencal critic was intolerant of the opinions of
other scholars and of deviations from his own decisions.[8]
He charged Maimonides with superficiality and misunderstanding the text.[9] The grounds of his criticism of laws
in the Code seemed to be that Maimonides read a wrong
meaning into Biblical verses, that he varied the intent of
Talmudic law, and made his own inferences from a Biblical law not found in the Talmud. He also attacked
Maimonides for choosing one of two alternate Talmudic views without giving a reason for his choice. Often

[8] Gross, *Abraham ben David*, pp. 49-55.
[9] Maaser (Tithes), V, 3; Biat Mikdash (Admission to the Sanctuary),
VIII, 1; Ishut (Womanhood), II, 13.

enough, ben David was unjustified in his censure, as
when he charged that the codifier included laws which
did not occur in the Talmud.[10] In these instances the
critic was mistaken. He also had variant readings of the
Babylonian Talmud which occasioned uncalled for attacks on Maimonides. Besides, the text of the Code used
by the Provencal Talmudist was not perfect. Abraham
ben David leaned heavily on Geonic opinion, while Maimonides inclined often to take issue with it.

* * *

We have noted in this part the disaffection of certain
scholars, some of great fame, to the writings of Maimonides. His critics were surprisingly few, and although
it may be assumed that they spoke with the sanction of
their academies and congregations, the opposition toward
Maimonides was personal, and restricted to differences
of opinion on several specific themes. The attacks in his
lifetime were only skirmishes; the real battles were to be
fought several decades after his death. Meanwhile the
philosopher remained calm. Perhaps he himself foresaw
the conflict that would break out later in every place
where there were Jews.

Like Caesar's division of Gaul, the anti-Maimonidean
controversy may be divided into three main parts. The
first and most eventful period, from 1230 to 1235, witnesses the fearless partisanship of such luminaries as
Judah Alfakar, Meir ben Todros, Solomon ben Abraham
of Montpellier, Jonah Gerondi, Nahmanides, Abraham
Maimoni, and others. Anathemas, incriminations, and a
vast amount of propagandist literature resulted. The dissension ended tragically with the burning of the Guide
and the torturing of the anti-Maimonists. The second

[10] Yibbum and Halizah (Levirate Marriage), V, 24.

stage of the conflict from 1288 to 1290 centered about the malevolent efforts of Solomon Petit to proscribe the reading of the Guide. This French anti-Maimonist journeyed to Palestine and there aroused the communities to antagonism against Maimonides. David Maimoni, grandson of the sage, together with the exilarch of Bagdad and the principals of the Damascus and Bagdad colleges, resolutely defended the achievements of the philosopher and pronounced rigorous bans against Solomon Petit.

During the third period of the controversy, from 1303 to 1306, the ghost of Maimonides is seen stalking about in the ranks of both liberals and conservatives who have, by this time, become divided into two hostile camps on the larger question of whether philosophy should be permitted or proscribed. Such outstanding scholars as Solomon ibn Adret, Asher ben Jehiel, Abba Mari ben Moses, Menahem Meiri, the Ibn Tibbon family, Jedaiah Bedersi and at least 100 rabbis, all leaders in their communities, took part in the struggle. It spread over Spain, Provence and France and ended only with the expulsion of the Jews from France in 1306 by order of King Philip IV.

PART II

THE SECOND CONFLICT

Chapter VI

THE BANNING AND BURNING OF MAIMONIDES'
PHILOSOPHIC WRITINGS

The opposition to Maimonides that arose about the time of his death assumed a violent form a quarter of a century later. Added to the criticism of his other-worldly beliefs and the dissatisfaction with the technique used in the Code, there soon developed a sharp aversion to his entire theology and to his absorption in Greek thought. As a rule the scholar is revered more after death than in life. But the generation that followed Maimonides took his words literally and his life critically. This fact alone tends to show how pronounced was the animosity against him.

Several reasons may account for the eruption of this virulent anti-Maimonist feeling a quarter of a century after his passing. (1) During his lifetime he overawed the Jewish world and commanded almost everywhere genuine respect on account of his Talmudic knowledge, his personality and his benevolent leadership. Some scholars grumbled, but hardly any denounced him. (2) The Guide, containing his philosophy, was translated into Hebrew the year of his death. It took several years for its contents to seep into the learned classes. (3) It was in the first three decades of the 13th century that the general anti-Aristotelian movement in church circles set the stage for the opposition to Maimonides. (4) What made matters worse was the fact that his followers spread his innovating ideas by writing and lecturing on them and in some cases popularized them in a way that made them abhorrent to the orthodox.

Three countries formed the stage for the conflict of 1232-1235, Northern or Christian Spain, Provence, and France. For many centuries Arabic culture and philosophy dominated in Spain. Since the eighth century Jewish contact with the Arabs tested the mental fibre of Israel. Until the Islamic philosophy appeared, the Jews guarded themselves in dealing systematically with ultimate realities. But the open discussion of theological questions among Arabs forced the Jews, their neighbors, to consider the perennial questions of revelation and reason. The Jews were influenced also by their surroundings to cultivate the arts and sciences such as poetry, rhetoric, logic, mathematics, astronomy, medicine, and metaphysics.

The Jewry of Southern France was strongly affected by the secular pursuits of their neighboring Spanish co-religionists. From 1100 to 1209 Provence belonged to Catalonia and Aragon; in the latter year it became part of France. When the Almohades overran Southern Spain (1148-1159) bringing ruin to the Jews, most of them emigrated to Christian Spain and to Provence taking along with them the culture acquired from the Arabs.[1] One of these fugitives from Andalusian Spain was Judah ibn Tibbon. The lively interest that Provencal Jews took in the whole intellectual life of the Arabs appears from the activity of scholars like the ibn Tibbons and Kimhis, who translated Arabic writings into Hebrew. Of course,

[1] Munk, *Melanges de philosophie juive et arabe.*

the Provencals cultivated Talmudic study;[2] in fact, their zeal in this respect was praised by the greatest authorities, even by Maimonides himself. Provencal Jewry was comparatively free from Jewish mysticism. The classic of Cabala, the *Zohar*, was apparently unknown in Provence during the 13th century. The other mystical writing, the *Bahir*, was banned by a synod in Narbonne, in 1240.

The Jews of Northern France as well as of Germany were least inclined to scientific culture and were given to traditional study of the oral and written law. Their mastery of the Torah was drawn upon by the Spanish and Provencal congregations.

The Agitation of the Anti-Maimonists

Owing to the lack of dates in the controversial correspondence, it is difficult to determine the order of some of the events. However, we have some limits for the conflict in these three outstanding incidents: the burning of the *Guide* and the *Book of Knowledge*, the Saragossa ban of Ab in 1232, and the writing of the *Wars of the Lord* by Abraham Maimoni in the early part of 1235. The mention of Samuel ibn Tibbon's provoking metaphorical interpretations by Solomon ben Abraham places the cause of the conflict before 1230, since Samuel ibn Tibbon died in Marseilles in 1230.[3] That the conflict had been brewing for several years appears from a statement of Abraham Maimoni that "at times it waxed hot and then waned."

The anti-Maimonists in the present conflict may be distinctly separated into two classes.[4] The first group

[2] Zunz, *Zur Geschichte und Literatur*, 1845, p. 481, note.
[3] Ginze Nistarot, IV (1878), p. 12.
[4] Otzar Nehmad, II, (1857), p. 189.

was led by Provencals who were dyed-in-the-wool liter-
alists. They regarded the visions of patriarchs and
prophets as actual, physical occurrences. They accepted
not only Scripture, but the Talmudic legends literally;
hence they embraced the doctrines of the Being of God,
of the World to Come, and of the afterlife in the grossest
material manner. Many of them had no knowledge of,
nor liking for, philosophic or secular study. They were
legal authorities only, like Solomon ben Abraham
and the pietist R. Jonah. The second group, the
Spanish anti-Maimonists led by Judah Alfakar, was
more liberal and even had scientific training. Differing
among themselves on the form of certain dogmas, they
were united in their opposition to the merging of Revelation with Greek philosophy. The quarrel did not spring
from the cabalists, although some of them participated
in it like Nahmanides.[5]

Although the first challengers of the Maimonidean
position came from the rabbis, the learned classes, the
people at large were well represented in the conflict. The
numerous poems written in the heat of the controversy
show that the people participated in the conflict, for
poems in that age were like the newspapers of our day.
They aroused or reflected public opinion. The burning
of Maimonides' books would not have been possible unless these acts had been countenanced by them. Again,
the synagogues which were popular institutions as well
as the academies of the learned were the meeting places
of the opposing groups, and the bans were proclaimed
publicly before the congregation. Some of the main
points at issue involved the religious conduct and reac-

[5] Jellinek in *Moses de Leon*, p. 14, thinks it was begun and led by
the cabalists.

tions of the mass of Jews. Could they be permitted to study science and philosophy without any restriction? Should they be taught the pure God idea? The entire discussion of resurrection and future life brought home to the people at large the problem of the purpose and worthwhileness of their efforts here on earth. The allegorization of Scripture and the rationalization of precepts were done not only to satisfy the intellectual curiosity of a few but to make the sacred texts more acceptable to the masses.

The chief instigator in the war against the Guide and the Book of Knowledge was the traditionalist, Solomon ben Abraham of Montpellier.[6] He was the teacher of the more famous Talmudist and moralist, Jonah Gerondi, who, under his master's direction aided the anti-Maimonist cause. However unfortunate were the consequences of Solomon's fanatic zeal, he was unquestionably a man of great learning, a rabbinic authority, and of considerable prominence. Seldom is he referred to without glowing epithets. The celebrated Meir ben Todros, veteran antagonist of Maimonides, extols him highly as "a faithful sprout, a fountain of wisdom and understanding, mighty in his efforts to restore the beaten paths and to repair the breach." The opinion of another polemist, the fairminded and learned Judah Alfakar, who gives a high estimate of Solomon and his theological ideas, may be given full credence. Nahmanides always speaks respectfully of his friend Solomon ben Abraham, and admonished the French rabbis to accord him every mark

[6] Israelitische Letterbode, III, p. 1; letter sent by Solomon ben Abraham to Nahmanides, II, p. 182; Kerem Hemed, V, p. 4. His legal opinions are mentioned by Meiri of Perpignan in the *Magen Abot*, p. 89.

of honor.[7] It is worth noting that Meiri mentions him in his historical introduction to his commentary on Aboth, among the few Provencal scholars.[8]

Besides Jonah Gerondi, David ben Saul aided his master Solomon. Little is known of David.[9] Abraham Maimoni cites a polemical treatise by him giving his own materialistic theological conceptions.

But the best known of this trio was Jonah Gerondi, (of Gerona) born in Spain, educated in France, famed as Jonah the Pious, and conspicuous as a Talmudist and writer of ethical works.[10] He died in 1264 at Toledo. He had gone to this city on his journey to Palestine and had been chosen head of the Toledo Rabbinical College. He was the teacher of the celebrated Solomon ibn Adret, a leading anti-intellectualist in the first decades of the next century, and of Hillel of Verona, an admirer of Maimonides. Jonah Gerondi was a cousin of Nahmanides, and they were further related by the marriage of the latter's son to Jonah's daughter.

The Argument of the Anti-Maimonists

It must be emphasized that in the conflict now to be described, the opposing sides stayed within the fold of

---

[7] From the fact that Nahmanides refers to him as Solomon of Barcelona, Michael (*Or Ha Hayyim*, p. 583) surmises that Solomon ben Abraham was born in Barcelona but had lived in Montpellier. Hillel of Verona describes Jonah, pupil of Solomon ben Abraham, as "R. Jonah the great of Barcelona;" *Kobetz*, III, p. 14b. They may have been associated together in Spain before coming to the Provence.

[8] *Bet ha Behira* on Abot, 1854, p. 18b; Acc. to the *Shaare Zion*, p. 41 he made commentaries on most of the Talmud.

[9] *Or Ha-Hayyim*, p. 346; acc. to Ashkenaze in *Taam-Zekenim* ed. Ashkenaze, 1855, p. 70, our David may be the one mentioned by Nissim Gerondi in his Commentary on Sanhedrin. Meiri mentions David as a pupil of Solomon ben Abraham.

[10] See Geiger, W Z J T, V, p. 91; *Yuhasin*, p. 221a; Israeli, *Yesod Olam*, ed. Cassel, p. 35; see for his epitaph, Luzzato, *Abne Zikaron*, 1841.

Judaism. The conflict did not reach the stage of a secession or a schism. In spite of the charges made against them, the Maimonists were dogmatists, as were the anti-Maimonists. But theirs was the error, if error it be, of reinterpreting the tenets of the faith in the light of the thought of the day. The anti-Maimonists protested against the overt dealing by the philosophers, either through the spoken or written word, with the account of Creation in Genesis I, and the Chariot Vision in Ezekiel I in any metaphysical way. These two subjects, known as Maase Bereshith and Maase Mercabah, must be taken literally.[11] Whatever mysteries they contain must remain incommunicable or at best reserved for the rarest few. The Talmud, argued the anti-Maimonists, warned against tampering with these two chapters, and the opinion of the Talmud binds every Israelite.

The traditionalists also opposed the secular studies of metaphysics Hokmat Elohut and natural sciences Hokmat Hateba. They fought strenuously against the harmonization of revelation and philosophy and the resulting evil, the loose interpretation of Holy Writ. Samuel ibn Tibbon, it is claimed, publicly preached that the narratives of Scripture, as well as Rabbinic dicta, should be allegorized.[12] As the Hebrew translation of the Guide, made in 1204, circulated far and wide, the people became alarmed at the mingling of Jewish and Greek teachings and the question of the proper sphere and function of philosophy became paramount. Is it necessary, as Maimonides held; is it permissible, as Jew-

[11] The mystics especially from this time on objected to Maimonides' definition of Maase Bereshith and Maase Merkaba as physical science and metaphysics.

[12] Ginze Nistarot, IV, p. 12; *Kobetz*, III, p. 16c.

ish precedent indicated; or is it forbidden, as the very orthodox contended?

The doctrine of corporeality played an important part in this conflict, as the eschatological belief did formerly. The anti-Maimonists had one special quality in their theology; it was corporealism or materialism. The belief that God was a physical being was deeply fixed in the minds of certain orthodox people. Prominent rabbis held it. It was supported by Scripture, Talmud and Midrash. Both Nahmanides[13] and Abraham Maimon[14] charge that the anti-Maimonists wrongly held to corporeality and that they are unjustified in attacking Maimonides for insisting on incorporeality. According to one controversialist, the corporealists began the quarrel by charging that the Guide explained away the anthropomorphisms in Scripture.[15] Maimonides they charged even had gone to the extreme of denouncing the believer in corporeality as a heretic.[16] Other traditional views which Maimonides was suspected of denying were the existence of an actual Gehinnom or Hell which was part of the materialist theology; the truth of legends which told of corporeal life and feasting in the hereafter; the lack of reasons for the precepts. His opponents contended that the novel methods and ideas initiated by Maimonides, although perfectly safe in his hands, had become a dangerous medium when used by a host of imitators who did not possess his versatility and piety. As we shall see, many other questions of doctrine and Biblical interpretation were hotly debated by the opposing sides.

[13] *Kobetz,* III, p. d.
[14] *Kobetz,* III, p. 16c, et al.
[15] Palakera, *Moreh ha Moreh,* Pressburg, 1837, p. 20.
[16] Teshubah, III: 7.

The animus against philosophy and the Maimonidean books was accentuated by a wide-spread neglect of Jewish precepts.[17] The worst thing about philosophic study is that it is sure to lead to religious infidelity. Men cease to pray; it is doubtful whether any saint can pass through the fearful desert of metaphysics unharmed. Jonah Gerondi criticizes the people for flouting rabbinic customs, and even mentions the religious laxity of the shohetim.[18] Evidence of religious decline at this time appears in the public preaching of Moses of Coucy (c. 1200-1260), brother-in-law of the anti-Maimonist Samson of Sens. This Talmudist traveled through Spain in 1236 urging the people to use the phylacteries and to observe a higher standard of ethics and morals.[19] He had a high regard for the Fostat sage and praised the Mishneh Torah for the enlightenment it brought Israel. Its author distinguished himself in every field of knowledge, and many people, says Moses of Coucy, were strengthened in their faith by his writings, which have spread through Christian and Islamic countries. He repeats, however, the usual criticism against the Code, that it lacks references to the sources, but he used it very extensively.

Solomon ben Abraham sought first to arouse Provence to anathematize the Maimonidean writings, and so he began the agitation in his own community, Montpellier. If he expected an easy undertaking he was sorely mistaken, for Provence was the home of scientific knowl-

[17] Ginze Nistarot, IV, pp. 12, 164, 165; *Kobetz*, III, p. 6c.

[18] *Shaare Teshubah*, ed. Warsaw, pp. 20a, b; 22, 29a, 30b.

[19] *Sefer Mizwot Godol* (Semag), Munkacz, 1905; Preface and Positive Command, no. 3; *Sefer Yuhasin*, p. 221b and *Shebet Judah*; ed. Wiener, Hannover, 1924, p. 95.

edge, philosophic study, and rational exposition of Scripture and Judaism. Montpellier did not offer him its support. The disputes often became so acute that physical injuries were inflicted upon the combatants. The other communities in Provence either remained unmoved by his appeals, or resisted him from the outset, as did Lunel and Narbonne, and especially Beziers.

The French Ban

Like Meir ben Todros before them, Solomon and his partisans turned to the Northern French rabbis for aid when he failed to impress his views on his fellow countrymen. Solomon sent Jonah to Northern France to persuade its rabbis to issue a ban, and the mission was successful.[20] The Northern Frenchmen showed their concern by sending a representative to ascertain the true state of affairs. When Jonah brought them a copy of the Guide with its elucidation of Peripatetic and Arabic metaphysics and with its untraditional expositions of Scripture, they became convinced of its pernicious effect and proclaimed a ban upon anyone who should read the *Guide* and the *Book of Knowledge*.[21] The ban was rightly taken by all Maimonists as an attack on the character and Jewish loyalty of Maimonides himself. The communities of Lunel and Narbonne retaliated by issuing a counter-ban against the anti-Maimonists. They began a pro-Maimonist propaganda in Spain, led by David Kimhi of Narbonne, and sought to anathematize the traditionalists. In defending the Maimonidean writings, Kimhi fought for his own self-preservation, for he advocates

[20] *Kobetz*, III, pp. 6b, 2c bottom.
[21] Ibid., pp. 8c, 10b.

views identical with those of the great sage.[22] He ventures to expound the Creation and Chariot Vision. He explains away the miracles and the phenomena in which angels appear. Concerning the resurrection described in I Kings, 17:17, he says that the child did not die but was unconscious. David Kimhi knew of the Guide only through the translation of Samuel ibn Tibbon. When the agitation against Maimonides became pronounced in 1232, Kimhi's commentaries were already known in Spain, and had already aroused the more conservative against him, as appears from Alfakar's criticisms of his esoteric interpretation of the Chariot.

The only statement on the controversy from the pen of Solomon ben Abraham, a letter to the Spaniard Samuel ben Isaac ha Sardi, expresses among other things, his fear of the results of Kimhi's agitation in Spain.[23] He charges Kimhi with misrepresenting his attitude toward Maimonides, and denies that he ordered a ban upon those who accept the Maimonidean theology. "As God lives, for whose great Name we entered this conflict, we take an oath, that never did we utter anything abusive or derogatory against the master and his Torah. His words are beloved and pleasant unto us. At every lecture we refer to his decisions, we discuss his views and endeavor to understand them, and always refer with praise

[22] *Yuhasin*, p. 219b calls him hakatan, the small one, after his father Joseph; See *Gallia Judaica*, pp. 384-385 for scholars who bear the name Petit and for the theory that Solomon Petit, anti-Maimonist, belonged to the Kimhi family. Perhaps this is point of Alfakar's taunt to Kimhi in letter beginning 'yigar adonoy beho hasatan, David hu hakatan' in *Kobetz*, III, p. 1c.

[23] Ginze, IV, pp. 10-13. Halberstam surmises that the correspondent may be Samuel ben Isaac ha Sardi, author of *Sefer ha Terumot; Gallia Judaica*, p. 326; Samuel went to the school of Nathan ben Meir at Trinquitaille and in that way may have met Solomon.

to his name for his numerous decisions."[24] It is surprising to see Solomon praise Maimonides. He evidently separated Maimonides the jurist from Maimonides the philosopher. He probably did so, too, out of deference to his surroundings where the sentiment favored Maimonides.

His only concern is about the progressives who reject traditional beliefs, who turn the Holy Writ into a cluster of metaphors, and who reject the creation story and the genealogy of the patriarchs. There are liberals who nullify the theological views found in the Talmud, and he states that he has often debated with them on these questions without success.

The Spaniard, Samuel ben Isaac, is especially pleased that Solomon had disclaimed any intent to assail Maimonides. He grieves over the dissension in Jewish ranks. The causes of the controversy are ill founded and do not warrant the severe rupture and the incrimination that has resulted. "It behooves every scholar," he avers, "to winnow and sift the reports and not to be too credulous of what he hears." Samuel counsels Solomon ben Abraham to take the initiative in making overtures of peace to the Maimonists.

The most celebrated theologian in the conflict, Nahmanides of Spain, was puzzled as to which way to turn. Although he urges his countrymen not to favor either side, or to come to any decision until both sides have been heard, he himself inclined toward the anti-Maimonists. He upholds the aims and efforts of Solomon ben Abraham. The fact that the French rabbis put

[24] Ginze, IV, p. 13. Abraham Maimoni however, in the Wars of the Lord (*Kobetz*, III, pp. 15-21) reveals the real objections of Solomon to Maimonides' theology which were as stated, incorporeality, his spiritual interpretation of the hereafter and his reasons for the precepts.

through the ban shows there is some basis for their fears and contentions.[24a] Writing from Gerona in 1232 to the Spanish province of Aragon, he characterizes the active Maimonist propaganda as insidious and pernicious. He warns the Spanish congregation to withhold drastic action, and not to issue a ban against the anti-Maimonists. Nahmanides' straddling did not help matters.

The Spanish Ban Against the Anti-Maimonists

In 1232 the Jews in the kingdom of Aragon, following the leadership of the Saragossa congregation, demonstrated their disapproval of the anti-Maimonist agitation and their wholehearted alignment with the Maimonist cause. The Saragossa rabbis, led by Bahya ben Moses, physician to James I, King of Aragon, sent a letter to the congregations of Aragon, informing them that they had excommunicated Solomon ben Abraham and his two pupils, Saul and Jonah, for assailing and banning Maimonidean and other philosophical writings.[25] The letter called upon other communities to follow this example. Maimonides is lauded for his vast learning, his clarification of the law, and his knowledge of profane literature. Instead of subverting he has enlightened and blessed Israel. The verse "The Torah which Moses commanded us is the heritage of the congregation of Jacob" is applied to Maimonides, "who drew us forth from the ocean of error and ignorance." The study of theology and metaphysics was always tolerated by the Talmudic sages. It was even considered imperative as a weapon to refute

[24a] *Kobetz*, III, p. 4d.

[25] Ibid., III, p. 5b; Bahya ben Moses and his brother Solomon aided the King as intermediaries in the conquest of the Mallorca Islands from Arabs. See Kayserling, *Die Juden in Navarra*, 1861, p. 159; Graetz, *History* (Hebrew), V, p. 33; Devir, II, p. 316.

the heretics. Jewish rabbinic learning demands familiarity with natural sciences. The Saragossa authorities scathingly denounce and excommunicate the trio for daring to ban anyone who peruses the writings of Maimonides or any other philosopher.[26] The otherwise mild Nahmanides condemns Bahya ben Moses and his family for usurping the powers of the Jewish community and acting in a high handed manner.

Beside this congregational letter Bahya ben Moses dispatched a personal letter to the Aragonion cities.[27] As a result four Aragonese communities assented to proclaim a ban against the anti-Maimonists, Huesca;[28] Monzon;[29] Calatyuad;[30] Lerida.[31]

The Burning of the Guide and the Book of Knowledge

The effect of the Aragonian bans was to bring the controversy to a sudden climax in the year 1232.[32] The copies of the Guide and the Book of Knowledge had reached France long before and now they were examined in Paris for heresy. The northern scholars gave an adverse decision on these books and decreed that any person found reading them was to be banned and his property confiscated. In their indignation they turned to the church authorities, who, animated by anti-Aristotelian sentiment that was prevalent at that time in Paris, condemned the Maimonidean philosophic books to the flames.

[26] The ban is signed by Bahya ben Moses and 10 others.
[27] *Kobetz*, III, p. 6b.
[28] Signed by 12 scholars.
[29] Signed by four scholars.
[30] Signed by Moses ben Solomon Alkonstantini, the father of Bahyah, and four others.
[31] Names of signers omitted.
[32] *Kobetz*, III, p. 14a, c, 17a; Hillel wrongly places the burning of the Talmud in this year; Jost, *Geschichte des Judenthums*, III, 1857-1859, p. 12.

Thus occurred the shameful public burning of the Guide and the Book of Knowledge. It was done at the instigation of the strict traditionalists, with the approval of the cardinal Romanus, the Judge of the heresy court. The light for the fire was obtained from the candelabra in the monastery. The Dominican priests kindled the fire and the burning took place in the market place before all the people. The intervention of the Dominicans[33] on the side of the anti-Maimonists may be variously accounted for. The support of the Church had been urgently sought by the traditionalists as a last move to give them the upper hand over the rationalists. The Church had itself begun a program of inquisition against heretics and the suppression of Maimonides' alleged heretical writings was a victory for the Church policy. In this connection it should be remembered that the Guide had come into vogue among Christians and the scholastics refer at times to the Jewish heresies. In 1210, the Physics and Metaphysics of Aristotle had been ordered burnt by the Dominicans. The Talmud and other Hebrew books had been burnt by the Church. The Guide was only another book found objectionable for spreading Aristotelian ideas.

Much uncertainty has crept in concerning the place of the burning. Abraham Maimoni gives the place as Montpellier,[34] whereas Hillel of Verona, writing about 60

[33] The terms used to describe the Dominicans is 'yehefim', barefooted priests.

[34] *Kobetz*, III, p. 17a; Acc. to Eppenstein (Abraham Maimuni; sein Leben und seine Schriften.) p. 28, note 2, hardly any copies of the Guide were to be found in Paris. Acc. to another view, Hagoren, 1898, p. 64, only the Guide and not the Book of Knowledge was committed to the flames in Montpellier.

years later, lays the scene in Paris.[35] Most historians today place the burning in Montpellier.

The anti-Maimonists had wrested only a pyrrhic victory from the progressives, and their act brought a reaction of feeling. Soon after the burning, some of the French rabbis who had proclaimed the ban withdrew their support from it. Within a year, on the complaint of influential Maimonists, those chiefly responsible for the burning were tried and sentenced to have their tongues cut out.[36] But these events did not end the conflict. The leaders of both parties came forward to defend their course.

[35] It is possible that the event of 1232 was connected in the mind of Hillel with the burning of the Talmud in Paris ten years later.

[36] *Kobetz*, III, p. 17a; Ginze, III, p. 179; Graetz, *History* (Hebrew), V, p. 65, surmises that the influential Bahya ben Moses had requested King James I of Aragon to penalize the Anti-Maimonists when he visited the ruler at Montpellier in 1234.

Chapter VII

DEFENSE OF THE SPANISH MAIMONIST VIEW- POINT

When the conflict reached this crucial stage, two prom- inent scholars of Barcelona, Abraham and Judah Hasdai eloquently appealed to the congregations of Navarre, Aragon, Castile and Leon to save the Maimonists of Provence from the drastic acts of their French op- ponents. The brothers had assisted Kimhi in his pro- Maimonist activity in Spain. Abraham had corresponded with the uncompromising anti-Maimonist Meir Abulafia of Toledo. His philosophic interests appear in his trans- lation of Maimonides' *Book of Precepts* and his *Letter to Yemen* from Arabic into Hebrew and in other such works.

For a long time they stayed out of the affair hoping that the conservatives would relax their hostility and a reconciliation be effected. They do not hesitate to place the guilt upon the ring leader Solomon ben Abraham who did nothing to stave off the dreadful turn of events. They heap the most abusive epithets upon him. "That worthless person is the source of contamination, the brother of enmity, the son of the hated consort; he and his disciples sinned and caused others to sin. He begot many vipers, serpents and scorpions; he brought forth lions, wolves and bears. He committed many trespasses, by means of the bans, wherein he himself was trapped. His withered soul is full of evil. He transgressed the many oaths contained in the epistles of the congrega- tions that reveal his reproach and shame. This wicked

man has demeaned himself and walked in the obduracy
of his heart and his thoughts. He has misled the young,
who imbibe his poisonous waters and incamp in the
shadow of his scorn. Through our sins and those of our
forefathers, this plague has crossed all boundaries and
spread into all congregations. In every district there
are well known men who will support the transgressors,
join their factions and maintain silence in the face of all
their false and rash utterances."[1]

They chide the Spanish communities for their neutral
attitude. The war over Maimonides is not a sectional
nor a personal strife; it is universal. The antagonists
of Maimonides have discredited the entire structure of
Judaism and deserve no quarters. The peace and harmony that the Spanish seek in their own land by refusing
to act against the anti-Maimonists are bought at the
cost of jeopardizing Jewish life in other lands. Only
the congregation of Burgos has evinced a fraternal spirit
in the harassed Maimonists of France and Provence. To
show their defiance of the ban against the sage's writings
the brothers resolved to read these writings publicly in
the synagogue upon every Sabbath.

Samuel ben Abraham Saporta

A more vigorous and detailed defense of rational
theology came from another Spaniard, Samuel ben Abraham Saporta, in an epistle to the French rabbis.[2] It is
possible that this letter brought about their changed attitude resulting in the withdrawal of the ban. He claims
that they would have been within their rights in banning
out and out heretics and scorners of Rabbinic traditions

[1] Ginze Nistarot, III, pp. 181-182.
[2] The Maimonist Moses Alashkar of the 15th Century refers to his
excellent defense of Incorporeality.

but certainly not in proscribing the wise books of Maimonides. He condemns as despicable the tactics of the anti-Maimonists in summoning the civil and ecclesiastic authorities to help them, and labels this exposure of internal communal trouble before the eyes of the world a desecration of God's name and treason to Israel.

He reminds the French rabbis that when the Code (*Mishneh Torah*) appeared in Provence the foremost among them praised it. "No one dared to open his mouth against it, or mutter against the doctrines he formulated. They did not then expound them falsely or pronounce them hateful. Why then do ye now, ye excellencies, dispute them? Why do you clamor against them? Why not thoroughly investigate before drastic measures are taken? Now all congregations in the North, South, East or West uphold the bond of these precious writings, and their reverence for our master, Maimonides, is like their fear of God. Let me know wherefore you quarrel with him."[3]

Samuel had studied the Guide thoroughly in order to find its alleged objectionable parts, but in vain. The book does not deviate in the least from the well-trodden highway of tradition. It is thoroughly impregnated with Hebrew lore, and if the French oppose it, it is because of their ignorance of its contents and of the author's motives. The anti-Maimonists do not grasp its profundities, and they consigned it to the flames with no more ado than they would the out and out heretical writings.[4] All the eminent scholars and saints of the Orient and of

---

[3] Ginze Nistarot, IV, pp. 43-44.

[4] Ibid., p. 55, he uses the phrase 'sifre Miros'; See Azariah de Rossi, *Imre Binah*, Wilna, 1863, Ch. 2, p. 70; also M G W J, 1870, pp. 138-139, for the meaning of this expression.

Spain, have emulated the sage's exemplary interest in science and philosophy.

Samuel denies that Greek philosophy is offensive or that it does not accord with Biblical and Talmudic study. Jewish opinion never condemned Greek philosophy categorically because of any heresies inherent in it. It had especially been permitted to Jewish leaders who came in contact with government bodies. If it harbored heresies it would certainly have been forbidden to everybody without exception. In fact, the true Jewish attitude is quite the reverse of that taken by the French rabbis: The Jew is taught to revere the Gentile sages, and to recite a benediction when he sees one of them. Among the men of the Talmud, physics, metaphysics, astronomy and geometry were favorite and familiar studies. Samuel cites the ancient controversy over the inclusion of Ecclesiastes in the Canon.[5] That had been opposed by some on account of its heretical contents; nevertheless sober opinion prevailed and it had become part of the Bible. Similarly, we should recognize the original and constructive scholarship of the Guide.

In posing the doctrine that God is incorporeal, Maimonides did not introduce an innovation in theology, and it is surprising that he should have been challenged for this. The distinguished geonim of the past and even his detractor, Abraham ben David of Posquieres, held this concept.

The Maimonean view that there are inferior and superior grades of prophetic communication is based on the explicit verse of Numbers, XII; 6, and is supported by a comment in the Sifre that only Moses received direct in-

[5] Shabbat, 30b; see Zeitlin, Canonization of the Hebrew Scriptures, pp. 130 seq.

spiration from the Almighty, but the later prophets had to depend on dreams and visions.

Samuel ben Abraham attempts to vindicate the eschatological beliefs of Maimonides which were a sore spot in this whole controversy. In his enthusiasm, Samuel ascribes to Maimonides orthodox views on hell, eternal punishment and the millennial banquet. He points to the mention of Gehinnom in Hilkoth Yesode ha Torah, V. 4 where the statement that "the worshipper of idols descends to the lowest level of Gehinnom" indicates that Maimonides had a material conception of it. In his Commentary on the Mishna he also treats of Gehinnom, although he does not particularize on the nature and extent of the punishment of the wicked.[6] The millennial banquet of preserved wine, Leviathan and the Wild Boar, all of which it had been charged were denied by Maimonides, were parts of his eschatological belief. The statement in Teshubah VIII: 3-4, that the term banquet (Seudah) is applied figuratively to the bliss reserved for the righteous and hence implies a rejection of belief in a real banquet, is explained by Samuel as referring to the state of the righteous soul after death.

The anti-Maimonists had charged Maimonides with violating time honored Jewish precedent by supplying reasons for Scriptural precepts. Samuel sees nothing improper in such original effort. It is unthinkable that Judaism should contain any ceremonies and ordinances devoid of reason and we dare not object to anyone's endeavors in this direction. Samuel also defends Maimonides' explanation of the sacrificial cult as a concession

[6] Comm. on Mishna Sanh., X.

to the people, on the ground that similar views are already expressed in the Midrash.[7]

Maimonides' explanation of the burning of incense in the sanctuary, namely, that it counteracted the odor of slaughtered cattle, is wholly acceptable. This reason does not lessen the sacred character of the sacrifices. The anti-Maimonists believed that this reason was contrary to the letter and spirit of the Mishnic statement according to which it was a real miracle that the flesh of slaughtered animals never deteriorated in the Temple.

The charge that the codifier violated Scriptural law in interpreting the *lex talionis* as monetary compensation, is not a serious one. Maimonides had forearmed his critics by declaring that the unwritten law so interpreted the laws of Exodus 21 and he feels safe in following it.

Saporta defends Maimonides for holding that angels were spiritual beings without physical form or quality. The angel that wrestled with Jacob appeared in a dream or a vision, and this precludes the presence of a corporeal being. Concerning the binding of Isaac, Saporta says that Maimonides did not deny the actuality of the event and nothing in the Guide indicates that he did. The only unreal and visionary element in the story is the conversation between the angel and Abraham. Samuel admits, however, that he had difficulty in understanding Maimonides' view of the talking beast in the story of Balaam. It appears that Maimonides regards the incident as visionary and at the same time avers that the beast received power of speech. In his *Commentary on*

[7] Ginze Nistarot, IV, p. 60.

Abot, V, 9, he explicitly alludes to the talking beast as one of ten miracles ordained at Creation.[8]

Maimonides did not deny the existence of demons in the Guide.[9] The creation of the universe does not require belief in its destruction, but, as Maimonides believes, the world is indestructible despite its creation in time and space.

Maimonides' treatment of the Messianic promises was hotly denounced by the French authorities who seem to have taken their own countryman Rashi as their model to interpret rabbinic legends. Saporta thinks that the philosopher's method should not alarm anyone, in view of the remark of the Amora, Samuel, that there is no difference between this world and the Messianic Era save that Israel will be free from foreign domination. The legend which tells of the natural growth of ready-made food and clothes in the Messianic era, would render this era most extraordinary and would conflict with Samuel's conception that normal life would continue. "All the great pre-eminent scholars agree that certain legends are metaphorical. Hence, I am greatly astounded, ye supreme excellencies, that ye have discarded all the ways of former geonim. The most extraordinary of all your utterances is that ye accurse all who expound the words of the masters otherwise than did Rashi. In truth not only the expounder do ye thus expose to reproach but the geonim themselves. For many explanations put forth by Rashi are not identical with those found in the commentaries of the geonim."[10]

---

[8] Ibid., p. 61.

[9] Ibid., Maimonides always refers to the belief in the existence of demons as heathen, Guide I, 7; III, 46.

[10] Ginze Nistarot, IV, p. 64.

Despite these champions of Maimonides, Spain had several influential anti-Maimonists and they and their followers had to be won over. This task was undertaken by David Kimhi (c. 1160-1235) the famous grammarian and Bible commentator.[11]

[11] For his life read A. Geiger, *Kebutzat Maamarim*, 1877, pp. 30-47. For bibliography, see the *Jewish Encyclopedia*, VII, pp. 493-494 and H. Cohen, *The Commentary of Rabbi David Kimhi on Hosea*, 1929, p. XII, note 2.

Chapter VIII

THE QUARREL BETWEEN DAVID KIMHI AND JUDAH ALFAKAR

By far the most prominent Maimonist, Kimhi, aged and infirm, left Narbonne and traversed parts of southern France, and the Spanish kingdoms of Catalonia, Aragon and a good part of Castile to arouse pro-Maimonist sentiment. One of his objectives was Toledo, the home of the inveterate foe of rationalism, Meir ben Todros, and the versatile Nasi, Judah Alfakar.[1] At that time Toledo boasted a highly cultured and influential Jewish congregation and the family of Alfakar occupied a leading position. Judah Alfakar was physician to King Ferdinand III and possessed wide secular culture. His support would be useful for either party.

At Avila, which was not far from his goal, Kimhi became seriously ill. He wrote to Alfakar to prevail upon the Toledo dignitaries to excommunicate the anti-Maimonists, informing him, too, that the French rabbis had receded from their opposition. Alfakar stoutly declined to yield to this request but formidably championed Solomon ben Abraham's cause. Although he deeply admired Maimonides' supreme mastery of Talmudic lore, he condemned the indiscriminate spread of the Guide among all classes and the sacrifice of Judaism to Greek thought.

The Nasi evidently regarded the aged commentator

[1] See *Kobetz*, II, p. 27a, for Maimonides' admiration for the Alfakar family. The city of Toledo was a center of Averroism; Michael Scot of Toledo made the first Latin versions of Averroes' Arabic commentaries on Aristotle. Perhaps Kimhi thought that it would be easy to enlist the Jews of Toledo in the philosophic party.

in the same class with Maimonides, a misleading philosopher. He alluded to Kimhi's attempts to scale the heights
of the Chariot and to abrogate the laws of the Talmud.
Kimhi is curtly advised to return to the lap of the Torah
and to give up his idle speculations. He and his partisans are blamed for the extreme hostility shown to Maimonides' writings.[2]

What aroused Alfakar most bitterly was the offensive
assertion of Maimonides that had Aristotle offered more
convincing proofs for the eternity of the universe, he
would have accepted them and would have harmonized
the creation story with the Aristotelian premise. Alfakar
conceded the right of the philosopher to harmonize, in
certain cases. In the matter of incorporeality, for example, the Bible describes God alternately in corporeal
and in spiritual terms, hence we may choose whichever
one accords with our rational ideas. But no alternative
views are found in the Bible concerning the origin of the
world. It uniformly teaches the divine creation. And
Maimonides went too far in asserting that any other
view was possible.[3]

Alfakar does not permit logic to tincture faith. Logic
may be fallacious, mere sophism. It is not needed to
confirm the teachings of religion. The harmful manner
in which metaphysics affects Judaism is seen from the
institution of the Sabbath. The purpose of the rest day
is to inculcate the existence of a Creator, by whose voli-
tion the world came into being. If, however, a creation

[2] *Kobetz*, III, p. 2cd; cf. Finkelstein, *The Commentary of David
Kimhi on Isaiah*, 1926, pp. LIII seq. for Kimhi's Allegorical Commentary on Genesis.
[3] Ibid., p. 1d.

did not take place or is declared to be necessary, the Sabbath and many other laws lose their sanction.[4]

Although averse to the mixture of philosophy and theology, he unstintedly lauds Maimonides for his vast learning and unblemished character. As the author of the Mishneh Torah he is a veritable monarch in the realm of law. He must not be unthinkingly criticized but judged with lenience. Alfakar charges most of the evil results of philosophic study to his followers, who did not possess his brilliance and faith and offered a strange fire on the altar of Judaism which the master did not command.

Judaism and Greek philosophy stand at opposite poles and are forever irreconcilable. The Guide fails completely to bridge the gulf between them. It is a perplexity and not a guide. It is basically wrong because it predicates the validity of revelation on the ephemeral thoughts of the Greeks. Greek wisdom must not be elevated to a par with revealed religion. From Zion and not from Hellas must the word of the Lord go forth. Alien thought may blaze a trail for Kimhi and his kind, but to himself it is an entering wedge to shatter faith. Samuel ibn Tibbon is scathingly rebuked for translating the Guide into Hebrew and thus placing a trap before the rank and file of the people.[5]

Under its attractive surface the Guide has pernicious elements. "Would that the book had never been written," avers Alfakar, "because we are vexed by the thought of the harm it will do in the future."[6] It turned Scripture into a book of metaphors, thus taking all reality

[4] Ibid., p. 2a.
[5] Ibid., p. 3b.
[6] Ibid.

from its contents. Such wonders as the sun's standing still, or the talking beast, were not actual phenomena, but visionary experiences. This view contradicts the Mishnic statement that "ten things were created on the eve of the Sabbath," among them the talking beast. How, also, can the rationalist explain the obvious wonder of the turning back of the shadow on the sun dial of Ahaz (Isaiah 38:8)? The authenticity of this event is established from the fact that the King of Babylon sent for Hezekiah to explain it. Alfakar's consistent anti-Maimonism appears in his defense of the material nature of the future world and personal life in the hereafter. A detail which reveals his frame of mind is his opinion on the longevity of early generations. Maimonides thought that only a few specially favored people, whom Scripture named, lived an excessively long life; the rest of the population lived the normal span of today. Alfakar avers that if it was possible for the few it certainly was possible for the entire species, and he accounts for Maimonides' view as a desire to harmonize it with the scientific theory according to which the length of human life is governed by the laws of physics and biology.

Kimhi boldly declares to Alfakar that the anti-Maimonist leader, Solomon of Montpellier, whom he hailed as a saintly scholar, is an ignoramus and a traducer. He stands self-condemned by the shameful conclusion of his agitation, the burning of Maimonides' writings. Christians have taken advantage of the situation and, pointing to a schism in Jewry, declare that the New Testament is the only true revelation. Kimhi pleads with his correspondent: "Will you and the exalted princes stand back when such things occur? At present, they have no other ally but you."[7]

Kimhi defends in a masterly fashion his own Jewish loyalty and the Maimonist position against all insinuations of heresy.[8] He has long sought an opportunity to discuss with Alfakar certain doubts which he does not care to commit to writing. Since Samuel ibn Tibbon's death, he has had no one to whom he could talk frankly. His assertion that dissensions over Talmudic laws will cease in the Messianic Era is quite correct, for one of the blessings of the age will be the clear understanding of all disputed laws. This opinion is not tantamount to a nullification of the Torah. "There is no Rabbi in Spain or France who is more observant of Talmudic laws, be it severe or lenient, than I." There is no cause for alarm in his speculations in metaphysics and natural sciences. History furnishes precedents of early scholars who engaged in these studies.

He is suspected for no valid reason. No consideration is shown him for his life long sacrifices and labors to carry aloft the banner of God. "I am old and decrepit while you live securely and sheltered in your homes in sumptuous style. You display no friendship nor mercy toward me and my needs.... If Solomon and his allies will make overtures of peace and recede from their position we will welcome them."[9]

Kimhi resented the charge that the Maimonists flouted Jewish traditions and beliefs. The fact is that they predominate over their opponents in the number of great

[7] Ibid., p. 42.
[8] Ibid., 3b, c, d.
[9] Ibid., 4a. At the end of the *Sefer ha Sharaahim*, 1838, p. 420, Kimhi also refers to his labors in behalf of Judaism.

scholars. They are pious, attend synagogue services daily and adhere to rabbinic teachings. They absorb themselves in study, day and night. Charity in its finest forms is practiced among them. Their philanthropists maintain students with shelter and provide others with free books. In the explanation of legends they follow Sherira, Hai, Isaac Alfasi and other Geonim of that stamp. The conception of a corporeal God stressed by the anti-Maimonists is not supported by Scripture or tradition. Surely then the Maimonists should not be reviled and condemned as disbelievers.

Several friends came forward and ably defended Kimhi. His townsman of Narbonne, Meshullam ben Kalonymus ben Todros, called upon Alfakar to be tolerant with the Maimonists.[10] Even if they are familiar with the Guide, they are nevertheless, God-fearing, and uphold the Torah. Meshullam suspects that the anti-Maimonists had incited Alfakar against the Maimonists. As a leader, he should not have committed himself to either side until he had thoroughly investigated the issues of the conflict. He suggests the rôle of pacifier and mediator to Alfakar. If Kimhi trespassed against him in word or deed, he, as an upright man, should not repay him in kind, but should be forgiving.

The notable Maimonist leader of Barcelona, Abraham ben Samuel Halevi, reprimanded Judah Alfakar for quarreling with Kimhi.[11] His forebears cultivated general knowledge and would have been the first to take up the gauntlet for Maimonides. Alfakar's long silence and his present unexpected hostility toward Maimonides are surprising. Abraham explains that Alfakar had been in-

---

[10] Ginze Nistarot, IV, pp. 1-5.
[11] *Kobetz*, III, p. 7.

trigued into it by friends. "Where are your mind's eyes? Will a man like you be so easily persuaded? The short time that I was privileged to delight in your company and sought shelter in the shadow of your wisdom and your love, I observed that you respected the works of the righteous teacher and were enamored of all his philosophic books."

Strange as it seems the anti-Maimonist Joseph ben Todros of Burgos whom we shall consider in the next chapter had criticized the Nasi for condemning Kimhi.[12] Alfakar replying in an apologetic vein reminds his correspondent that Joseph had used severer language against Kimhi in his letter to Provencal Jews.

But in the end he capitulates to the earnest request of Kimhi's admirers.[13] He withdraws from the fray and ceases his attacks. "I will remember all the afflictions of David (Kimhi) and will no longer quarrel with him. The fire of my erstwhile zeal will be extinguished by the showers of goodwill."

[12] Ginze, IV, 9; Ginze, III, p. 168. It appears that Joseph ben Todros too changed his attitude toward Kimhi.
[13] Ginze, IV, pp. 5-6.

Chapter IX

DEFENSE OF ANTI-MAIMONISM

Contrary to the hopes of the rationalists Alfakar's surrender did not stifle the anti-Maimonist sentiment in Spain. The veteran Meir Abulafia of Toledo, his brother, Joseph of Burgos, and the poet, Meshullam ben Solomon, thundered their protest. We have told how Abulafia opposed the Maimonidean theory of resurrection as taught in the Code thirty years previously and had tried to arouse Provence and France against the sage. He now shows little appreciation for the Guide. In principle it adheres to the faith but actually it nullifies many essential teachings. It is an obnoxious book and is full of inconsistencies resulting from the author's desire to hold on to theology and philosophy. Without exonerating Maimonides, Meir puts a greater guilt upon his followers who went too far in their extravagant rationalization. Solomon ben Abraham is lauded as a hero for venturing to stem the tide of heresy. He calls upon Nahmanides to halt the efforts of the Spanish Maimonists to issue a ban against their opponents.[1]

Meir's brother, Joseph of Burgos, capital of the Province of Castille, wrote to the Provencal anti-Maimonists approving their position.[2] He was forced into the conflict by certain Provencals who had reprimanded him for not blocking the agitation against Solomon ben Abraham in Spain. He cites the unflinching loyalty to Judaism,

[1] *Kobetz*, III, pp. 6, 7.
[2] Ginze, III, pp. 150-171; The mystic Moses de Leon dedicated his book Shekel hakodesh to him; See Zunz, *Zur Geschichte*, p. 433.

pure and undefiled, that has characterized his family. His father, Todros ben Kalonymus, warred openly against the abominable heresies and exterminated them root and branch. He swears to follow his example. He is especially provoked because David Kimhi visited Burgos and enlisted support for the Maimonists there. He accuses Kimhi of obtaining the congregational letters of Burgos in aid of the Maimonist cause dishonestly. These letters were not approved by the congregation and were sealed without the knowledge of the local rabbis. Among the signatories are ignoramuses who have become the militant forces of philosophy, who 'ride the chariot' and speak with temerity against the French rabbis. It appears that Joseph and his father-in-law, Nathan, enforced an excommunication enacted against Kimhi by the French rabbis and expelled him from the city.[3]

In Joseph the anti-Maimonists found a welcome champion who pointed out the pernicious effects of bringing philosophy into the Bible and the Jewish school; the resulting infidelity of the age, the general criticism against the Mishneh Torah because it does not include Talmudic dialectic, the ineffectiveness of the Guide in solving the problems it set up and the praiseworthy initiative of Solomon ben Abraham. He deplores the widespread appearance of the Torah's critics because they undermine the foundations of tradition, make naught of the visions of the Bible, regard as metaphorical the contents of the Torah and Talmud, ridicule the miracles and impugn historic teachings concerning Paradise. Philosophy is their Eureka, their salvation. He, however, sets up Kabala, tradition, as the way of Torah-true Judaism.

Joseph's attitude in the controversy was similar to

[3] Ginze, III, p. 168.

that of the renowned physician, Judah Alfakar. Although
claiming to have read *sefarim Hitzonim,* non-sacred
books, and to hold Maimonides in unbounded esteem for
his brilliant works and for his irreproachable character,
he gravely feared the spiritual hazard involved in the
unrestricted spread of Maimonides' revolutionary methods. He maintained that Rabbinic Judaism should be divorced completely from philosophy and that the theological doctrines should be preserved in their original
form. He commends the French rabbis for enacting the
ban, which like the revolving sword at Eden, will guard
Judaism against all trespassers who would desecrate the
sanctities of the faith. This prohibition had a precedent
in King Hezekiah's concealment of the Book of Medicine.[4] It accords, also, with the Talmudic point of view
which execrates anyone who teaches his son Greek philosophy. Even the early Mohammedan rulers had an aversion to philosophic speculation because it led to heresy.

Despite these feelings he found that the anti-Maimonists had perpetrated a grievous wrong in inviting the
mediation of Christian authorities; in letting them burn
the Guide. This was an act of treachery, by which the
fate of Israel was placed in the hands of Gentiles who
welcomed an opportunity to wreak vengeance upon Israel. The prudent and tactful way would have been to
overcome the opposition by peaceful measures. But like
Alfakar, Joseph holds the Maimonists finally accountable
for this heinous deed, because they had driven Solomon
ben Abraham to despair by their vituperation and perse-
cution. If Solomon had overstepped the bounds by agi-
tating against Maimonides, he should have been forgiven
because his motive was to check religious decline and

[4] Ibid., p. 157; *Berakot,* 10a; *Pesahim,* 56a.

demoralization. "If he (Solomon ben Abraham) does dispute with Maimonides, why do you go to the extent of stigmatizing him as a rebel? Do you regard the contents of this sealed book (the Guide) as of Sinaitic authority, guarded and fully panoplied? Do you trust yourselves to select what is satisfactory in the Guide? Are all his words established forever?"[5]

The Maimonists are hypocrites who pretend reverence for the Torah while they offer strange fire on the altar; they are the rich and influential who flagrantly disregard the law and its teachings. They prate about harmony but actually they are responsible for the religious conflagration. Not the Provencal Maimonists but the French masters have followed the norm of Judaism, and the weight of public opinion is with the latter.

Joseph is not so blinded by hate that he cannot see the good points in the Mishneh Torah, noteworthy for its systematization, the inclusion of detailed and remote bits of knowledge and its brevity. Maimonides' fore-runners made partial codifications of certain branches of Jewish law, but he is the only one who codified the entire law, oral and written. Strangely this anti-Maimonist even admits the pre-eminent value of the philosophic Book of Knowledge, comprising the first of the fourteen divisions of the Mishneh Torah, calling it a "crown of gold." He sees nothing incongruous in placing it at the beginning of the compilation. The tree of knowledge should properly be planted at the root of faith. This view of Joseph's is inconsistent, since the Book of Knowledge is usually coupled with the Guide as objectionable to the anti-Maimonists.[6] But the Code as a practical guide to jurispru-

[5] Ginze, p. 172.
[6] Nahmanides also draws a distinction between these two books in favor of the Book of Knowledge, *Kobetz*, III, p. 9b.

dence is criticized by Joseph for reasons already familiar to us.

If the Code, intended for students, is inadequate, how much more unsatisfying is the Guide, filled as it is with mysteries? "Even where the author sets out to reveal, he quickly conceals; he never begins a subject and finishes it...it is as though a hand touched his lips, that the arrows of his profound thoughts should not pass his mouth." Instead of the *Guide for the Perplexed*, it should be called the *Perplexity of the Guides*.[7] The author's purpose to reconcile the lore and miracles of the prophets with human reason is a worth-while but insuperable task.

The Maimonists have foolishly created a cult of worship for the Guide. Certainly it is not infallible and we may question the truth of its contents.[8] Joseph ben Todros rhetorically asks the Maimonists, "Have you explored the depths of the sea of Greek philosophy that you are perplexed? Have the alien writings disclosed to you the gates of the shadow of death? Have you reached the limits of metaphysical speculation? Have you seen their proofs that you resort to the Guide as a place of refuge?"

The best testimony to the danger that lurks in philosophy is the case of Maimonides himself. Lion-like he stood at the portals of the temple of learning, excluding the unfit and forewarning the novice not to cross the fields of metaphysics without first arming himself with the knowledge of the sciences. Maimonides even intended to withhold from his translator the third part of the Guide. His doubts about the wisdom of publishing the Guide gave way to the conscientious motive of telling

[7] Ginze, IV, pp. 163-164.
[8] Ibid., p. 168.

the truth even if it were rejected by ten thousand and apprehended by only one person. It is clear, then, that he opposed the indiscriminate spread of the contents of the Guide. But in the most brazen manner his precautions are ignored. The ignorant and immature enter the 'Vineyard,' distraught by the beauteous scenes viewed from afar.[9] Even the translators of the Guide into Hebrew are not spared. The crime of Samuel ibn Tibbon and Judah Harizi lay in the fact that they made it accessible to the multitudes. Harizi by translating incorrectly made a dangerous book worse.

The writer offers the case of one who reasoned that if a sick person could be cured by a physician's prescribed diet, certainly he, being in good health, would benefit even more by the prescription. The fallacy of this logic proved fatal to him. For as the sick cannot eat the heavy foods of a healthy person, so the latter cannot sustain himself on the diet of a sick man. The religionists of the Torah are the healthy ones. As long as they have not indulged seriously in speculation, they do not require the ministration of Maimonides' Guide. And, if they peruse this book without any need for it, they are sure to bend under the strain.

Judaism does not require any strengthening from metaphysics or the natural sciences, because it is a matter of revelation and tradition. "Let us, therefore, understand and know that our reason cannot dictate to us to turn to the left or the right. And he who overreached the universal boundary to pervert all that is straight, to compose rationalistic nonsense on the precepts, to devise a speculative structure for the Torah, has overstepped the

[9] Ibid., p. 155.

mark, thus bringing retribution upon the world. This is the way of heresy."[10]

Every person must follow the prophetic teachings and accept the affirmations of the sages even if they be not understood. As the blind person depends upon his guide to lead him aright, so must the individual rely on tradition to make clear any doubtful passage of Scripture.

Joseph refuted the old contention offered by the Maimonists that philosophic knowledge is useful as a weapon against heretics. If philosophy weakens the foundations of Judaism it certainly cannot be used defensively. No matter how brilliantly stated, the heretic cannot be persuaded by argument to accept the old doctrines. He is just as firm in rejecting them as the believer is in affirming them.

Philosophic heresies are more reprehensible than the deviations of the Karaites. The latter adhere rigidly to Scripture, although they reject Talmud and may be said to stay within the fold much more than philosophers who repudiate the written law. The argument of the Provencal Maimonists, that they are able to preserve Judaism intact despite their secular interests, that heresy has not invaded their land, and that the Torah flourishes in their midst, may be true, says Joseph ben Todros. But what of the future? He foresees a time when people will not be able to resist the seductive charms of philosophy and will become alienated from Judaism.

Meshullam ben Solomon Dapiera

The nature of the controversy may be gleaned from several lengthy polemical poems written by the anti-Maimonist, Meshullam ben Solomon Dapiera, a Provencal

10 Ibid., pp. 159-160.

poet, among others.[11] He shows the strength of the anti-Maimonean position by claiming the partisanship of the renowned Nahmanides and the latter's cabalistic teachers, Ezra and Azriel. The congregation of Beziers was apparently a stronghold of the Maimonists, for the poet Meshullam thus apostrophizes: "arise, O France, gird on thy armor; against Beziers, let us kindle our wrath." As long as he possesses the true faith, he will not turn to a false oracle.[12]

He charges that the Guide made radical innovations in Jewish thought, but more especially he pours venom upon its translators for popularizing the Guide and distorting the original notions of Maimonides. The translator Harizi tried to sweeten a bitter potion. He put a stumbling block in the way of perverted people. The philosophic views are too modern, unsupported by the hallowed teachings of the past. "What have you to do with Plato and the philosophers who beget iniquity and weariness?" As against the philosophic party he upholds the conception of corporeality and finiteness, the miracles of Scripture, the dividing of the Red Sea, Revelation at Sinai, the Manna, the talking beast, all the legends of the Talmud and whatever wonders are ascribed to God. The reasons given by the rationalists for incense, mixed seeds, sacrifices, and others are not correct.[13] The poet attacks the rationalists who claim that the dead resurrected by the prophets were merely cases of suspended animation and another view imputed to Maimonides that at death the

---

[11] Steinschneider, *Moreh Mekom ha Moreh*, p. 9; see also Marx, J O R, XXV, 1935, pp. 389-406; Brody, Moznaim, III, 1935, pp. 402-413; and for an Elegy by Meir Abulafia on Maimonides, pub. for first time, see Brody, Tarbiz, VI, 1935, pp. 1-9.

[12] *Moreh Mekom ha Moreh*, p. 12.

[13] Ibid., no. 32; p. 11.

soul of the wicked person becomes extinct. Meshullam
follows the tradition of assigning the wicked to eternal
punishment in a physical hell. He argues against minimizing the effectiveness of prayer and for the old notions
of angels.

In reply to Meshullam, an anonymous poet pleaded for
tolerance toward the philosophers and extolled Maimonides[14] as one who affixed to his writings the seal of truth.
Valuable knowledge can be obtained from the Guide, the
Book of Knowledge, and the Eight Chapters, although
these are not without some defects. The philosophizers
do not renounce the faith when they compared prophecy
to a dream, nor do they condemn any one who, relying on
Scripture and rabbinic sayings, ascribes finiteness and
corporeality to God.

Another poet goes into ecstasy over Maimonides. He
would roll himself in the dust of the philosopher's grave
as a sign of homage. His writings bear the stamp of
divinity. He removed the tarnish from Scriptural precepts, even confirming his opinions with the Talmud.
He explained the most abstruse matters in a simple and
clear style. He gave a great impulse to study. Academies and scholars multiplied under his influence. This
Maimonist sarcastically declares that perhaps the book
is not honored because its publication was not heralded
by strange phenomena such as at the Revelation at Mt.
Sinai. He charges the anti-Maimonists with failure to
understand the Guide because it is an intellectual work;
they prefer the Midrashism. So, too, the legalists study
ancient laws but are totally ignorant of the newer intellectual currents.[15]

[14] Ibid., p. 14, no. 39.
[15] An attack on Talmudic study was made by the mystic Isaac ibn
Latif.

Still another anonymous poet extols Maimonides for his mastery of the natural sciences and metaphysics.[16] He mentions especially his correct presentation of the nature of the soul as a spiritual entity, of incorporeality, and his theory of prophecy. The Code and the Guide will flourish forever, and we should steadily read them as a means of self-development and self-perfection.

Many short epigrammatic poems, some no longer than three or four lines were written by the partisans. As examples, we cite these three. Judah Alfakar, the anti-Maimonist, apologizes to the ghost of Moses, son of Amram, for this new evil-doer that bears his name. Maimonides is a prophet of Baal opposed to the true prophet of God. On the other hand, Jedaiah Bedersi, spokesman for philosophy, says of Maimonides, he is either man or angel. If he is man, he was conceived by an angel; or else he is an angel, born on earth. Abraham Maimoni pictures the fire that burnt his father's books as making them immortal, even as Elijah was translated alive to heaven in a fiery chariot.[17]

16 Ibid., p. 2, no. 6.
17 Moznaim, nos. 1, 12, 15.

Chapter X

JONAH'S RETRACTION AND NAHMANIDES' COMPROMISE

Nahmanides Defends Jonah from the Slanders of Beziers Maimonists

The tension of the theological conflict appears from the personal attack upon the family purity of Jonah Gerondi by the Maimonists of Beziers. The charge that his uncle's great grandfather had a concubine, the mother of his children, involved not only the legitimacy of the learned Jonah Gerondi but also Nahmanides.[1] The latter was so vexed by this slander that he sought out Samuel ben Isaac of Spain to issue a ban against the Beziers calumniators.[2] He requested the same thing of his Beziers sympathizers in several letters bristling with revenge to Meshullam ben Moses of that city. The excessive humility and forbearance that he manifests throughout the controversy forsakes him when his personal and family honor is attacked. He regrets that he had not been more aggressive and severe against the Maimonists when the controversy started. He defends the marriage of his forebears and states that it had been validated by the Rabbinical Court which had investigated the matter and

---

[1] Ginze, IV, pp. 15, 22-23; Ha Goren, I, 1898, p. 58; Nahmanides had written in a responsum to Jonah Gerondi that the children are legitimate and can inherit; see *Zedah l'Derek* of Menahem ben Zerah, 1859, Maamar, III, Kellal, I, Ch. 2, pp. 63-64. On concubinage in Middle Ages, see Burke, *History of Spain*, Vol. 1, pp. 404-405; Concubinage was practiced in Spain and Italy where no children were born of the first marriage.

[2] Ginze, IV, p. 16, note 4. He is the same to whom Solomon ben Abraham had written defending his position.

found no taint in the family. The entire thing is nothing
but a conspiracy against Jonah because of his adherence
to the anti-Maimonist cause. They thought in this manner
to intimidate him. "They hated openly the one who re-
proved them, because of the evil leaven in their midst,
for he anathematized and doomed them. And now the
dogs begin to bark, when they see that his hand is heavy
upon them, and his sword devours them for their infidelity and heresy, *kefirut* and *minut*.

Nahmanides proposes a trial before Meir ben Todros
of Toledo or any of the French rabbis,[3] and suggests
Beziers, where these slanderous charges were born, as
the place of the trial.

Jonah Deserts the Anti-Maimonists

With the burning of the Guide and the Book of Knowledge the highest point in the controversy was reached.
After it the passions began to cool. The collapse of the
anti-Maimonist movement came when Jonah Gerondi,
realizing the frightful consequences of the struggle, experienced a change of heart. He retracted and openly
confessed in the congregation of Paris. "I am smitten
with shame and remorse that I opened my mouth against
our holy master, Moses ben Maimon and his writings.
I hereby confess wholeheartedly that Moses and his
teachings are true; that we are the deceivers. I undertake henceforth to visit and prostrate myself over his
grave in the company of ten persons; to visit the grave
for seven days and to repeat daily, 'I have sinned against
the God of Israel and against our master, Moses ben
Maimon, for I have spoken perversely against his
books.' "[4] After thus acknowledging his guilt, Jonah visit-

[3] Ibid., pp. 18-24.
[4] These facts are given by Hillel of Verona, see *Kobetz*, III, p. 14.

ed Montpellier and then Barcelona where he publicly made the same retraction.

He established a school in Barcelona, Continuing his journey to the grave of the philosopher in Palestine, he came to Toledo. He stayed here longer than he had expected, owing to the importunities of scholars that he settle among them. He died a sudden and terrible death. As he breathed his last, he called for Maimonides.

Nahmanides Seeks to Mediate

Nahmanides attempted to mediate between the two parties.[5] Both his general theological affirmations and his polemical letters make it difficult to state exactly where he stood in the controversy.[6] On the one hand, he was associated by many ties with the leading anti-Maimonists. Solomon ben Abraham was a personal friend and Jonah Gerondi, Solomon's aide, was related to him. At the same time, Nahmanides idolized the memory of Maimonides and called upon all Jewry to pay him his full measure of esteem as the unique master of Judaism and the most benevolent leader of his day. Nahmanides constantly urged unity and since the anti-Maimonists were the aggressors, he certainly would have been pleased to see them cease their antagonism.

Although comparatively young, he denounces in no uncertain terms the boldness of the French rabbis in anathematizing the masterful writings of the philosopher and calls upon them to definitely revoke it. In the first place, the ban should never have been enacted. If it had to be done, it should have been limited to the Provence, because Spain is free of the objectionable philosophy and

[5] *Kobetz*, III, pp. 8-10; MGWJ, 1860, pp. 184-195.
[6] In his Commentary on the Pentateuch he often criticizes Maimonides' rational exegesis.

should not have been included with Montpellier and other Provencal towns in the ban. Under no circumstance argues Nahmanides should the Book of Knowledge, a part of the Code, have been prohibited because it could not be put in the same class as the Guide. Every public measure, he states, must be acceptable to public opinion, otherwise it will defeat itself. Where it is certain to be resisted, it were better not to enact it. Furthermore, deference should have been paid to a man of Maimonides' genius and prestige and a ban against his writings will need some explaining to communities like Yemen where his name is invoked in the Kaddish, the mourner's prayer. They idolize him for his responses and his benevolence in easing their economic and political distress and they will resent the restriction of his writings. He will submit to the ban as long as it is in force, but petitions them to withdraw it.

Maimonides surely did not deserve to be defamed by the French rabbis. They should have respected his achievements in the realm of law. He was a tower of strength to Israel; a strict adherent of the ritual. In some instances he even adopted a more rigorous view than the Talmud. All opposition to the Mishneh Torah, a key to the entire Halakah, is unwarranted and must be given up. Its greatest merit is the systematic and clarifying presentation of the varied body of law and belief. For example, the subject of repentance did not receive an organized treatment in Talmud, Midrash, or even in Geonic writings. His contemporaries, the sages of Lunel and Abraham ben David of Posquieres, evinced no hostility toward it. They disputed the opinions of the sage, but never assailed the Code on the ground of heresy.[7]

[7] *Kobetz*, III, p. 9d.

Its philosophic section, the Book of Knowledge, incul-
cates reverence for religion. Nahmanides denies there
is any doctrinal disagreement between Maimonides and
the orthodox, or between him and the French rabbis who
vilify him for presenting the conception of an incorporeal and formless God (without *zurah* or *tabnit*). This
idea is consonant with Hebrew teaching. It has been
espoused by the Geonim and Spanish savants.[8]   The
eschatological views in the Book of Knowledge which
vexed the anti-Maimonists are defended at great length.
According to him Maimonides believed in the reality of
Hell, in the hereafter and that different degrees of suffering awaited the sinful. Maimonides omitted all details
relative thereto because no one can know just what takes
place there. On the other hand, extreme caution must
be exercised in using the Guide. Maimonides himself
urged that it be not studied save under certain stipulations, particularly, that people occupying themselves with
it be mature in age and steeped in rabbinic literature.
He also stated that all philosophical ideals must accord
with the views maintained by his Talmudic precursors.

   Although personally Nahmanides disliked the formulated philosophy of the Greeks, he praised the work of
the sage of Cordova for two reasons: first, because he
was marvelously endowed with mental powers, and sec-
ondly, because he created a bulwark of security and defense for the Jewish people. He saved the unwary from
the Greek abominations. He inspired scholars, launched
academies and restored to the fold many who were lured
away by philosophy. The Guide served as a place of
refuge to those few who had lost their faith. Its author

   [8] A citation from the *Sefer ha Rokeah* by Eleazar ben Judah, 1160-
1238, of Worms is given in which this doctrine is defended in the name
of the Geonim Saadia, Hananel, Nissim and Nathan.

had been animated by a desire to counteract the subversive tendencies of Aristotle and Galen. In view of
all this, how could he be charged with undermining Judaism, or how can the anti-Maimonists insinuate that like
Alexander Jannaeus, he had turned heretic. "It is not
for you, excellencies of the Talmud, that he labored, but
for the doubting ones."

Of old, Greek learning was permitted in Israel, the
sciences, especially medicine, and such knowledge as
the Jews needed in the courts of the kings. When Israel
was scattered over the world they lost their speculative
writings and resorted to Greek and other alien learning.
Maimonides' absorption in philosophy did not affect his
religious steadfastness or moral character. In all France
or Spain there appeared none so well versed in all
branches of wisdom. He was revered for his saintly virtues, adamant faith, profound humility, noble aristocracy,
charity and benevolent interest in the congregations.

Nahmanides admonished his correspondents to desist
from the controversy and "not to try to compel all Israel
to become saints." His friend, Solomon ben Abraham,
the instigator of the conflict, should be treated with the
proper respect, due a man of learning. He shows his
abiding veneration for the great sage in calling upon the
communities to request Abraham Maimoni to serve as
arbiter in the controversy.[9]

In this inconsistent position of Nahmanides in
acknowledging the greatness of Maimonides, yet joining
the anti-Maimonists, and also in the distinction he draws
between the Guide and the Book of Knowledge, we have
an anticipation of the anti-philosophic struggle of 1303-
1306.

[9] *Kobetz*, III, p. 10d.

Chapter XI

ABRAHAM MAIMONIDES

Perhaps the most notable literary and theological contribution in this controversy came from the distinguished philosopher's son, Abraham (1186-1237). He succeeded his father as Nagid in Egypt in December, 1204, and wielded considerable authority as decider in religious matters. This is clear from the replies he made to Daniel ben Saadia's inquiries on the code and the Book of Precepts, as well as from other responses. His *magnum opus, The Highways to Perfection*, embraces many fields of Jewish learning and indicates great piety.[1] Like his father, Abraham practiced medicine and served as physician to the Sultan Alkamed, the brother of Saladin. Abraham inherited not only the honor enjoyed by his venerated father but also the latter's humility, uprightness, intellectuality and ardor for the Torah. Maimonides describes him as "modest and meek, in addition to possessing goodly qualities; a subtle mind and beautiful disposition. He will, with the help of God, become one of the great ones, without any doubt."[2] If he was an inconspicuous figure in Jewish history, it may be because he was overshadowed by the prominence of his father. He shared the latter's familiarity with secular learning and his rational treatment of Jewish theology.

[1] Eppenstein, Abraham Maimuni, sein Leben und seine Schriften, Jahresbericht der Rabbinerseminars, Berlin, 1912-1913; *The High Ways to Perfection of Abraham Maimonides*, published by S. Rosenblatt, N. Y., 1927.

[2] *Kobetz*, II, p. 31; Nahmanides (*Kobetz*, III, p. 10d) and the poet Alharizi (*Tahkemoni*, p. 352) are among the many who paid warm tribute to Abraham Maimoni.

Unconfirmed reports reached Abraham, who had been living in Egypt, that the anti-Maimonists in Montpellier with the assistance of Christians, had committed the Guide and the Book of Knowledge to the flames. In January, 1235, a communication from Acco gave him a detailed account of the venomous attacks upon his father's writings, including the reprisals inflicted on the anti-Maimonists who had their tongues cut out. As a result he wrote the extremely important polemic *"The Book of the Wars of the Lord,"*[3] which shows Abraham battling as a good rationalist against his father's detractors. Two years after writing this book Abraham died. The polemic, addressed to the Jews of Provence and Spain, defends his father's eschatology, his spiritual conception of the Godhead and metaphorical interpretation.

Abraham particularly refutes two polemical articles: a letter by Solomon ben Abraham to the French rabbis, and David ben Saul's statement, especially his materialistic conception of God, neither of which unfortunately has been preserved. He is rather impatient of these rabbis, frequently referring to their ideas as stupid and impossible. Abraham declares that theological disputes should properly be avoided because they do not concern the people at large. Only a select minority can attempt to deal with religious concepts. The mass of the people justifiedly seek clarification and instruction only in practical matters of law and ritual.

He contrasts the present-day animus of the anti-Maimonists with the favorable reception of his father's writings in Southern France during his life-time. The Guide and Book of Knowledge quickly gained circula-

3 Ibid., III, pp. 15-21.

tion. They were approved by a group of French authorities, among them the tosafist Joseph (ibn Baruch of Clisson), and his brother Meir, on their way to Palestine.[4] These had read Al Harizi's translation and thoroughly approved his father's rationalizing methods, but prevented the spread of the book among their pupils.

The *Wars of the Lord* is valuable historically because it furnishes us with the motives of the anti-Maimonists, particularly the motives of Solomon ben Abraham and David ben Saul.[5] Abraham assails their aversion to philosophy. Knowledge is at a premium in Judaism. It preceded revelation; man exercised his intellectual faculties, long before Judaism was promulgated. The stress that Judaism places upon reason is patent from the legal stipulation that a minor or a feeble-minded person is exempt from the commandments. In the prayer-book the pious Hebrew petitions God for understanding and knowledge. The prophets of Israel repeatedly allude to the importance of knowledge for upright and reverent living.

This array of evidence proves the un-Jewish and abnormal standpoint of the anti-Maimonists who frown upon intellectualism as heresy. When philosophy con-

---

[4] Ibid., p. 16c. Alharizi mentions the two brothers as belonging to the congregation in Jerusalem; *Tahkemoni*, p. 353.

[5] Abraham lists the following documents (not extant) that were sent to him from Acco, with a report of the burning in Montpellier.

   1.) The ban by the Lunel Maimonists on the Provencal anti-Maimonists.

   2.) Letters by Lunel and Narbonne Maimonists to Spanish congregations.

   3.) The letter they sent to Spanish congregations beginning mi ze bo m'edom.

   4.) The ban of the anti-Maimonists put through with Christian help.

   5.) Solomon ben Abraham's letter to the French rabbis.

   6.) A statement by David ben Saul giving his views.

flicts with Judaism, as, for instance, in its postulate of a beginningless world, we must, of course, accept the Jewish conception. In many instances, they agree as in the doctrines of God's unity, incorporeality and infinity. The anti-Maimonists are not able to grasp such philosophic conceptions of God. The Guide and the Book of Knowledge are not the proper food for their simple and unsophisticated minds.

Solomon ben Abraham assailed the Maimonidean view of incorporeality. He conceived God as a material, finite and enthroned Being. Against this Abraham cited Scripture and Talmud to demonstrate the logic of the sage's fine and exalted theory. Our conception of God depends, of course, on our attitude toward Biblical and agadic interpretation. If we construe all descriptions of God sensually, the anti-Maimonists are right. But in that case we expose ourselves to erroneous views bordering on idolatry.

Abraham Maimoni cites such foremost scholars as Saadia, Hai, Samuel ben Hofni, Nissim, Hananel, Isaac ben Giat, Alfasi, Joseph ibn Migash and Abraham ben Ezra, who utilized philosophic ideas in their endeavor to clarify and define Judaism.[6] They all held that God was not corporeal or finite. The anthropomorphic expressions in the Bible must be explained metaphorically because the belief that the Deity is corporeal is just what forms the great heresy of the Christian religion.[7] The Mohammedans borrowed the conception of an incorporeal

---

[6] Ibid., p. 15d. These scholars combined Talmudic learning with theological study; Two other classes of Jews are (a) the Talmudists who devote themselves solely to Talmudic dialectic, (b) and the Jewish masses who follow their teachers blindly.

[7] Ibid., p. 20d.

Deity from Judaism and thus marked a great departure
from their own primitive faith.

Abraham also devotes considerable attention to the
extreme view of Saul ben David who believed that God
occupies a throne in the uppermost celestial regions, separated from the rest of the universe by a par-
tition.[8]   Abraham replies that he heard clandestinely
that the phrase *m'ahorei hapargud*, 'behind the curtain,'
is a figurative one. Certainly we have a right to explain
figuratively any Talmudic or Scriptural passage that is
so clearly poetic.

According to Abraham Maimoni the fallacy of the anti-
Maimonists lies in the assumption that corporeality refers only to bodily substance, and not to fire or light.
The fact is, that any substance that has dimension, that
is tangible or visible may be termed corporeal. Therefore, when David and his partisans localized God in the
highest heavens and conceived him as ethereal they cor-
porealized Him and were guilty of spreading teachings
contrary to Judaism.

Furthermore, how can the corporealists defend the belief that the Divine Glory, which is twice as large as the
seven heavens, entered the caves of Mt. Sinai where He
appeared to Moses. Abraham Maimoni further shows
the absurdity of a localized and finite Deity by asking
where the Divine Glory dwelt before the Throne was
created and before heaven and earth were made. God,
the creator of everything and all space, cannot be local,
in any sense. Since He is not finite, He is not corporeal;
since He is not corporeal, He cannot occupy the Throne,

8 He bases the notion on Hagiga 14b where Elisha Aher says, "I heard
from behind the curtain," and such verses as Psalms, 97:2, "Clouds and
darkness are round about Him," he takes literally.

nor abide in fire (celestial elements) nor in the clouds.
Phrases such as "sitteth in heaven," "rideth heaven,"
"who sitteth on high," "blessed be the glory of the Lord
from his place," are intended to convey the thought of
God's majesty and magnitude. "My sainted father," says
he, "made this clear in the Moreh."

The logical result of extreme literalism is found in the
erroneous Christian teaching that God is a father and has
a son. Fortunately, Judaism has escaped the embarrass-
ment of conceiving God corporeally, because it holds that
the "Torah speaks in the language of man."[9]   In this
connection Abraham Maimoni explains metaphorically
the legend that "God will make a dance for the pious in
Paradise. He will stand in the center and every one will
point his finger and say, "Behold, this is our God....."
A literal construction is impossible. The dance symbolizes the joy of the immortal soul. His presence among
them alludes to their intimate knowledge of Him. The
pointing of the finger indicates their thorough comprehension of the Godhead, unattainable even by the angels.
The phrase "on that day," means the World to Come.

Towards the end of his life Maimonides had already
been harassed for his spiritual and symbolic characterization of the Hereafter. Solomon ben Abraham and his
coterie also assailed him on this ground. Maimonides
took literally an alternative opinion that in the World
to Come there would be no eating nor drinking. Hence
he excluded from it all materiality, a step which virtually negated reward and punishment and resurrection.
The anti-Maimonists maintained that the body must share
in the perfect bliss of the hereafter. Abraham frankly
asserts that the material promises for the Future World

[9] *Kobetz*, III, p. 21a.

were intended for the Messianic Era.[10] These two eras
are often used interchangeably by the sages. The Messianic Era will not be the scene of the transcendental
life. Cosmic and human nature will be the same except
that excessive joy and abundant material blessings will
come to Israel.

At the same time the polemist offers an esoteric interpretation of the eschatological banquet. The monster,
Leviathan, represents the evil inclination in man. It is
used synonymously with serpent to symbolize the earthly, brutal, and sinful nature; the eating of the Leviathan
represents man's final conquest of the evil in him. Such
a method must be pursued wherever prophetic or rabbinic utterances are contrary to human experience and
reason.

Abraham also argues with the opposition in the manner of the Talmudic dialectic. He points to the glaring
contradiction between Rav's statement that in the future
world there will be no eating and drinking, etc., and
Joshua ben Levi's which tells of the preserved wine being used in the World to Come. He asks Solomon ben
Abraham, "Why do you accept the opinion of Joshua ben
Levi and reject that of Rav? Is it possible that Rav was
altogether mistaken concerning the Hereafter? If Rav's
view is the correct one, then all contrary midrashic conceptions must be dropped. If, on the other hand, the
antagonist rejects Rav's view in favor of a materialistic
millennial notion, he, Abraham, claims the same priv-
ilege of interpreting the future life as he sees fit.[11]

Abraham justified his sainted father's denial of Hell
by pointing out that there is no clear tradition concerning

10 Samson of Sens offers the same explanation.
11 Ibid., p. 19b.

it. The Talmud contains diverse opinions on the subject, among them being the bold statement that there is no such place as Gehinnom, but that the heat of the sun will destroy the wicked. As for Paradise, we do know that it will be unlike anything on earth. The Paradise in which Adam lived is not the eschatological Paradise.

"Other objections raised against my father's works by Solomon in his letter to the French rabbis are preposterous and not deserving of answer," except his criticism of the reasons for the Biblical ordinance given in the third part of the Guide. These reasons, says Abraham, were not offered by his father as final and will never be satisfactory to everybody.

We have completed the story of, perhaps, the greatest of the anti-Maimonist conflicts. The desperate efforts of the opponents of the Guide availed them nothing. Even when Maimonides was assailed for his studying philosophy, the highest admiration was shown him for character, authority and for the Code. The tragic burning of the Guide more than anything showed the bigotry of the orthodox and the unworthiness of their contention. Their agitation fell to pieces. Jonah Gerondi retracted. Nahmanides pleaded for a compromise. Alfakar yielded to Kimhi. Abraham Maimoni bravely reasserted his father's principles.

PART III

THE THIRD CONFLICT

Chapter XII

A. *RATIONALISM AND THE CABALA*

Rationalism could not die. In fact, it grew mightier than ever in the 13th century. A great philosophic revival occurred in which Jews played a big part. Averroes, the 12th century commentator of Aristotle, became extremely popular among Jews and Christians.[1] His theology excited the Church to opposition. So we find that the popes anathematized the writings of Aristotle, Avicenna and Averroes in 1231, 1245 and 1263. One bishop, Etienne Tempier of Paris, took action in 1270 and 1277. The Averroistic system raised doubts on creation, Providence and Future Life. The famous scholastics Albertus Magnus and Thomas Aquinas wrote treatises to reconcile Aristotelianism with Christian doctrine. It appears that their efforts were not satisfactory to everybody, for we find that Aquinas was suspected of infidelity to the Church by the General Chapter of the Franciscan Order in 1282.

The Bishop of Paris, previously mentioned, had drawn up in 1277 a list of 219 objectionable teachings that had crept into the church through the scholastics. It does not surprise us then that Jewish conservative sentiment should in the last quarter of the century crystallize into an

[1] His commentaries on Aristotle were translated from Arabic into Hebrew, among others by Jacob Anatoli, 1232, Judah Cohen of Toledo, 1247, Moses ibn Tibbon, 1260, Samuel ibn Tibbon, Shem Tob Palakera, Kalonymus ben Kalonymus, 1314, Levi ben Gerson, wrote a commentary of Averroes, cf. Renan, *Averroes et l'Averroismes*, 1861.

anti-philosophic movement. The fire of hate against the Guide and philosophic literature that smouldered for half a century was kindled again in 1290 throughout Europe and in Palestine by a mystic, Solomon Petit of Northern France. The 13th was the century of the Cabala and we must take note of the inter-relations between this movement and rationalism to get a setting for Petit's agitation and to know that many mystics had a high admiration for Maimonides.

Jewish thought in the 13th century moved in three broad streams; the talmudic-traditional, the rationalistic and the cabalistic. Of these, the Cabala, springing from a source hidden in the far past, had been swelled by centuries of additions until at this time it had reached its floodtide. Another aspect of Jewish spiritual activity, its influence was so pervasive that it affected the rabbinist, Karaite, philosopher, scientist, statesman and even Christian teachers. When we deal with the Cabala, we are faced with an age-old deposit, of layer upon layer of irrational thought derived from the many cultures with which Judaism had come into contact.

The mystic movement expressed itself in two widely different forms. One was speculative and methodical; it dealt with standard philosophic questions; some mystics even used the ideas of Averroes. The other was superstitious and practical; it studied the various names of God and religious symbols for the purpose of using them in magical rites. The latter form was most prevalent in Germany and France where Jews did not engage in worldly studies and mysticism was divorced from systematized philosophy. The cabala in its first form flowered in Spain, where it came in contact with the strength-

ening forces of Mohammedan culture which had imbibed
so deeply from Plato.

The prominence of the Cabala in this century raises
the question whether it may not be causally related to
the anti-Maimonist sentiment of the time. Did the spread
of rationalism produce cabalistic activity as a reaction
or counter-movement and was the anti-Maimonean movement sponsored by cabalists? In many ways the cabalists
conflicted sharply with the rationalist rabbis. The former
ignored the hard rigid method of the philosopher's logic.
They rejected conventional forms and modes for expressing ideas; they dethroned reason and exalted faith.
Not the postulates of the intellect but the emotions of
the heart were to be sought. Through symbols, through
the sensuous picturization of God and His angels, the
creation of a thousand intermediaries between the Infinite *Ensof* and man, its moral treatment of the parts of
man, of the sanctuary and natural objects, by all these
means, repulsive to the intellectual mind, a romantic
element was injected into Jewish thought.

It offset the rigid Talmudism and rationalism of the
day. Many pious and thoughtful leaders to escape from
the wide spread of Greek thought looked into the Torah
for a purer, native and more racially Jewish philosophy.
It would be unjust, however, to infer that the cabala was
militantly anti-intellectual. In the conflicts of the 13th
and 14th centuries, we do not find the mystics in the
front ranks fighting against the Guide and the Book of
Knowledge.[2] Some of them probably were close to these

---

[2] In the conflict of 1232, Solomon of Montpellier and Jonah Gerondi
were orthodox Talmudists and not known as cabalists; Nahmani was a
cabalist, but a half-hearted anti-Maimonist. Meir Abulafia may have
been a cabalist, we do not know for certain. Toward the end of the
century, more mystics became definitely anti-Maimonist. In 1303-1306

writings. It was a cabalist, Nahmanides, who saved Maimonides in the hectic days of 1232.

At this point we will only cite the broader principles
upon which mysticism and rationalism were divided in
the 13th century. The former borrowed the teachings of
Neo-Platonism, the latter held fast to the cool intellectualism of Aristotle. Some mystics sensed that the correct
distinction between the two lies in their methods; that
philosophy pursues divine knowledge through examination and contemplation of natural phenomena and that
mysticism obtains divine knowledge through the names
and powers of God as discoverable in the ten spheres, the
alphabet and the numbers.[3] The problem was this: which
is more authentic, natural science and syllogistic reasoning, or the theology built on letters, names of God, angels
and so forth?

This distinction is further marked by Jewish thinkers
who had taken the creation story and the chariot vision
to represent physical science and metaphysics respectively, while the mystics claimed that they represented divine
lore which is discoverable only by the pious. If, they
argued, these two terms stood for human inquiry into
the physical and mental worlds, why would such information, obtainable by reason and experience, be secrets
sodot and why would the Talmud prohibit them?

An essential difference between the two schools is
that philosophy considered universal knowledge and revealed religion as dissimilar things that had to be combined. Rationalism, therefore, was a conscious harmonization movement. The cabala regarded all learning,

---

Abba Mari ben Moses did not pass as cabalist and Solomon ben Adret
shows slight mystic tendencies.

[3] Jellinek, *Philosophie u. Kabbala,* pp. 21-22.

secular and spiritual as springing from one source, divine revelation.

Externally considered, the Cabala was emotional and ecstatic, rationalism was logical, empirical and demonstrable. The Cabala was erotic and sensual.[4] Rationalism was idealistic. There are other fundamental respects in which they may be differentiated, notably in the matter of the world's origin. The latter as taught by Maimonides held firmly to the belief of a creation from nothing; the cabala taught that the world was potentially eternal. The world was in the Endless *Ensof* as flame is in the coal.

The cabalists protested against the transcendence of God and overcame the difficulty of a chasm between intellect and matter, strangely enough, not by making God corporeal, but by connecting the infinite and endless One and this mundane sphere, by means of the ten spheres, which were parts or powers of the Godhead, from which all existence emanated. In this way they surmounted the difficulty of a God who is pure intellect affecting a material world. The spheres of the rationalists were astronomical bodies. To the mystics they were parts of the Godhead.

The mystics regarded the Torah as primeval or pre-existent, an aid to God in creation. The rationalists see it as a revelation against the background of historic events and forces. The Spanish mystics, like the rationalists, explained away the anthropomorphisms in the Bible. They ascribed to Him neither human organs nor any kind of attributes. They denied corporeality with their mouths, but actually spoke of him in terms of substances, space, parts and dimensions; they constantly addressed him as

[4] Recanati, *Biur*, Venice, 1545, pp. 212, 213-214.

such in their prayers. The results of the esoteric treatment of anthropomorphisms were very much unlike those obtained by rationalistic exegesis. The former gave literal interpretations, whereas Maimonides, for example, who refused to humanize God, rejected the corporealisms as mere rhetoric.

A further practical distinction was in their attitude toward the precepts. The mystics desired the strict retention of the precepts and believed in the inherent efficacy of every ceremonial act; the rationalists had ethicalized the precepts and given them a disciplinary and instrumental value. All formalism in creed and ritual, for which both the Talmudists and rationalists were criticized, melted away under the spiritual subjectiveness and fervor of the cabalists. In other words, the merit of the Cabala was that it could not be condemned as unJewish, or as leading to religious decline. Thus cabalism was a centripetal and rationalism a centrifugal movement. Cabala always kept its original meaning of tradition or transmission; it denoted the legitimate legacy of the past, whereas *"philosophia"* was always an alien concept.

The mystics and rationalists diverged in their attitude toward Scriptural interpretation. Neither believed it should be taken literally. The former accepted the truth of the literal with a symbolic meaning, the sense of Scripture could be extended indefinitely; the latter rejected the literal, thus shaking the historical basis and divine inspiration of the Torah. In a way, the results obtained by both schools could not be satisfactory.

The Cabala assumed the pre-existence of souls; it adhered to the doctrine of transmigration, angelology, de-

monology and astrology. It used many forms of magic.
All of these things the philosophic mind frowned upon.
The Cabalist offered resurrection and immortality to the
pious and the upright; the philosopher promised survival
only to the intellectualists, declaring that it is the reason,
sekel, that endures. The Cabala stressed the independent
nature and fate of the human soul; whereas Averroistic
philosophy taught that every person's soul is only a part
of a world-soul. The Cabala sought union with God by
theurgic means, incantations, names of angels and the
over-powering of ever-present evil spirits, the rationalists
sought it through intellect. The former held that evil
was a real, active, positive agent that emanated from one
of the manifestations of God; rationalism held that evil
was inherent in the universe, only as the negation of
what exists. The Cabala made much of the mystery of
sex, both in relation to human and divine matters. Maimonides avoided that strain.

That in some circles the mystics were accused of de-
parting from the norm of Judaism appears from the fact
that they are charged with heresy in propounding a God
who is Ten in One. Their opponents compared this to
the Christian dogma of the Trinity.[5] This charge arose
because the mystics regarded the ten spheres as divine
powers or parts of the Godhead, while the rationalists
made the spheres created parts of this universe.[6]

Just as certain rationalists found the Talmud too con-
fining and unsatisfactory, so some mystics held the Talmud in disfavor. It must not be the be-all and end-all of
religious virtue. Knowledge of the secret lore is the

[5] Jellinek, *Auswahl Kabbalistischer Mystik,* pp. 19, 49.
[6] Recanati asserts that the ten spheres do not negate Divine Unity,
Biur, p. 98c.

highest wisdom. Perhaps it is not too extreme to say that the cabala formed a sort of apocalypse of philosophy.

The mystics of the 13th century like Abraham ben Samuel Abulafia, Menahem Recanati, Azriel, Joseph ibn Abraham Gikatilla, and Isaac ibn Latif, took a definite stand toward Maimonides and philosophy. They knew the philosophic writings of the Jews and some of the current Gentile thought. All of them spurn rational theology and think it is much inferior to their own esoteric system which is truly prophetic. They admitted the Bible has to be reinterpreted, but the added meaning must be mystical and not philosophic. Some of them tried to adapt rational theories to their own ideas. Abraham Abulafia[7] and Joseph Gikatilla[8] wrote commentaries on the Guide along cabalistic lines. Isaac ibn Latif is as clear and logical in presenting cabalistic notions as any of the philosophers.[9]

B. *MOSES BEN HASDAI TAKU*

The most important and pronounced mystic for our purpose was the German, Moses ben Hasdai Taku, (1250-1290), who vigorously came out against rationalism and whose book, the *kitab tamim*, gives the best background for Solomon Petit's anti-Maimonist agitation.[10] The success of Petit in Germany and North France was to be expected, for the cabala flourished there under the aegis of Judah the Pious and his pupil, Eleazar of

[7] Abulafia's commentary is unpublished. The manuscripts are in the library of the Jewish Theological Seminary of America.

[8] His hasagot on the first fourteen chapters of the Guide are published with the *Sheelot Saul hakohen*, Venice, 1574.

[9] See Ha-Shahar, II, (1871), pp. 81 seq.; also Klatzkin, *Anthology of Hebrew Philosophy*, 1926, pp. 120-125, for extracts from ibn Latif's writings; Schonblum, *Rab Pe'alim*, 1885.

[10] Otzar Nehmad, III, (1860), pp. 58, seq.; see MGWJ, LIV (1910), pp. 70-81, 600-607.

Worms. The call to uproot heresy was certain to find willing ears. Moses Taku does not condone Maimonides, but he selects Saadia as his chief target.[11] He charges him with being the first to inaugurate philosophic speculation in Judaism and accuses him of heresy. Until Saadia appeared, no one dared to make innovations in Scripture or in rabbinic legends. His *Emunot v'Deot* bred a host of unorthodox writers. By disputing the plain teachings of Scripture, the Gaon had done the same thing that Christians and heretics did in order to undermine Judaism. Moses Taku voices his abhorence of the rationalists in the following language: "What shall we do concerning these rash and unreliable persons? Shall we hearken to any of them? If one of them stopped the sun in mid-day and even if Joshua, the son of Nun, and Elijah the prophet returned, we would not hear him." The rationalists understand astronomy but not the creator of the planets. Between the lines we see that the critic imposes a restraint upon himself in not assailing Maimonides. He cannot, however, overlook Maimonides' association with alien philosophers who rejected the Torah outright.

Taku condemns as detrimental to Judaism, all profane knowledge, the sciences and philosophies of the world, because they are an entering wedge, if not the very hammer that shatters the sacred body of religious teaching. The Talmudic sages realized the danger that lurked in profane studies and prohibited them to the immature and the otherwise unfit. He cites the incident described in the Talmud of a youth who died while speculating on the theophany in Ezekiel.[12]

[11] Otzar Nehmad, ibid., p. 68.
[12] *Hagiga*, 13b.

Like other scholars of his type, he found endorsement for his aversion to metaphysical inquiry in the Psalmist's words, "It is the glory of God to conceal the matter." The matter is, of course, the classic and mysterious questions of cosmology, the origin and constitution of the physical universe, technically called in Jewish theology, Maase Bereshith. He contended that in antiquity Maase Bereshith represented a system full of esoteric knowledge, which disappeared with the close of the Talmud. The thinnest stream of that sea of recondite learning has filtered down to modern times. It is foolhardy to attempt to discover all that rich knowledge concerning the origin and operation of the world. The mystery and elusiveness of such study arouses all kinds of speculation and many there are "who pretend to be wise and fabricate views which they declare to be the exposition of the creation story." The conflicting views current among thinkers point to their ignorance of its real meaning.

A clear hint that a sacred lore once flourished, is found in Kiddushin 71a where we read, that the "Ineffable name of forty-two letters should not be communicated save to one who is pious, meek, middle-aged, etc., etc." Custom therefore reserves theosophy for the few.

Ancient Jewish science embraced the beliefs that creation resulted from the Divine Will; that the Creator had measurable dimensions above the highest heavens; that He is concealed from everybody's ken; that His own spiritual creatures like the seraphim and hayyot cannot behold His majesty and form; and, that God decreed that the sphere enclosing the constellations should revolve diurnally.

Moses ben Hasdai took issue with the philosophers on the doctrines concerning God. He affirmed the corporeality of God, citing many of the materialistic Talmudic legends in support of his view.[13] He attacked the favored and unorthodox view of Maimonides that all anthropomorphic expressions in the Bible are metaphorical. As a literalist, Moses Taku could not avoid entertaining a corporeal conception of God. He finds that it is conveyed in Gen. 1:26. His reasoning is queer: since man is corporeal, the God in whose image and form man is said to be, must be corporeal. He argues further that if God is not corporeal, if He exists without attributes, then he cannot share the emotions of pleasure and pain. If so, he is not affected by man's goodness and piety. This in turn abolishes the belief in good and bad, reward and punishment, Paradise and Hell.

Moses does not ignore Scriptural verses which contradict his views of a finite God, and explains them after a fashion. Isaiah 40:18, "What likeness will you compare unto him?" does not in the critic's view question the corporeality of God, but rhetorically states the magnitude and brilliance of His glory. It conveys the thought that God is immeasurably great, far beyond human comprehension.

The representation of God as a Being who fills heaven and earth, all space, is obviously difficult to reconcile with statements that describe Him as occupying a circumscribed area. The difficulty is resolved by assuming that God can alter his location even as do the planets, or, again that He is like the ocean whose overflowing waves fill the caves of the coast. Saadia is attacked by Moses Taku for rejecting the Amoraic legend that God moves about in the eighteen thousand worlds that He created.[14]

[13] Otzar Nehmad, pp. 60, 65, 77.
[14] *Aboda Zara,* 3b.

One dares not discredit anything found in the Talmud.
God can be present in one spot without His presence
in the highest regions being affected. "It is madness to
speculate how God limits His glory (makes himself
finite). We cannot judge nor know His greatness nor
fearful deeds."[15]

Angels, too, are material beings. Multitudes of them
were created at the beginning of the world. He speaks
especially of the larger angels, Sandalphon, Zebul and
Galizur.[16] All Scriptural stories of angels are therefore
real.

Moses Taku finds heresy in the scientific view that the
cosmos exists and operates according to natural law or
by blind necessity. In particular he holds up to ridicule
the notion that the earth is kept in space by the gravita-
tional or centripetal force of other, larger revolving
spheres.[17] Against this, he argues that if the non-reli-
gious theory is correct the people should experience the
sensation of the earth's movement. Again, if the velocity
of the spheres sustains the earth in space, how shall we
explain the existence of this earth before the creation
of the spheres on the fourth day. So, too, we must deny
the miracle of the cessation of the sun's motion, for if
this actually happened the earth would have dropped to
destruction. Neither is it correct to say that God is an
immanent power in the spheres and thus is the cause of
their motion. No! God, dwelling outside this world in

[15] Otzar Nehmad, p. 71.
[16] Ibid., p. 59, see Guttmann in *Moses ben Maimon*, I, p. 196, for
objection of Thomas Aquinas to limiting angels to the number of spheres.
[17] Otzar Nehmad, III, p. 68. Moses Taku states the queer notion that
the knowledge of the planetary movements came from the antedeluvians
whose longevity enabled them to observe celestial phenomena.

a remote celestial realm is Himself the active, intelligent mover and administrator of the universe.

He believes in the literal teaching of the words "He hangeth the earth over nothingness," and concludes that God alone keeps the earth suspended in mid-air. It is just as easy to assume that this is done by the fiat of God as to hold with the philosophers that He is the cause of its revolution. He assails Maimonides for teaching that the highest sphere, that of Reason, is moved perpetually by God and that this motion propels all other celestial bodies. Such teaching contradicts the Biblical account of creation, wherein we are told that "God finished His work on the seventh day." From this it appears that the divine command brought all the planets into being and once for all ordained them in their courses.

Taku disagrees with Maimonides' Neo-Platonic notion that there are only ten spheres: the seven planets, the eighth sphere in which are the twelve constellations, the ninth in which are the hayyot and celestial throne, and the tenth in which is the sphere of the intellect.

The present world will be destroyed and then rebuilt, contrary to the philosophic view that it is indestructible.

Other doctrines on which Moses ben Hasdai entertained anti-Maimonidean theories were prophecy and eschatology. In karatic[18] and progressive circles where anthropomorphism was rejected, the notion was current that God communicated with the prophets by means of intermediary forms created for that purpose. Moses Taku believed that God spoke personally and directly to the prophets.

[18] Ibid., p. 80, he attacks the Karaites, especially their opposition to the Talmud.

Chapter XIII

THE AGITATION OF SOLOMON PETIT

Solomon Petit, who led the anti-Maimonist agitation at the end of the 13th century, was clearly a man of Moses Taku's mental outlook, but he was also a man of action. After collecting endorsements of German and French rabbis who favored a ban against the Guide and Book of Knowledge, he went to Italy for the same purpose. In 1288 he appeared in Acco to carry on his nefarious work.[1] This city attained its highest importance during the crusades. There must have been an active Jewish community there. Possibly, it was the haven of many European rabbis who made the pilgrimage to the Holy Land.[2]

Solomon Petit is otherwise known in Hebrew history and literature only because he is mentioned by Isaac of Acco as his teacher.[3] Isaac of Acco in turn was the disciple of Nahmanides. It has been surmised that this anti-

[1] *Kobetz*, III, p. 23a, opening of Palakera's statement; also p. 13d; many Jews from France settled in Acco in the 13th century, and might have encouraged Petit. See Mann, "*Jews in Egypt and in Palestine under the Fatimids*, I, 1920-22, p. 175; II, pp. 370, 371, 383.

[2] Toward the end of the 12th century Benjamin of Tudela found about two hundred Jews there under the leadership of several rabbis. The Tosafist Samson settled there. In 1230 Acco was visited by the merchant-rabbi Shem Tob ben Isaac of Tortosa, and in 1268 the theologian Nahmanides preached to the local congregation on the New Year Day. Following the political vicissitudes that came upon the city in 1291 when the Sultan al Malik al Ahsraf captured the city from the Christians, the Jewish community dispersed.

[3] Gross in Gallia Judaica thinks he is the same as Isaac ben Mordecai still living in 1343.

Maimonist belonged to the Kimhi family because the name Petit was borne by its members.

Petit met with little success and the controversy raised by him was of much less importance and severity than the one started by Solomon ben Abraham in 1232, when the Guide and Book of Knowledge had been publicly burnt. The literature on the Petit controversy is meagre owing to the destruction of anti-Maimonist documents ordered by the Oriental bans. The only light comes from the bans pronounced upon Petit,[4] from Hillel of Verona and from Shem-Tob Palakera. These sources reveal that considerable antagonism was shown to the Guide by the orthodox rabbis. They had no use for it because it taught philosophy, which was taboo to them. More definitely, they could not accept Maimonides' idea of an incorporeal, transcendental God. In the opinion of the Maimonists the foes of Maimonides are self-seekers; they put themselves forward as champions of orthodoxy for selfish ends.[5]

As in the quarrel of 1232 so now an aggressive defender of Maimonides arose in his own family, David Maimoni, a grandson, who had left Egypt for Acco to fight the activities of Petit. He succeeded his father, Abraham Maimoni, as Nagid in Egypt in August, 1238, ·

---

[4] See Ben Abraham in Ha Goren, 1898, p. 79; The anti-Maimonist bans of Petit are not extant. There were four bans against Petit of which we know:

    1.) David ben Samuel of Mosul in Iyar, 1288, in Ginze Nistarot, III, 117-124.

    2.) Samuel ben Daniel of Bagdad, Tishri, 1289, in Ginze Nistarot, III, 125-128.

    3.) Jesse ben Hezekiah of Damascus, Tammuz, 1291, in *Kobetz*, III, 21-22.

    4.) The congregation of Safed in same year, *Kobetz*, III, 22.

[5] *Kobetz*, III, p. 24a.

at the surprisingly early age of sixteen.[6] He, too, served as royal physician. A eulogy by the congregation of Rome at the time of his death shows the glamor cast on this generation by his renowned sire. David's call for help against Petit elicited the prompt proclamations of the ban against him by the heads of the communities of Mosul, Bagdad, Damascus and Safed. They show the extent and intensity of Petit's opposition as well as the great admiration felt for Maimonides. The exilarch David ben Daniel of Mosul, writing in May, 1288, lauds profusely both the Code and the Guide, and impugns the malicious motives of Petit, who does not understand the Maimonidean writings. Such is the way of the world, the one who is destitute of the knowledge of a certain thing, will despite his shortcomings, seek to do mischief. The charge of heresy is only a pretext. The real object behind Petit's challenge to the Maimonidean writings is to obtain power and publicity.[7] He is another Korah bent on deposing the Moses of his day. The exilarch denounces the reactionaries as mere publicity seekers, who desire to associate their names with eminent scholars. They know that the ignorant public will consider them persons of great learning for having dared to controvert great leaders of the faith. He asserts the usefulness of the Mishneh Torah as a legal code. The Talmud is so formidable and complex that people of early days, hard-pressed as they were, could not master it. Then, too, the non-legal material interspersed in the Talmud, made it unhandy as a Code of Laws. Codification had been attempted without success until Maimoni-

---

[6] Mann, p. 328.
[7] Ibid., p. 118.

des made his Code. "No court requires any other law book to frame its decisions for litigants."

The Guide, too, is a welcome book. The exilarch David shares Maimonides' conception of the immateriality of God and the figurative character of anthropomorphic language in Scripture. The Guide apprizes us of the correct way to understand Scriptures.

The great sage quite properly concerned himself with philosophy because Israel must lead the world in it as it does in religion. Deut. 4:39 is quaintly interpreted as a command to individuals to cultivate the universalistic studies[8] "Thou shalt know"—ascertain the truth as far as possible: "This day" — astronomy and this created world; "In the heavens above" — study of the super-sensible, the souls, intellects and angels; "and the earth" —physical sciences.

The exilarch issued a ban signed by himself and his rabbinical court against Petit and upon any one who will speak disrespectfully of the Maimonidean writings; or who will take any step official or unofficial to proscribe these writings; who will harbor or distribute any anti-Maimonist literature or who will seek the aid of Gentiles against the writings of Maimonides. The ban will not be lifted from any violator unless he repent at the grave of the sage in the presence of ten men. The only person who can lift the ban is David, the grandson of Maimonides.

David wrote to the Jews of Bagdad for help against Petit and in September, 1289, Samuel hakohen ben Daniel, head of the Bagdad Academy, replied, offering to suppress the anti-Maimonist agitators. He demanded the prompt withdrawal of all anti-Maimonist bans and

[8] Ginze, III, p. 120.

documents. Anyone who did not comply with this request within three days after the receipt of Samuel's notice was to be excommunicated. This missive was accompanied by another in which the formula for the severest ban is given. Solomon Petit is offered an opportunity to recant; if he refuses, the ban will go into effect. The Bagdad authority calls upon other communities to take similar action. It appears that Jesse ben Hezekiah, exilarch of Damascus, issued a severe warning to Petit to cease his activities.

But these efforts forced Solomon Petit to return to Europe where he sought again the moral support of German and French rabbis in carrying out his plans. He collected many letters of approval and even succeeded in winning over some Maimonists. He then returned to Acco in 1290 but was forthwith excommunicated by the exilarch Jesse ben Hezekiah of Damascus in July, 1291.[9] His decree imposes the severest penalties upon anyone who will show disrespect or antagonism toward the Fostat sage. The harboring of any anti-Maimonist literature was forbidden.

"For the glory of the God of Israel, of His sacred Torah, and of its scholars and supporters, we, Jesse, son of Hezekiah, the Nasi, exilarch of all Israel, and his court, have been aroused to build a fence in order that the intruder shall not make a breach against the sages of the Torah. For, we have heard the talk of the people that there is one instigating against the great Gaon, our mas-

---

9 This ban is similar in form to the Christian bans of the period; Kobetz, III, p. 21; *Minhat Kenaot* of Abba Mari, p. 182; Kerem Hemed, III, p. 169. Annexed to this decree are the names of the exilarch and the date Tammuz 1286, followed by the signatures of his twelve colleagues. Of the 12 signers only one, Perahia ben Nissim is known as the author of Novellae on Tractate Sabbath; *Or Hayyim*, p. 568; *Die Babylonische Geonim*, p. 124.

ter Moses, son of the rabbi, our master Maimoni of
blessed memory, who opened the eyes of the dispersed
by means of his books so honored and precious among
all who know the faith, the Yad ha hazaka, which he
called the Mishneh Torah, and the Guide of the Perplexed, in which he embraced all religious philosophy
that he might wage battle and refute the heretic and all
who disbelieve our true and sacred Torah. Now, the instigator came and heaped upon this book, things which
are not true. We, accordingly, admonished and took con-
certed action against anyone who should continue to de-
fame the Guide or agitate against it. We did not wish
to punish unless we had issued warning, as our perfect
Torah commanded us. And now, not only is he not deterred nor affrighted by our anathema and excommunication, but has added transgression to his sin and has
traveled to the distant isles (France and Germany) and
returned with letters which he alleges contain the signatures of rabbis. These decree that the people stop reading the "Guide of the Perplexed" and that it be banned
forever. Some of the signers had formerly agreed with
our admonitions which we had sent them and had affixed
their signatures to letters that anathematized and banned
anyone who should speak disparagingly of the Gaon, the
aforementioned master, Moses, or of any of his writings.
We are in possession of those letters. Now that we see
that the instigator refused to listen to our words and
maligns the "Guide of the Perplexed," we need not re-
strain ourselves any longer. We have, therefore, decreed
to excommunicate by name ..... and any man or woman, great or small, who shall speak evilly against the
Gaon, our master Moses, of blessed memory, or against

his book "The Guide of the Perplexed," either in the
presence of one person or before many, who shall say
that it contains anything heretical or who shall say that
one who reads it is led in the path of heresy, whether
that person says these things to one person or to many or
who shall stop the reading of it, or who orders that it be
(banned) either orally or in writing. Anyone who possesses a writing, a copy, an agreement, or a letter signed
by these men, or unsigned, but containing any of the
previous mentioned stipulations, is obliged to relinquish
them from his possession and power and deliver them
and their copies to the Nagid, our master David, son of
the Nagid, our master Abraham, of blessed memory; or
to one of the sons of the Nagid. They must be delivered
within three days after our decree is promulgated in the
presence of ten Israelites.

"Anyone who, from whatsoever place, shall bring letters containing even one of the things alluded to and
prohibited above, shall not be permitted to copy them,
and certainly not to show them to any person. But he
must at once be informed of our decree that the article
must be given to the Nagid our master, David, or to one
of his sons. If none of them should be found in the city,
then the one who has these letters should bring them to
ten reputable Israelites of the city who support the
Torah of the Lord and the words of the Gaon of blessed
memory, our master Moses, of blessed memory, and
they should forthwith be destroyed.

Anyone who shall violate even one of these above-
mentioned decrees shall be under the curse, the anathema, excommunication and ban. Those who indulge, aid
and support him will be deemed like him. Anyone who

shall endeavor to preserve these letters which we have prohibited and which we have ordered to be delivered to the Nagid, he, too, shall be under the curse, etc. Anyone who shall through cunning, contrive to preserve any such letters or copies thereof which we have ordered confiscated, shall be under the anathema and excommunication.

"If, heaven forbid, there should be among those now found in Acco, or of such who shall come there, one who possesses a letter containing any of the forbidden things and one who shall defy our decree and not deliver it to the Nagid or to any of his sons, or to ten reputable residents of the city who adhere to the Torah and to the words of the Gaon our master, Moses, so that they be destroyed forthwith, we hereby allow any person to do all in his power to take them from his possession, even to resort to the Gentile courts. He who shall uphold our decree, may the God of the Universe preserve and bless him."

Most dramatic was the action of the Safed rabbis who standing at the grave of Maimonides read the ban and swore by his spirit to enforce it. They reiterated the story of Petit's efforts in Europe and Palestine and demanded the turning over of all anti-Maimonist documents to David Maimoni.[10]

[10] *Kobetz*, III, p. 22.

Chapter XIV

THE MAIMONIST HILLEL OF VERONA

Hillel checked the agitation in Italy

Echoes of the anti-Petit bans proclaimed in the Orient were heard in the West. Mention of them is made by Hillel ben Samuel of Verona and the Spanish writer Shem Tob Palakera, both of whom brilliantly defended the Guide and the Book of Knowledge.

Next to the Oriental leaders we are especially indebted to Hillel (circa 1220-circa 1295) for shedding considerable light upon this quarrel. For three years he studied in Barcelona under Jonah Gerondi, the repentant antagonist of Maimonides. [1] He studied medicine at the University of Montpellier. Although a rigid adherent of Jewish precept and traditional learning, he was enamored of the philosophic views of pagans, of Averroes, who had become popular in Northern Italy, and of Maimonides. Hillel played the rôle of a disseminator of secular study among Italian Jews and was the first to study Aristotle through Latin channels. His metaphysical interest appears certain from a treatise on the soul, *Tagmule ha Nefesh,* a commentary on the 25 propositions in the Guide, and other theological works.[2] Hillel's special

---

[1] *Kobetz,* III, p. 14b.

[2] These articles are published in the Tagmule ha Nefesh. Hillel translated from Latin into Hebrew the neo-Platonic work, — Liber de Causis, which greatly influenced Gentile and Jewish thought in the Middle Ages. *"Rewards of the Soul,"* deals with Greek and Arabic psychology and with eschatology. This treatise shows the central position occupied by this problem in Medieval thought. We cannot lose sight of the fact that the Maimonidean controversy began over resurrection. Hillel defends the Maimonidean view that reward and punishment are spiritual; Paradise and Gehinnom are not physical regions.

science was medicine and he had translated Latin medical books into Hebrew. His public lectures on the Guide did much to popularize this work and philosophy generally.[3]

Hillel checked the anti-Maimonist movement in Italy. He corresponded in 1291 from Forli, Italy, whither he had retired in old age with the papal physician, Maestro Isaac Gajo, who resided in Rome. Maestro Isaac served as physician to the Popes from 1279 to 1291. Besides his medical skill he was master of the physical sciences and theology. Hillel wanted his friend to use his influence against the anti-Maimonists. From the correspondence between them we learn much concerning the conflict of Montpellier in 1232-1235, the burning of the Guide and Jonah's connection with it. Hillel learned of Petit's malevolent mission from a chance visitor. "If I had known, I would have left my affairs and hastened after him to Ancona. I would not have let him go until I brought him to the refiner's pot before the sages of Israel and Gentiles to ascertain what heresy he and the false witnesses found in them. I also heard that with these letters he banned, anathematized and incited to strife the congregation of Acco and made brother turn against brother."[4] He therefore cautions his friend to prevent any drastic action from being taken in Rome against the monumental works of Maimonides and not to be misled by the rabbis who endorsed Petit's anti-Maimonist plans.

There exists an interesting report sent to David Maimoni in Acco, of how the Pope Nicholas IV interfered

---

They describe a spiritual state. Hillel repudiates the eschatological absurdities found in certain Jewish sources.

[3] Husik, History of Med. Jew. Phil., 1930, pp. 312-327, gives an excellent study of Hillel's ideas.

[4] *Kobetz*, III, p. 13b.

in the controversy.[5] Two Jews, Isaiah and Meir, had succeeded in getting the Pope to issue a proclamation against the partisans of Petit which was read in the synagogue at Rome. It stated that the Pope had read the Guide, most probably in the Latin translation, and found nothing harmful in it to faith. In fact, Maimonides was praised as a bulwark of monotheistic religion. Anyone who will traduce the great philosopher will be penalized by a fine of 100 silver pieces.

Let us note Hillel's opinion of Maimonides. Antagonism to the Guide may be due to honest difficulties encountered in its study, or to fanatical opposition to philosophy. As to the first, Hillel acclaims himself the best expert on the Guide and informs Isaac that if he has any difficulty with its ideas to seek his aid. He will explain everything satisfactorily. "For, praise God, I say truthfully and without boast but in praise of my Creator, who graciously bestowed it upon me, that there is today no man in Israel who knows all the mysteries of the Guide, its roots and branches, better than I do, especially the second and third parts that are the most important parts of the Guide. All his meanings are clear to me, because the books which he used for sources, namely the books of natural science and metaphysics, are known to me, as well as their commentary by a distinguished master."[6]

He has collected and elucidated all controversial parts of the Guide, including a set of absurd questions on the Guide by Nahmanides who found that it contradicted Talmudic and Midrashic writings.

Hillel proposed to call a synod at Alexandria to which

[5] Hakedem, III, pp. 111-114; Mann, *Texts and Studies*, 1931, pp. 422-423.

[6] *Kobetz*, III, p. 14d. He refers here to Averroes.

the congregations of Germany and France will be invited to send representatives. That synod should decide definitely on a trial of Maimonides' detractors. The court trial may be held in Venice, Marseilles or Genoa. If the arguments of the malcontents be reasonable and valid, the writings in question will be banned; if not, the antagonists must surrender. The judges in the trial should be the authorities of Babylon and their decision should be final.[7] Should the German and French critics of Maimonides refuse to go to trial they will forthwith be excommunicated. He thinks that Oriental Jewry should assume the rôle of Maimonides' defender in token of their historic influence and service to the cause of Judaism.

He is rather proud of the part he is playing in the controversy and he promises to write to the Nagid, David Maimoni, grandson of the philosopher, and to other celebrated authorities of Egypt and Babylon urging them to act against such rabbis as impugn the sage's writings. Hillel was gratified to learn from his friend in Rome that he did not join the anti-Maimonists, that Maimonides had many admirers in Italy, and that the authorities of Bagdad and of Damascus had made short shrift of Petit.

Quarrel between Hillel and Zerahiah

Apparently there was no unity in the ranks of either party. This is seen in the case of Hillel who though he suppressed the anti-Maimonist propaganda and genuinely admired Maimonides had a long quarrel with Zerahiah, also an advocate of Maimonidean rationalism.[8] Zerahiah

---

[7] Ibid., pp. 14d, 15a.

[8] Otzar Nehmad, II, p. 229. His views were similar to those of his contemporary Levi ben Abraham; He translated the *Pirke Moshe*, a medical book by Maimonides into Hebrew; See Otzar Nehmad, III,

was a prominent scholar who translated several Aristotelian works from Arabic into Hebrew. The quarrel between him and Hillel arose over the rationalistic exegesis of the Bible. Hillel was decidedly averse to the interpretations given in the Guide of the appearance of angels and of the wonders, and he protested to Zerahiah against the tendency to convert the Bible into a book of tales. Zerahiah in turn belittled Hillel's vaunting familiarity with the Guide. He had a poor opinion of the latter's metaphysical method. "You have shown yourself in these matters as one of the Germans, who never saw light. You have put forth an array of fallacious views betraying ignorance of philosophic literature. If in such easy and simple matters you stumble, what can I hope further?"[9] He had at one time regarded him as a sage like Hillel of the Talmud; now however he finds him destructive and captious. Hillel should give up his philosophical speculations and go back to the realm of unquestioning piety and mystic lore which suit him better. "Return to the land of thy fathers,..... Wrap thyself in Talit and Phylacteries, read the Book of Creation and Ben Sira. Study the Shiur Koma and Book of Secrets. Give up the books of science and secular knowledge."[10]

Zerahiah classes Hillel among the followers of Nahmanides and not of Maimonides. His opinion of the former is not very complimentary. He may be a roaring lion in the field of rabbinic literature, but his voice is of no importance when it comes to physics and metaphysics.

---

pp. 109-111, Hemdah Genuzah, I, pp. 45-46, and Steinschneider for his translations.

[9] Otzar Nehmad, II, p. 137.

[10] Ibid. He cites also his replies to queries on the Guide sent to his relative, Solomon of Barcelona, who may be identical with Solomon ibn Adret.

"He did not know the direction and the abode of light, nor the true purpose of the Guide, for he was not conversant with it. If he perused it, he was not disposed to penetrate its doors and chambers. One who understands the true purpose of the sage will not be astonished at any of his words, certainly he will not assail him, nor make open war against him."[11]

In order to avoid protracting the unpleasant dispute, Zerahia proposes to Hillel that they hold a debate in Rome and that a body of learned and representative men decide who is right.

The focal point in this polemic was the antagonism of Hillel to the metaphorical method of Maimonides. Hillel maintains that Scripture must be accepted in its simple literal sense, while Zerahia upholds the two-fold method of interpretation, the figurative and the literal. The prevailing rationalistic attitude at the time was that the double interpretation did not impugn the veracity of the Bible; the simple meaning was for the masses, the figurative one for the thinker, and the two converge to teach the same object. Such stories as the binding of Isaac and of Jonah and the whale are believed by the people at large and by many Talmudists to be factual, while the more thoughtful take them as fiction.[12]

Zerahia is at a loss to explain how Hillel could say that only the use of the literal method would be consistent with the saintly and pious character of Maimonides. Hence, we, too, must so understand Scripture. Zerahiah points out many instances of metaphorical exegesis in the works of the sage and maintains that, at all

---

[11] Ibid.; See Gudemann, *Hatorah veha Hayyim*, II, pp. 134-138, where similar severe opinions by Zerahia concerning Abraham ibn Ezra and David Kimhi are given.

[12] Otzar Nehmad, p. 138.

events, his greatness is beyond question despite any form of interpretation he may have used. Zerahiah further counsels his perplexed friend to be consistent in his expository method, to follow either the rationalist or the traditionalist view throughout in his treatment of a passage or episode, and not to apply one method to one part and another to the other.

Hillel holds the view that a real, physical encounter took place between Jacob and the angel (Gen. 32:25-33).[13] Yet he does not conceive the angel as having been corporeal. He theorizes that the motion of the angel stirred up physical forces in the air which impinged upon Jacob and struck him in the thigh. Zerahiah belittles this ingenious explanation. A prophetic experience is either real or imaginative. If angels are incorporeal we cannot conceive of them as the causes of forces having tangible effects. We cannot combine corporeality and angelic being. The story, argues the rationalist, symbolizes the conflict between the spiritual and natural forces in man, and the injury to the thigh is intended to convey the seriousness of the struggle.

The story of Abraham and the three angelic visitors (Gen. 18:1-ff.) is construed by Hillel as partly factual and partly prophetic. The prophetic or unreal part is the appearance of the three angels. Zerahiah rejects this divided interpretation and says that if their appearance was visionary, it is difficult to explain the preparation and the serving of food. The whole episode must have been either real or imaginative since Hillel himself concedes that part of the story was visionary.[14] The only conclusion is that it was all so.

[13] Ibid., p. 131.
[14] Ibid., p. 134.

Likewise, the rationalist takes Gen. 19:1-23, the story
of the promiscuity of Lot's daughters, as a vision. Hillel,
on the other hand, construes it literally and condemns
Lot for the shameful part he played. In taking the nar-
rative as metaphor, Zerahiah regards Lot as a saint and
eminently worthy of being rescued from the fate of the
other inhabitants of the doomed cities. The mention of
Lot as the divinely ordained inheritor of certain lands
proves that his action was not reprehensible, for the
simple reason that the entire episode was conceived
as an allegory.

The speech attributed to the beast in the story of
Balaam is taken literally by Hillel. The angel made the
air suitable for the production of intelligible sounds made
by the tongue of the beast, which is the natural organ
of speech. It is conceivable that this could happen even
as air might cause the strings of a harp to vibrate and
produce meaningful sounds. The alternative is to regard
the occurrence as a miracle like the division of the Red
Sea, the rescue of Daniel, and the opening of the earth
to swallow up Korah.[15] Zerahiah strenuously opposes
placing the incident of the talking beast on the same level
with these supernatural wonders, notwithstanding the
fact that it is enumerated as one of the ten marvels, pre-
ordained at creation. The entire episode, he maintains,
is metaphorical.

Hillel protests against the use of the term secrets,
sodot, to describe natural laws and phenomena. The
term is a misnomer. Such clear and well-known scientific
principles as are found in Greek philosophy cannot be
called "secrets." In doing so, Maimonides merely makes
abstruse what is simple and creates mysteries where

[15] Ibid., p. 129.

there are none. To this accusation Zerahiah replies that Maimonides described scientific and metaphysical knowledge as mysteries only from the standpoint of Scripture; where it is not openly taught, but must be derived in a recondite way. The special distinction in Maimonides' use of the word *sodot* is that it comprises *only* the principles of physics and philosophy, which are universally accepted. This shuts out the possibility of applying the term to the mysteries of the gematria, the talisman, the divine names, and all the nonsense found in the *Book of Creation*, the *Book of Raziel*, and in the *Shiur Koma*.

Chapter XV

SHEM TOB PALAKERA

Commentator of the Guide

Another effect of Solomon Petit's agitation and the issuance of the bans against him was to call forth a virile defense of Maimonides and his writings by Shem Tob ben Joseph Palakera of Spain.[1] The bans had been sent to Barcelona, perhaps to Solomon ibn Adret, where Palakera lived. In the Letter, inspired by the bans, Palakera refers not only to the adversary and fool, *mekatreg and peti* (Solomon Petit), but to the French rabbis and their narrow views. Palakera was an outstanding philosophic writer of the 13th century (1225-c. 1290), and lived in the intellectual atmosphere of Aristotle and Maimonides. Like them, he is contemptuous of the unprogressive teachers.[2] He has an important place in this controversy of 1290 because although he did not appear as an active participant, he wrote very clearly on the points at issue between the Talmudists and philosophers; praised Maimonides and his works and criticized the anti-Maimonidean standpoint. He believed sincerely that Greek philosophy was in harmony with the Torah and tradition. In the preface of his book the *Sefer ha Maalot* he proposes the familiar theory that classic philosophy had its antecedents in the patriarchs and in Solomon. In the *ha Wikkuah* he endeavored to establish the point that philosophy is a twin sister of faith and should be

[1] *Kobetz,* III, pp. 23-24; *Minhat Kenaot,* pp. 182-185; see Ashknaze, Taam Zekenim, p. 73; Malter, J O R N. S., I, Shem Tob ben Joseph Palaquera.
[2] *Sefer ha-Maalot,* p. 67.

equally prized. In the *Sefer ha Nefesh* he sums up the religio-philosophic psychology of the Middle Ages. In the *ha Mewakesh* we have a delightful half-prose and half-poetic story of the patient seeker after truth, a sort of Werther. One after the other he meets and consorts with the rich, the strong, the artisan, the physician, the good man, the grammarian, the poet, the devotee of the Torah, and lastly his ideal, the philosopher, first in the person of a naturalist, then in that of a metaphysician.

His book, Primer of Philosophy, *Reshith Hokma*, is important for its classification of learning, and because it describes exactly what medieval scholars understood by (a) natural and (b) metaphysical studies. Preceding these are the sciences of logic and the many forms of mathematical study. Natural science treats of the common elements in all simple and compound bodies, their essential nature, number and relation to each other.[3] The by-products of physical science are cognition, dream interpretation, the talismanic art and alchemy. Metaphysics covers the following fields of investigation: the study of existents, of their unity and multiplicity, agreement and difference, potentiality and actuality, cause and effect; the existence of God, of other eternal spiritual substances, and the dependence of corporeal substances and heavenly bodies on spiritual substances. The theological off-shoots of this field of inquiry are prophecy, miracles, world to come, reward and punishment, and the immortal soul.

Palakera condemns the opponents of philosophy for their narrowness in attacking such studies as are not

[3] *Reshith Hokma*, Berlin, 1902, pp. 50-51; See Efros, Palquera's Reshit Hokmah and Alfarabi's ihsa Al' ulum, J. Q. R., XXV, 1935, pp. 227-235.

related to religion proper, like mathematics, logic and astronomy. He advises against absorption in the Talmudic dialectics and regards the study of Alfasi, the Code of Maimonides and the Commentary to the Mishna as sufficient.[4]

His devotion to Maimonides is obvious from the Moreh ha Moreh, a commentary on the Guide written in 1280 which ranks, scientifically, superior to those which followed.[5] He is sickened by the struggle against Maimonides and bids the anti-Maimonists bear in mind the "frightful fate of Korah." Palakera is generous in his praise of the Mishneh Torah's systemization of the varied laws of Scripture and Talmud. For this alone the philosopher merits the greatest honor.[6]

He illustrates his faith in the universal efficacy of Maimonidean teachings by a striking example. The one who fears injury to his eyes from the sun's light will shut the windows in order to keep out the light. But he cannot stop the sun from shining upon the earth. Even so it is impossible to suppress the brilliant light shed by Maimonides, although his books be banned and burned.

He finds nothing objectionable in the Guide, nothing innovatory. Maimonides' predecessors possessed the same knowledge of the problems that divided the orthodox and the liberal, but they merely hinted at them, while he solved them, once and for all.

Palakera finds the Guide useful in three ways: (1) to refute the disbelievers, (2) to save the faithful from being lost in the perplexities and pitfalls of philosophy. The 'proofs' of philosophy are often presented with such

---

[4] *Ha Mevakesh*, p. 102.
[5] *Moreh ha Moreh*, 1837.
[6] *Moreh mekom ha Moreh*, 1885, pp. 5, 24.

certitude and finality as to make religious affirmations suffer. Maimonides wrote the Guide to show the inadequacy of the proofs. (3) To uproot the entrenched idea of a corporeal God entertained by many rabbinical authorities who were led to this gross conception by a literal acceptance of Scriptural and agadic anthropomorphisms. "I have seen many of them, one is esteemed a great rabbi and a prince who spoke derogatorily of our Master (Maimonides) for rejecting the materiality of God. I asked him, 'Do you believe that the hand of the Lord is like the hand of man?' He answered: 'It was a real hand.' When I heard this reply, I kept silent, for I knew I could not win him to the right view. For he was like an untamed cow, he reached maturity and old age without knowing the Lord. He grew up on that knowledge from his youth. That is why the Guide devotes so much space to the attributes of the true character of God. But one correct statement he made, that he does not need the Guide for the Perplexed, because he is not perplexed about the Torah. Would that all who are like him would act similarly and not refer to Maimonides. Why do they come into the deep sea when they cannot swim?"[7]

Most shocking is not that the people at large attack Maimonides but that esteemed scholars, who ought to realize his genius should do so. Palakera would restrict the study of the Guide to those whose faith has been shaken as a result of combining sacred and profane studies. Where a person's faith is not impaired or in danger, the Guide will only do harm.[8] So, medicine is useful for the sick but not for the healthy.

Philosophic study, says Palakera, is not indispensable.

[7] *Kobetz*, III, p. 23c.
[8] *Moreh ha Moreh*, p. 6.

It is just as well if one can center his entire heart and
mind on the study and practice of Judaism. On the other
hand there is nothing wrong if one cultivates philosophy
as a secondary interest prompted by a sincere desire to
ascertain its truth. The early rabbis followed that course,
for Samuel, the sage of Israel, exchanged philosophic
ideas with Gentile thinkers. Philosophy must not, however, precede the study of Torah. If it does, the scholar
is apt to reject Judaism altogether or to entertain incorrect views of it. He lays down a further rule that the
Guide must be reserved for persons who are over forty
years of age, of wide Jewish learning, and familiar with
the subject matter of the sciences. This fear, that acquired ideas of youth prejudice us against new knowledge, was felt by Maimonides. Another restriction on
philosophic study is the limited capacity of the average
individual. "Why," asks the writer, "has the fool the
price wherewith to acquire philosophy, but has no
heart?" The Guide must be studied, if at all, in the
original Arabic; to understand it fully other philosophic
writings in Arabic must be studied. The Hebrew translations are incorrect and give the superficial reader a
wrong idea of Maimonides' theology.[9]

Palakera defends Maimonides against the charge of
holding that human perfection can be acquired through
universal branches of learning.[10] He claims that the
master had in mind only material perfection. The higher
perfection can be achieved only through spiritual channels, through contemplation and comprehension of the
Supreme Being. The eternal bliss of the soul must be
understood as the culminating reward of the soul's high-

[9] *Kobetz*, III, p. 24d.
[10] *Moreh ha Moreh*, p. 19; Guide, I, 34.

est intellectual activity. The active Intellect functions
like the sun. It enables the human mind to think just as
the sun makes it possible for the eye to see.

Palakera takes issue with Maimonides' assertion that
the common people should be taught the pure concept
of God, i. e., that He has no attributes.[11] That, thinks
Palakera, is a dangerous step. Popular trust in God depends upon the belief that He possesses powers and
qualities, that He has an interest in man's welfare. The
multitude should therefore be permitted to hold the usual
orthodox views concerning the divine attributes. For it
is impossible that the average man who knows little or
nothing about logic and metaphysics should grasp the
essence or the true nature of God.

The Debate

Palakera presents the cause of philosophy in an hypo-
thetical debate between a religionist and a philosopher,
and shows that the findings of philosophy do not conflict
with revelation.[12] The religionist argues that philosophy
opposes revelation, creation, miracles and individual Providence, that it is forced to explain Judaism in line with
the heresies and infidelities that result from Greek
thought. It is not enough to cast away the un-Jewish elements in philosophy and to choose the good. Since philosophers as a class and on principle disbelieve in the
Torah, all their works must be tabooed.

The religionist argues further that philosophy is superfluous as a confirmation of religious beliefs. Their Mosaic origin gives them the stamp of finality. Acceptance
of them is based on the testimony of faithful people who

---

[11] *Moreh ha Moreh*, p. 20. Granted that God is incorporeal, philosophers differed on the advisability of teaching this doctrine to the masses.
[12] Jellinek, *Iggeret ha wikuah*, 1875.

experienced the events told in Scripture. Certainly direct evidence is more reliable than intellectual hypotheses or logical conclusions. This is the familiar argument that Judah Halevi developed so forcefully in the *Kuzari*. The religionist contents himself with accepting the dogmas in their traditional sense without entering into subtle definitions.

The philosopher retorts that Judaism is tolerant to the truth regardless of the source from which it derives. Scripture devotes considerable space (Exodus XVIII) to the idea of Jethro, an idolator. As honey is drawn from the bee, so one should receive the truth as far as possible, from whatever source, even from infidels. But philosophers are not infidels, they acknowledge the existence of God and His unity.[13]

The articles of faith are in themselves not convincing; they need the support that accrues from intellectual insight. Anything traditional may be discredited in various ways, by argument or by contradictory statements occurring in other ancient books. The philosophers even denied such perceivable things as motion and space; how much easier it is to combat the authenticity of hoary traditions. Hence, philosophy is essential to establish the absolute value of Jewish doctrines.

The Torah itself has commanded us to employ reason in its study. This is assumed in the case of Abraham who had no tradition to follow in arriving at the conception of an exalted God and hence must have arrived at it through his own reason. The Pentateuch reiterates the command to *know* God. The prophets give us the theophanies of Isaiah, Ezekiel, and Zechariah; in the Holy Writings we have thought-provoking books like the

13 Ibid., p. 6.

Psalms, Job, Ecclesiastes and Proverbs. Furthermore, the Talmudists engaged in the study of geometry, astronomy and logic.[14] The Midrash tells of the beauty of Greek civilization. The forbidden books alluded to in the Talmud are not philosophic works as many have supposed, but magic and kindred pseudo-sciences.

When the religionist contends that secular study often leads to the neglect of religious observance, to unethical conduct, and to the repudiation of the Torah, the philosopher replies that not every one is qualified for intellectual life. Even eating too much honey is harmful. As for the indecent conduct that stigmatizes certain thinkers, this has nothing to do with their intellectualism; it is caused by their disposition. For that matter we can find religious scholars of unsavory character.

The liberalist concedes that the prophet ranks higher than the philosopher. But in so far as philosophers as a class desire to discriminate between truth and falsehood, they are worthy of our consideration, whether Jewish or not. Whatever is true in their writings we may accept; the false, should be rejected.

The demonstrable proofs of philosophy were advisedly omitted from Scripture because they belong to select individuals only, while Scripture was promulgated for the multitudes.

The philosopher clinches his argument against the traditionalists by showing that, after all, philosophy coincides with the teachings of revelation in many ways; in the Ten Commandments which inculcate the existence of God and creation; both teach that God communicates with the prophets by means of angels; that God only should be worshipped; that there is a summum bonum;

14 Ibid., p. 15.

that the soul is immortal and receives retribution; both demand the practice of mercy, charity and other social virtues.[15] The only point of difference is the belief in miracles which rationalism considers contrary to nature and therefore impossible.

Solomon Petit's agitation failed because it was put down so promptly by the bans of the Oriental authorities. Besides, the increase in the number of rationalists at this time shows that the bans of the conservatives became a dead letter. A whole generation of scholars grew up to whom the Aristotelian philosophy was not a new venture but a natural fact of Judaism.

[15] Ibid., p. 16.

PART IV

THE FOURTH CONFLICT

PHILOSOPHIC VERSUS RELIGIOUS EDUCATION

Chapter XVI

THE PHILOSOPHIC HERESIES

The conflicts that we have described were climaxed by a bloodless battle over the right to study philosophy which raged in Northern Spain and Southern France, or Provence in 1303-1306. The earlier conflicts had centered around a different cause. Specifically, it was the theology of Maimonides, and the traditionalists had fought bitterly to destroy the Guide for the Perplexed and the Book of Knowledge. But the war against Maimonides failed. Even from the first it was always emphasized that the opponents had nothing against Maimonides personally. His fame and his books were vindicated.

The struggle we are now to study was anti-philosophic, not anti-Maimonist. Far from attacking Maimonides, the active leaders often asserted their respect for him. The conservatives of Provence and Spain now turned against philosophy in general and against the rationalist interpretation of the Bible which had become very popular. Yet Maimonides dominated the arena in this long and bitter quarrel, for both sides frequently referred to him, the one to show that he encouraged philosophy, the other to show that he restricted its study to the educated minority.

167

The main theatre of the conflict was Provence, situated between France and Spain. In certain matters of custom and law, Provencal Jews differed from their neighboring coreligionists. For our purpose, it is essential to remember that in Provence the two cultures of the adjacent countries, Talmudism and philosophy met. Provence was the home of Abraham ben David and the ibn Tibbons; and here where the two cultures were diffused the clash occurred.[1] The zeal of Provencal Jews for scientific and metaphysical learning was unusual, and its effect upon Judaism appeared in a critical examination of Holy Writ. Some of the congregations stood out more conspicuously as centers of Jewish and liberal learning. A correspondent of Abraham ben David pictured the foremost Provencal communities of Montpellier, Lunel and Nimes, as follows: "The first is the temple mount, the second is the hall of the temple, the last is the inner chamber, the seat of the Sanhedrin, whence the law goes forth to Israel."[2] It is worthwhile noting that the vast Orient from Egypt to Persia drops out completely from this controversy. Its communities and teachers take no part in it. The cause for this may be the unimportance of Oriental Jewries in this period due to their diminished numbers and their loss of intellectual leadership. The centers of Jewish life had moved to Europe where Jewish civilization had taken root and was now flourishing.

As in the controversy of 1232-1235, so now the battle lines were clearly defined. On one side stood a solid phalanx of noted scholars who placed full faith in the oral and written Law, to whom sacred literature repre-

[1] See E. M. Hulme, *Renaissance and Reformation*, p. 67, for the state of general culture in Provence.
[2] *Temim Deim*, 1896, no. 7, p. 3b.

sented the epitome of human wisdom, the alpha and omega of all knowledge. These spurned the liberal studies. On the opposite side were ranged the devotees of philosophy who insisted that it had a rightful province within the domain of Judaism. They respected philosophy, putting it forward, not as an enemy of religion, but as another vehicle for the articulation of truths revealed by God. These were the admirers of Maimonides.

Between these two broad views there were shades of opinion. Some traditionalists said that the natural wish to explore the sensible and supersensible realms might be gratified under certain limitations. If the individual had saturated himself with rabbinic learning, he might, upon maturity, be permitted to enter the *Pardes,* "the paradise of fools," as the study of philosophy was called. A distinction was drawn also between the original writings of Gentile authors and the works of Jews. Some wanted to prohibit the former only and allow the latter; others urged a contrary course. At one time in the controversy, the question was raised whether the objection extended to suspected Jewish studies, like the rationalization of Scripture, or applied simply to books on science and philosophy. Thus, although the active leaders theoretically opposed philosophy, they did not set out to suppress it entirely, but only to curb its promiscuous study. One thing was certain, the enemy of Judaism was Greek philosophy.

If there is any vagueness about the cause of the strife that divided Jewry in the first decade of the 14th century, it is cleared up by the *Sefer ha Yoreah,*[3] a short treatise in which Abba Mari ben Moses, instigator of the

[3] *Minhat Kenaot,* 1838, pp. 125-130.

dissension, revealed the state of mind of those opposed
to independent inquiry. The extreme orthodox scorned the
rationalist method and its obnoxious deductions as
flounderings of a mind in error — a mind given to speculation. Philosophy was the natural parent of heresy.
By kindling interest in all the sciences, general and exact, it touched man's conscious life at every point. Hence,
philosophy easily gained adherents and usurped the
crown of supremacy. Having gone so far, it exploited
Scripture for further evidence of the truths and theories
of philosophy.

Besides the fact that intellectual inquiry could not
establish the validity of religious claims, it created a
hazardous situation for Judaism. It involved the surrender of the doctrines such as individual providence,
creation, and miracles.[4] When the philosopher, for instance, laid great stress upon furnishing metaphysical
proof that God exists, he appeared to be rendering Judaism a service. Actually, the existence of God cannot be
made patent to the naked eye, nor proved by argument.
One did not need a ladder to climb to the skies to behold
Him. Faith and personal experience much more than
logic, offered adequate assurance of His existence. So,
too, it is foolhardy to try to prove on a scientific basis
the manner of the world's origin, Providence, the nature
of the soul, or life in the hereafter. Even the occasional
employment of philosophic aid became in the long run
an entering wedge which insidiously helped to weaken
the foundation of Judaism.

Before stating the objectionable teachings that provoked the orthodox it is important to know that all
through the 13th century a battle raged over Averroism

4 Ibid., p. 127.

among Christians. Averroes, a contemporary of Maimonides, was the most famous medieval commentator of Aristotle. His deductions conflicted with Christian doctrines and his followers were accused by the more conservative in the Church of over-devotion to philosophy and science. Their idea of the unity of reason, or of one universal reason, took away the foundation of belief in personal immortality. The idea that matter is eternal and the world therefore uncreated negated the Biblical story of creation. With this went the idea of God's providence, of human free-will and responsibility. The Averroists put forward the theory of the double truth, that philosophy and theology are both right, although incompatible. The most noted teacher of these Averroistic ideas was Siger of Brabant who was tried and condemned by an inquisition to life imprisonment. Solomon ibn Adret and especially Abba Mari refer frequently to these heretical beliefs as the inevitable conclusions of Aristotle's philosophy. Abba Mari speaks sadly of the people's hunger for Aristotle's *Physics* and the *De Senso et sensato*. He cites Averroes' Commentary on Aristotle's work *De Coelo,* wherein proofs are given for the eternity of the heavenly bodies, thus rejecting creation.[4a]

Allegorization:

The preaching of heresy, *kefirah, minut* which Abba Mari blamed directly on the vogue of secular learning drove the traditionalists to issue their protest. The scandalous preaching took the form of public lectures at synagogues and at wedding ceremonies.[5] Many of the rationalists were teachers who propagated their ideas in

[4a] Ibid., pp. 123, 127.
[5] Ibid., pp. 31, 175; *Malmad ha Talmidim,* pp. 124b, 129a.

the classroom or as private tutors. They were thoroughly familiar with and taught sacred as well as scientific subjects. As we might expect they often published their alleged irreligious views.

The main charge against them seemed to be that they turned scriptural texts into philosophic allegories. The traditionalists rejected such interpretations as subversive of Judaism. The Bible stories require no elucidation other than that which is obvious. Their real worth lies in their inculcation of the doctrines of Judaism. If the Bible was not to be believed literally, they argued, skepticism concerning the reliability of revelation resulted. With one bold stroke the rationalistic method wiped away the genuineness of Biblical personalities and events. Indeed, Jacob Anatoli, whose *Malmad ha Talmidim* had been caught in the thickest of the battle, held that there was no actual utterance by God at revelation. A voice, not divine, created solely for that activity, had been heard. And even this voice the people did not hear distinctly: only Moses did. If, then, as the rationalists asserted, the patriarchs were not real human beings, but philosophic types, what became of early Hebrew history and of all the religious principles predicated on their lives?

Although the Midrashic and Geonic writings contain many allegories of Scripture, there is a wide difference between this early activity and that of the rationalists. The former had a Jewish basis and motive, and was national and pietistic. Even when Maimonides allegorized, he invested the episode or figure with a greater ethical importance. Not so with the rationalists of this century whose treatment of Holy Writ may be described as a kind of scholastic typology. The difference between it and allegory consisted in this: allegory may or may not accept the historical truth of the stories of Scripture: whereas typology demands that the things it deals with be as true as the applications it makes. Now the question can properly be raised: Did the rationalists believe in the reality of the Scriptural facts, using them in addition as symbols or types of other things? Or were the traditionalists justified in their fears that the rationalists took the texts only as allegories, hence fictitious?

Rational Typology:

Jacob Anatoli in his *Malmad ha Talmidim* allegorized the Bible very freely. En Duran, a younger brother of Abba Mari,[6] enumerated in his reply to Meiri's letter some of the bizarre metaphorical interpretations which transfigured Biblical characters, making of them philosophic personifications.[7] Abraham and Sarah were form and matter.[8] Lot was intellect, his wife matter.[9] Maimonides referred to Plato's view that form was male and matter, female, which was based on the notion that woman contributes the matter and man the form of their offspring. Isaac was the active soul; Rebecca, the intelligent soul. Leah was the perceptive soul, and her five sons the five senses: Reuben — sight, Simeon —

[6] Steinschneider, *Jewish Literature*, 1857, p. 93.

[7] Kaufman, Simeon ben Josephs Sendschreiben an Menachem ben Salomon, *Zunz Jubelschrift*, 1884. The name of the letter in Hebrew is Hoshen Mishpat. This document is extremely valuable and gives the course of the conflict; Cf. Kaufmann, *Die Sinne*, pp. 12-15, 17-18; and the symbolic interpretation of Isserles, *Torat-ha-Ola*, I, p. 7, III, p. 5.

[8] *Minhat Kenaot*, pp. 41, 50, 51, 54, 61, 69, 77, 118; Jost, *Geschichte des Judenthums*, 1857-1859, refers this not to Scriptural stories, but to the legend of Abraham and Sarah in *Baba Batra*, p. 58a. For numerous references to this notion, see Steinschneider, *Jewish Literature*, p. 293, note 10.

[9] *Minhat Kenaot*, p. 41; *Malmad ha-Talmidim*, p. 19a, p. 25b.

hearing, Levi — feeling, Judah — smell, Isaachar — taste. In addition, she had a sixth son, Zebulun the *common* sense. Dinah was the functioning of sensations induced by the imagination. Dan is the correct imagination; Naphtali, the imagination of impossible things. Zilpah was the appetitive power; Asher, seeking; Gad, deprivation (self-denial). Rachel was the spirit of God, ruah-el, the intelligent soul; Joseph the practical faculty, and Benjamin the theoretical faculty. Joseph's sons, Manasseh and Ephraim, also represented the practical and the theoretical.[10] The twelve tribes were taken to mean the twelve constellations.[11]

Kederlaomer was the imaginative power that retains sense impressions after their stimuli have ceased. The five kings were five powers of the soul and the four kings represent the four elements (Gen. XIV).

In the rationalization of the story of Moses' birth, Exodus 2:1: "And there went a man from the house of Levi" symbolized the birth and formation of man; "man" was form; "a daughter of Levi" was the perfect matter; from the union of these two (ben hachomot), the physical and spiritual worlds, comes the human being.

Exodus 2:2: "And she bore a son" alludes to the birth of the intellect; "She hid him" means Moses waited until he reached his fullest development before he appeared before Pharoah; the name of Pharoah's daughter, Batya, was explained as Active Intellect (daughter or effect of God); Pharoah was allegorically taken to mean God.[12]

In Exodus 2:16, the priest of Midian was the judging

---

[10] Hoshen Mishpat, pp. 158, 160.
[11] Ibid., pp. 16, 41 and 54.
[12] Hoshen Mishpat, p. 160.

soul; his seven daughters, the seven faculties of the soul, or the seven sciences; sheep were the people who are led like sheep by the shepherds, their leaders; Zipporah was divine knowledge. Gershom and Eleazar represented the practical speculative faculties. Amalek betokened the evil impulse.[13]

Exodus 3:1, relating how Moses tended the flock of Jethro and led it into the wilderness to the mountain of God at Horeb, was paraphrased as follows: Moses led the Hebrew people (sheep) according to reason (ha midbar) and attained the pinnacle of perfection (mountain of God).[14]

The Garden of Eden was a name for science and philosophy; so we find that the rabbis actually described philosophy as Paradise. The intellect was the Eden of pure forms. In this Eden was the Garden where grew all trees. The tree of life represented metaphysics; the tree of knowledge, political knowledge. Man was ordered not to indulge in the latter, although he need not reject it completely. But when he ate to excess of this tree he was severely punished.[15]

Anatoli interpreted allegorically, not as factual, the three sons of Adam, Cain, Abel and Seth. They represented respectively, acquired intellect or practical knowledge, unselfish exercise of will, and union with the highest soul through the acquisition of knowledge.[16]

The seven-branched candlestick (Menorah) symbolized the seven planets; and its formation from a single mass of gold conveyed the philosophic idea that the universe

[13] Ibid., p. 151.
[14] The same interpretation is given by Isserles, *Torat ha-Ola*, p. 54b.
[15] *Minhat Kenaot*, p. 142a.
[16] *Malmad ha-Talmidim*, p. 22a.

was one solid substance, containing no vacuum.[17] The tabernacle, ark, mercy seat, cherubim, the veil and the table all bore intimations of the divine governance of the world. The table with its two groups of six loaves of bread represented the twelve constellations of the zodiac. The twelve stones on the Ephod had some representative connotation. The breast-plate set with its four rows of stones was an emblem of the four seasons of the year, and its twelve names of tribes the twelve constellations.

As punishment for the cowardice of the spies, God kept Israel in the desert for forty years, until the evil star should change its position. The star of Moses was helpless against the star of Amalek, which explained why he ordered Joshua to fight Amalek. He ordered Phineas to resist the Midianites also because his own star was not in the ascendant. Neither could the great deliverer oppose the thirty-one kings of Palestine. Another reason offered for the people's stay in the wilderness was that Moses communed with God through the thick cloud, representing his own material intellect. When the cloud lifted (Number 9:17) the spiritual glory of God descended and the people advanced.[18] From all this it seems that the alleged crime of the allegorists was the same as that charged against some of the higher critics of the Bible in recent years, namely, that the early figures of Bible history never lived and that the stories about them are myths and fables.

The Urim and Thummim and the Astrolabe

Among the specific cases of heresy was stressed the identification of the Urim and Thummim which the high-

[17] Ibid., p. 137a.
[18] Hoshen Mishpat, p. 160.

priest wore on his breast plate (Exodus 28-30) with the astrolabe, an ancient instrument, used for astronomic observation and astrological purposes.[19] Abraham ibn Ezra criticized Rashi for taking the Urim and Thummim to be a sacred article containing the ineffable name.[20] He did not himself say what it was, but only that it was a deep mystery. Nahmanides, quoted Ibn Ezra's view as being that the Urim and Thummim is a metallic instrument, which, of course, he rejected. According to Nahmanides the Urim and Thummim communicated the divine will and its power was beneath that of prophecy but superior to that of the bat kol. (divine voice).

Abba Mari related that on a Sabbath in July, 1305, he expounded Numbers 22:7, "with the rewards of divination in their hand" to mean the astrolabe. The official reader differed with him and explained that the astrolabe was used by the Talmudic sages to determine the new moon, thus including it among the Jews' religious articles.[21] Abba Mari, however, cited Maimonides to the effect that the Scriptural prohibition of sorcery, *Me'onen,* was directed against those who determined by the stars what time was propitious for certain events. Abba Mari included the astrolabe in that category, repudiating it as an instrument used to determine the new moon. This the rabbis ascertained by calculation and observation.

It seems that Ibn Adret permitted the consulting of the astrolabe on Sabbath,[22] a thing prohibited by Abba

[19] *Minhat Kenaot,* pp. 105, 106, 107, 119; Hoshen Mishpat, p. 159. S. Gandz, The Astrolabe in Jewish Literature, H U C Annual, 1927, pp. 469 seq.

[20] Ibn Ezra on Ex. 28:6; Gen. 31:19. He wrote a book on the Astrolabe; Jacob ben Machir, protagonist of rationalism in this controversy, translated a work on the Astrolabe written by Ibn Al-Saffar.

[21] *Minhat Kenaot,* p. 106.

[22] In response to a Perpignan inquirer; Ibn Adret, *Responsa,* Levow, 1811, I, no. 772.

Mari and others. The anti-intellectualist, Asher ben Jehiel, refrained from passing an opinion on the astrolabe. "I do not know what to answer. I do not know the instrument, and it is a time to keep silent."[23]

Rationalizing the Precepts:

The orthodox took even more vigorous exception to the rationalization of precepts. Reasons for the Biblical laws to the orthodox way of thinking, were not ascertainable by the Jew who lived in benighted lands, separated from the fountain of inspiration, the center of learning, Palestine. Perchance the secrets would be divulged in the blissful Messianic age when Israel, free from vexation, would regain the knowledge of forgotten lore.[24]

But the rationalists, following Maimonides, insisted that every ritual act must be intelligently explained. Thus, for instance, they attached no mystery to the use of salt at sacrifice. It was simply a preservative. The injunction against seething a kid in its mother's milk meant, symbolically, that one should not use the unripe fruit of philosophic inquiry. Certain foods were prohibited for health reasons. The laws of impurity and other rites were explained historically or psychologically.

In imitation of Maimonides, Jacob Anatoli graded the precepts, according to the objects they subserved. Their highest object was to sustain the right spiritual life and comprised belief in God's existence and unity, and in the duty of loving and imitating Him by the practice of

[23] *Min. Ken.*, p. 111.

[24] In this ingenious way, Abba Mari explains the statement "God will reveal the reasons for the laws to Israel," and the view that the "Torah is destined to be renewed," namely, not that new laws will be formulated, but that the lost knowledge of ancient Israel will be restored.

honorable conduct.[25] A second class of less essential precepts, such as phylacteries, fringes and mezuzah had for its purpose the stimulation of interest in the principal duties and beliefs of a Jew. A still lower class required the performance of occasional duties like fasting and blowing of the shofar in order to restore the moral and intellectual equilibrium of man.

Doctrinal Heresies

The rationalists denied the creation of the world, God's knowledge of and Providence over this earth and man's life, the existence of an after-life, the miracles, such as the revelation at Sinai, the sending of the manna, the dividing of the Red Sea, and the standing still of the sun.[26] In other words supernaturalism was rejected. Any one who accepts the undemonstrable teachings of religion is put down as a fool. The entire Torah they characterized as mere legislation enacted by Moses, and not as divine revelation *Torah min ha Shamayim.*

We find criticism of the view that the soul is intellect and that the apex of human development is the intellectual life;[27] also of the philosophic theory that the celestial spheres are made of a fifth element or substance purer than the matter of our mundane sphere, with the implication that the former is primary or eternal.

The orthodox favored the theory of divine attributes[28] in order to preserve the concept of a real, personal God. The philosophic party, however, ridiculed the popular belief in the corporeality of God and the angels. They cast doubt on the doctrine of resurrection by circulating the theory that the revival of the son of the Zarephite

[25] *Min. Kem.*, p. 155a.
[26] Ibid., pp. 31, 41, 46, 59, 69, 120, 151, 152.
[27] Hoshen Mishpat, pp. 154-171.
[28] Ibid., p. 142.

(I Kings 17:17) was a case of resuscitation rather than
resurrection. They rejected without qualification the belief in devils,[29] asserting that "one should only accept
that which is perceived by the senses, understood by the
intellect, or handed down by tradition." They joined the
precept ordering the covering of the blood of sacrifices
with the superstition that demons fed on blood. According to their own lights, of course, demons stood for
impulses and forces planted by God in our natures
for our own good, but sometimes abused by us.

Rationalizing Talmudic Legends

The legends of the Talmud fared no differently at the
hands of the rationalists. They bore down with particularly strong denial on the Talmudic statement that the
letters *Men* and *Samek* of the Ten Commandments were
suspended in mid-air.[30] The intellectuals also rejected
the opinion that the ark occupied no space in the temple.[31] One legend, the allegorization of which caused
considerable stir, was that of the Amora Benai and his
visit to the graves of Abraham and Sarah.[32] The opening of the three judgment books, for the righteous, the
wicked and the average man on New Year (Rosh Hasha-
na 16b) and the statement in Abot II, I, were declared
metaphorical and not real fact.[33] The other eschatological view that the righteous will wear crowns in the world
to come and will partake of the leviathan and preserved
wine were construed figuratively. The legend of a huge

[29] Ibid., p. 184a.
[30] *Shabbat*, p. 104a; Perles, R. *Salomo ben Abraham ben Adereth*,
1863, p. 72, note 65.
[31] *Megillah*, 10a.
[32] *Min. Ken.*, p. 69; Hoshen Mishpat, p. 147.
[33] *Malmad*, p. 175a.

stone hurled at Israel by Og, king of Bashan, expressed the conflict between the good and evil impulses.[34]

A distressing consequence of the popular absorption in philosophy was the neglect of the proper study of the Bible and the Talmud. The rightful lore of the Jew is the Torah. Since the dawn of history it has been his greatest concern. True, some of the doctors of the Talmud possessed the wisdom of other nations, and the subjects debated in the Talmudic tractates presumed a knowledge of many sciences; nevertheless the Torah always was their principal passion.

Another disastrous result of the allegorical exegesis was the reduction of religious ceremonies to a nullity. Rationalism seemed to dissolve Judaism. Indeed, many traditionalists voiced their misgivings that a growing contempt for ceremonial Judaism might be laid directly at the feet of misleading interpreters of the Bible.[35] The Scriptural ordinances of the dietary laws, succah, lulav, phylacteries and many other observances were flouted. Scepticism grew about the power of prayer. Such was the ominous danger that lurked in the new rationalism.

On the ground that greater havoc would result from an open break between the two parties, some rabbis like Menahem Meiri of Perpignan preferred not to offer resistance to the alleged heresies. A few refused to take sides for personal or political reasons. Others, however, quickly joined ranks to seek an antidote for the heretical poison in the body politic of Israel.

[34] *Berakot,* p. 54a.
[35] *Malmad,* pp. 50, 55 and 175; *Min. Ken.,* p. 46; Palakera, *ha Wikkuah,* p. 15; Geiger, *Zeitschrift,* V, pp. 101, 106, 115.

Chapter XVII

THE VIEWPOINT OF THE RATIONALISTS

Samuel ibn Tibbon

The innovations thus far discussed were taught by a group of intellectuals whose place in Jewish thought will provide a clearer background for the struggle. These intellectual leaders were not anti-religious or anti-Jewish. They did not fall in with the critics who caused so much trouble to the Church by their denunciations of the clergy, of its doctrines and institutions. The only one among them of this type might be Joseph ibn Caspi, whom we shall consider in a later chapter. The Jews could not condemn or brand any disbeliever in their midst as a heretic with the same effect that the Church did it through the Pope or the church synods. The Jews had no such centralized organization and no final authorities. The thing that came nearest to the Church's heresy laws was the ban. The ban was not very effective, for despite the impressive ceremony that attended its proclamation, it was often local, temporary and personal.

Several of these teachers who called down upon their heads the wrath of the orthodox, like Samuel ibn Tibbon and Jacob Anatoli, died about three-quarters of a century before the conflict; yet they are important because they and their views are often referred to. Besides epoch-making translations, Samuel ibn Tibbon (1150-1230) wrote a commentary on Ecclesiastes[1] and philosophic

---

[1] This commentary is still unpublished; The Ms. is in the library of the Jewish Theological Seminary of America.

discourses under the title Yikawu ha Mayim.[2] In the latter he was aware that he was treading on dangerous ground, but he believed that the end justified the means.

Of course, he did not pin his faith on the Bible as a literal record. He explained the Talmudic opinion that the Torah spoke in the language of men to mean that Scriptures sometimes used exaggerated or hyperbolic phraseology such as a person may do, or as is found in poetry. The anthropomorphism of the Bible, or the ascription of human parts to God and the intelligences must be understood in this way.[3]

It is worth noting that ibn Tibbon following Maimonides and David Kimhi devoted himself to study the creation story and the chariot vision, the great mysteries, the exposition of which was held to be sacrilegious and was regularly denounced by the traditionalists. The chariot visions of Isaiah and Ezekiel were said by Samuel ibn Tibbon to represent not a real throne, but a figurative description of the divine governance of the world.[4]

He candidly declared that he trod in the footsteps of Maimonides and dealt with subjects that the Talmud proscribed in order to strengthen Judaism which was losing ground on account of the people's interest in philosophy. Ignorance of these matters only lessened the world's esteem for Israel, and belied its boast of being "a wise and understanding people." He praised Maimonides for venturing to set forth the philosophic ideas of incorporeality, of the Intelligences, and the meaning of the precepts. He defended his own loyalty

2 *Yikawu ha-Mayim*, 1837; The title is from Gen. I, 9 and means 'Let the waters be gathered together.'
3 Ibid., pp. 20, 21.
4 Ibid., pp. 122 seq., 46-53.

and piety, and disclaimed any motive to assault the citadel of Judaism.

This secret knowledge had been transmitted cautiously from hoary antiquity. The prophets and sages had concealed it. But now it had become public knowledge. Everywhere Scripture was weighed in the balance against philosophic principles, and there was no longer any virtue or logic in withholding the result from the masses of the Jewish people.

At the top of man's thinking life must be metaphysical study. This Samuel ibn Tibbon found asserted in Jacob's dream. The ladder was man's reason, which stood on an earthly base, but reached to the heaven, which was transcendental knowledge.[5]

It is interesting, too, to mark that in his formulation of Jewish tenets, he named the existence of God, providence, retribution and immortality among the doctrines, but omitted revelation. Furthermore, in making a doctrine of immortality, and not of resurrection, he ignored the tradition that reserved reward and punishment for the resurrected body.

The predilection of the family for translation appeared in Samuel's son Moses, (d. 1283). He lived in Montpellier and like his father made the scientific works of the Greeks and the Arabs accessible to Jews. In his theology and Scriptural exegesis he followed Maimonides and his uncle, Jacob Anatoli. The stories of the Bible were parables filled with an inner meaning. In line with this attitude, his opinion on the Song of Songs rendered it pure metaphor and poetry as the title *Shir*, song, indicated.[6] This collection of songs enacted the drama of the longing and the possibility of man's reason to unite with

[5] Ibid., p. 174.
[6] *Commentary on Canticles*, 1874, p. 8.

the Active Reason. The Commentary gives us a valuable chapter on medieval psychology and theories of knowledge. Man's soul is conceived as female (Shulamit). The beloved (dod) is the Active Reason which stimulates man's hylic or potential reason. The 'daughters' are the faculties of the soul.[7] In "Jerusalem" the matured soul reached perfection.

Activity of this kind shows the marked trend of secular influence in Israel and accounts for the clash between the traditionalists and the liberals in the first decade of the 14th century.

Jacob Anatoli

The partiality of the Tibbonide family for secular studies had its exponent in Jacob ben Abba Mari Anatoli,[8] scientist and philosopher (c. 1194-1256), son-in-law of Samuel ibn Tibbon. During the controversy that raged in Provence and in Northern Spain in 1232, he lived in Naples, receiving a yearly stipend from the Emperor, Frederick II (1194-1250),[9] for his translations. Frederick's Sicilian court was a center of intellectual activity. The patronage extended by this ruler to scholars proved how a premium was set on culture and science in those days.[10] Michael Scotus, the scholastic with whom Anatoli associated in the service of the Emperor, was mentioned repeatedly by Anatoli in the *Malmad* as his co-worker. Anatoli could see no point in the criticism directed at him for voicing the views of a

---

[7] Ibid., p. 12.

[8] Jacob ben Abba Mari was the great-grandson of Anatoli ben Joseph, Dayyan of Alexandria, correspondent and admirer of Maimonides, *Kobetz*, I, p. 28a, II, pp. 36-37.

[9] *Malmad*, p. 92; Anatoli cites Frederick II's reason for the sacrifice of domestic and not wild animals. This sovereign employed also the Jewish scholar, Judah Cohen of Toledo.

[10] Munk, *Melanges*, p. 488.

Christian scholar. The test of a statement should be not its author but its intrinsic value. He cites the broadmindedness shown by Moses in recording in the Bible Jethro's advice on the administration of justice before the giving of the ten commandments.

Anatoli was in the habit of preaching rationalistic sermons at weddings. Some of his discourses were especially designated as appropriate for such occasions.[11] For a time he lectured publicly every Sabbath, but on the advice of friends who wanted to avoid trouble he ceased this practice.[12] He collected his short lectures on each Section of the Pentateuch and published them under the name *Malmad ha talmidim* (The Goad of the Scholars). They became popular and spread throughout Spain, France and Italy. Its Jewish sources were Maimonides, Abraham ibn Ezra and Rashi. It was permeated also with the intellectualism of Plato, Aristotle, Averroes, and the church fathers. The mention of Anatoli, long deceased, in the polemical correspondence of 1303-1306, shows the powerful influence of his life and views. The book of this "aged king" was bitterly lashed in orthodox circles because it sent forth venom in the form of philosophic allegorization; by others it was highly regarded and was studied in school and synagogue.[13]

Anatoli stoutly denied that Maimonides rejected the doctrine of resurrection. The sage spoke with holy inspiration and followed faithfully the direction of the prophets and holy writings. The anti-Maimonists, so

11 *Malmad*, pp. 34b, 124b, 129a. This is interesting because the anti-philosophic agitators Abba Mari and others, refer a number of times to heretical views preached at weddings.

12 Ibid., p. 6b of Preface.

13 *Min. Ken.*, pp. 44, 70, 139; Gross, R E J, IV, (1882), p. 199, takes the "aged king" to refer to Samuel ibn Tibbon.

Anatoli rebuked them, would even have attacked King David, author of the psalms, if he had lived in their day.

He severely indicted the traditionalists for their shallow acquaintance with holy writ, which they read superficially as children do, without thought. They are content, he says, to skim over the text twice and the Targum once as the sages commanded.[14] But the intention of the ancients was not merely to read, but to digest and assimilate holy writ. Every Sabbath and festival day was to be an occasion for studying the text; to understand its true meaning. But the people rush through the reading of the weekly portion as though they were eager to finish an unpleasant task. This is really an abuse of the Torah, for one of the blessings reads, "O Lord, make the words of thy Torah sweet in our mouths." A delicious food should be eaten slowly and appreciatively, and not at once swallowed. So, too, one should linger and ponder over the words of the Torah. It seems, thinks Anatoli, that the sole object of the people on the sanctified days was to fill their stomachs.[15]

Anatoli, likewise, reproaches the people for their insincere and superficial observance of ceremonies. The blowing of the Shofar, for instance, had ceased to have a spiritual meaning. The people were concerned with it only as an instrument, with its beautiful shape and the clearness and volume of its sound. They had lost sight of the meaning of the fringes *tsitsith* and looked only for a prayer-shawl that would appear attractive. Public worship, too, lacked the fullest concentration, devotion and understanding. "If one were to beseech a human sov-

[14] Jonah Gerondi stresses this in the *Sefer ha Yirah* (Book of Fear), Warsaw, p. 8a.
[15] *Malmad*, p. 5.

ereign in such disgraceful manner, no one could save him from his sentence." The prophetic writings were read very infrequently and then treated only as stories fit for old people. The thought-provoking Solomonic writings were not fully appreciated.

Anatoli asserted that authentic philosophic teachings agreed perfectly with the truths of the Torah, and he stressed the need of a critical and more logical study of the contents of Scripture.[16] He pointed to Solomon as a classic instance of a thinker and scholar whose search for deep moral and religious values was evidenced by Proverbs and Canticles. The fact, too, that the Book of Ecclesiastes, despite its skepticism, had been included in the canon, attested that the synagogue favored honest investigation, provided, of course, as in the Book of Ecclesiastes, there was a foundation of faith.

The rabbinic injunction, "Withhold your children from philosophy" *higayon,* and the prohibition against studying Greek philosophy were not to be taken categorically.[17] They referred only to the young and others who were unprepared. Anatoli admitted that philosophic study called for a person of unusual attainment, one of calm temper, excellent qualities, piety and, of course, the basic knowledge of Scripture and Talmud.

Anatoli appears to have been out of sympathy with the rabbis whose impractical hair-splitting arguments were of the greatest moment to them. In their opinion metaphysical study was time-wasting as well as perni-

[16] Ibid., p. 3a.

[17] The term higayon is variously explained. Acc. to Rashi it means Scriptures. The medieval philosophers took it to mean Logic and then also philosophy. Acc. to writer in *Beth ha Midrash,* ed. I. H. Weiss, it refers to hagiogrypha like Ecclesiastes and Canticles which were allegorized; See Ginzberg, *Unbekannte Sekte,* pp. 70-71.

cious and they despised it as the invention of fools. He had quarreled with one of these rabbis who objected to his study of the sciences from Arabic writings with his father-in-law, Samuel ibn Tibbon. The charge that metaphysics and the natural sciences foster heresy and therefore should be discarded is false and cowardly. He insists that the only substantial basis for the spiritual life was metaphysics, the true wisdom, paradise, spoken of in rabbinic literature. He made so bold as to say that metaphysics was even called Torah, and to prove his point he cited the command, "be diligent in the study of the Torah, and know how to answer the heretic." How else could one answer the heretic save through philosophy? The sciences, like astronomy and mathematics were useful in stimulating and training the mind to be capable of metaphysical study.[18] The Jews had a preference for the Greek language, as appeared from the homily that the beauty of Japhet (Greece) shall dwell in the tents of Shem.

Isaac Albalag

Among the disseminators of advanced views was Isaac Albalag, whom later writers often branded outright as a heretic. Although he was not referred to in the correspondence, his views furnished a sound example of the theology attacked by the traditionalists and were clearly stated in his translation of, and commentary on the *Mukasid* of the orthodox Arab theologian Algazali, made in 1292.[19] Enamored of Aristotelian philosophy as the queen of all knowledge, and the Talmud as her lady-in-waiting, he defended the Greek thinker against the at-

[18] Ibid., p. 6a.
[19] H. Auerbach, *Albalag u. seine Uebersetzung des Mukasid al-Gazzalis*, 1906.

tacks of Algazali.[20] He even censured Maimonides for
not coming out more candidly in favor of philosophy. He
entertained no fear of philosophy's subversive effect on
religion; the former was reserved for the few, the latter
for the multitude. That was why the Bible omitted all
philosophic matters. One should not be surprised at any
contradiction between intellectualism and faith, for he
considered each supreme and independent in its own way.
Did Scripture confirm his metaphysical views, all well
and good; did it fail to do so, he accepted it none the
less as prophetic intuitive truth. Each depended upon a
different process of comprehension. Philosophy perceived the sensible through the intellect; religion perceived the intellectual through the senses.

In such wise he subscribed to the doctrine of the two-
fold truth which admitted the literalness of Scripture
as a matter of faith and held that philosophy was a purely
intellectual pursuit. This doctrine was prevalent in non-
Jewish circles.[21] The synagogue frowned upon it. The
Jews were either harmonizers, or like Judah Halevi and
Crescas, they tried to refute Aristotelian teachings. Albalag, therefore, differed from Maimonides, who had to
establish the tenability of Scriptural teachings from the
philosophic standpoint. He exceeded the rationalism of
Maimonides with his theory of the world's beginning.
For instance, whereas the latter did not dare to postulate
the doctrine of an uncreated world, Albalag drew from
Scripture the hypothesis of the world's eternity.

Albalag was the first of the rationalists who openly
took the field against obscurantism or mysticism, which
had penetrated into Jewish life. Far better, he thought,

[20] ha-Halutz, IV, pp. 92, 93.
[21] Lange, *The History of Materialism*, pp. 218-219.

for one to endorse the literal meaning of Scripture than mystic interpretations, that are neither philosophic nor prophetic.[22]

That he himself did not construe the Bible literally is obvious. But he realized that the mass of the people could not comprehend God save as a corporeal, local and finite being. They lacked the power to grasp a metaphysical concept. Hence, Scripture, purporting to bring a blessing to man, must address itself to the masses. It promised material rewards and penalties when it meant to offer spiritual ones; it spoke of this eternal world in terms of time. Of course, the wise knew that there were 'mysteries of the law' that disclosed the true character of retribution, God and the cosmos.

Levi ben Abraham

The free-thinker Levi ben Abraham (1250-1320)[23] was directly responsible for the anti-philosophic outbreak. Born in Villefranche near Perpignan, he moved at the age of eighteen to Montpellier where he was instructed in the sciences by Moses ibn Tibbon. He wrote his alleged heretical books in 1276. When, in 1304, the scholarly Samuel Sulami had moved from Narbonne to Perpignan he invited Levi to his home to act as tutor. After considerable wandering he established himself at Arles in 1315. In his solution of the current problems, he followed Abraham ibn Ezra, David Kimhi and Jacob Anatoli, drawing most of his rational theology from Maimonides. His rôle in Jewish thought may best be described as a popularizer of the Guide. His encyclopedic work was much broader. Without influence or position,

---

[22] ha-Halutz, IV, p. 88.
[23] Steinschneider, *Gesammelte Schriften*, pp. 228-233; Leo Back, zur *Characteristic des Levi ben Abraham ben Chajjim*, M G W J, (1900), pp. 24-41, et al.

and as it appears, very poor, he, rather than any of the more independent rationalists, became the target of traditionalist criticism. In general, the innovations introduced by the followers of Maimonides were adopted by Levi ben Abraham and were the reason for his being *persona non grata.* A few examples will serve to illustrate his rationalistic method. He explained Exodus 33: 2: "There is a place with me," to mean that there is a degree of highest knowledge concerning God which is attainable by man. "And you will stand on the rock", signified that Moses should understand the form, *tsurah* the source of all things.[24] He submitted all the names of the deity to examination and offered the traditional as well as the newfangled meanings for them. The name, Ehye asher Ehye, he said, certified that God is always the same, after creation as before it; he found in it expressed also the philosophic truth that the Intellectus, Intellectum and Intellect are one in God. The essence of God, of course, remained a mystery, but He stood clearly revealed in His works.

He saw in the Scriptural account of Abraham both unadorned fact and a myth woven about Abraham and Sarah as form and matter. The twelve tribes corresponded to the twelve constellations. God created the world according to fifteen principles,[25] the ten pure forms and five physical elements; "Bereshit" the first principle, the highest emanation, governed the creation of heaven and earth. The ten spheres, first to be formed, approximated the ten Words, *maamorot,* by which God created the world. In his insistence on the doctrine of the creation from nothing, Levi ben Abraham differed from

[24] Back, p. 33.
[25] Isaiah 26:4; be'yah means with God, Yod (10) plus he (5).

other rationalists. "Nothing" did not have the relative or Platonic sense of primary matter, but of absolute nothingness. In fact, it would be more correct to say that the world came *after* nothing, rather than *from* nothing.

Levi ben Abraham believed that God ruled the world through intermediaries or angels, who though they emanated from Him, were not to be addressed in prayer. Without a system of angels it would be impossible to account for the control of pure spirit on this material world, or for the rise of multiplicity and change from God, the one and absolute. The Metatron of rabbinic literature was the active intellect which endowed matter with a variety of forms.[26]

Unlike Maimonides, Levi ben Abraham followed Abraham ibn Ezra in believing that stars exercised some control over human affairs. Long life depended on the stars and on natural vitality. Prayer and piety were powerless to prolong life. The most the intellectual and moral person could do was to ward off sudden death. Prayer for the sick was only a wish that God spare the stricken one from sudden death; for, in medicine as in navigation and agriculture, success depends on the presence of many natural factors.[27]

Levi's opinion of prayer is interesting as it involved the psychology of his day and what we know as the power of mind over matter. We can see why the orthodox objected to it. The act of prayer required concentration and stimulation of the reason to enable it to associate with pure forms. Genuine worship does not express

[26] Metatron is connected with the word matrona, mother and source of all things.
[27] Back, p. 68.

itself in words or supplication, but in the elevation of man's reason. With his reason in the ascendant man could rise superior to his material impulses and desires, and suppress them which is the purpose of prayer.

As Levi inherited his ideas from liberal predecessors, so he became the inspiration of an entire school that advocated his views. In this struggle he found support in Samuel Sulami, Jacob Machir, Jedaiah Bedersi, Joseph Caspi and Moses Narboni.

Chapter XVIII

THE ANTI-PHILOSOPHIC AGITATION

Abba Mari ben Moses

The thought-system of his contemporary Levi ben Abraham and of the other men considered, aroused Abba Mari ben Moses of Montpellier to instigate the controversy. To him we are indebted for most of the material relating to it. Not much is known of his personal life. He was born in Lunel; his father and grandfather were distinguished men, the latter having borne the title Nasi. His great-grandfather was the illustrious Meshullam ben Jacob of Lunel (d. 1170), whose desire for a broader culture obviously he did not inherit. After the French expulsion in 1306, he removed to Arles, later, about the end of December, 1306, going to Perpignan where many Jewish refugees had settled. In his old age he visited Barcelona, but it is not certain that he died there.[1] Judging by the homage paid to him, he certainly ranked high as a Talmudic scholar. He seemed to have been without a philosophic trend of mind, although he refers to the pseudo-Aristotelian work, *Book of the Apple,* and to Averroes' commentaries. He quoted several times from the Guide.

The simple religious affirmations that preface the *Minhat Kenaot* show the limited theological scope of his vision. He differed with Maimonides in his doctrinal formulation, reducing all Jewish beliefs to three prin-

[1] See Gross, Notice sur Abba Mari de Lunel, R. E. J., IV, (1882), pp. 192-207. Zunz, *Geschichte der Synagogal Poesie*, p. 498 ascribes to him a dirge for the 9th of Ab; This poem, it is surmised, Abba Mari wrote after the French expulsion which began in Ab, 1306.

ciples: the existence of God, creation and providence. If one were permitted to add to these three, he would have to include many more than the ten required to make up the thirteen principles of Maimonides. He was like Maimonides, however, in removing all corporeality from God. His sole reason in instigating the controversy was to rescue Judaism from the menace of the allegorists and secularists. He admits that the trouble is not widespread, nevertheless it must be checked. Not willing to set himself up as a champion he sought for some one of recognized scholarship and influence to assume the leadership of the movement. In Solomon ibn Adret, he found his man. The close and respectful association between the two is clear from the elegy composed by Abba Mari on the death of ibn Adret in 1310, which he addressed to the Barcelona congregation.

Abba Mari ben Moses himself was loud in his praise of the Guide, although he knew it to be permeated with Greek philosophy and scriptural rationalization. He lauded Maimonides as the "paragon and pattern in whose footsteps we may walk without fear of stumbling." This defense of Maimonides was not a pretense, but resulted from a genuine admiration for the erudition of the sage. Yet, it does not appear that he embraced any of the untraditional ideas of the Maimonidean philosophic works, nor did he show any special acquaintance with the great theological writings of the Jewish masters.

Abba Mari had a friendly word, too, for Aristotle, whom he styled the father of philosophy, and whom he revered for demonstrating the existence, unity and incorporeality of God. Aristotle was handicapped by lack of divine inspiration and, relying altogether on the evidence of his senses, he naturally denied creation and miracles. He received no behest from God to believe otherwise; "but if a Hebrew philosopher should be found who maintained the view of Aristotle and his proofs for the eternity of the world; who furthermore would publish works to show that Scripture may be accommodated to those erroneous opinions, or who would deny the miracles recounted in Mosaic or prophetic writings — I will not say that such a person and his book should be proscribed, but that he should forfeit his life."[2] The good teachings in Aristotle are like a jar of honey, about which a dragon is wrapped. There is danger in Greek philosophy because it rejects creation and divine guidance of man's life. In pointing to the miracles at the Exodus as a proof of creation, Abba Mari naïvely remarks "If Aristotle and his associates had been in Egypt and at the Red Sea at the time, they would not doubt the creation; he would have evidence against his own books and his theories for eternity."[3] The age of miracles did not end in the Desert or in Palestine. Israel lives in the midst of the greatest miracle, unappreciated because it is continuous and ever-present. Its survival in a world of hate and barbarous cruelty toward him is the wonder of the ages and evidences the special providence of God.

Abba Mari championed the religion of faith and trust in God, *Emunat ha Emunah* as against the religion of reason. He took for his precedent, Abraham, who fully submitted to God's word as when he was ordered to circumcise himself and to bind Isaac, acts that might well have aroused reasoned opposition. In contrast to the

2 *Min. Ken.*, p. 15.
3 Ibid.

allegorists, Abba Mari stressed the realities of Abraham's life; he explained that the precepts have reasons which will be disclosed in the Messianic era, meanwhile they must be observed; the Sabbath is a sacred institution grounded in the truth of the doctrine of creation. He supplements the philosophic proof for God from the regularity of the planetary movements and the need of a prime mover, with an argument from the unity and wonderful construction of the human organism.

Abba Mari drew a sharp distinction between the sciences and metaphysics and declared himself in favor of the former. The sciences, mathematics, astronomy, physics, and especially medicine, were utilitarian and had a place in the wisdom of the Talmudic sages. Their scientific knowledge, transmitted to them by a chain of succession from the prophets, thoroughly harmonized with Hebrew teachings. But metaphysics, comprising all transcendental knowledge, was neither practical nor urgent, and the Talmud clearly wanted to suppress it. "One should not lecture on the chariot vision to one person nor on creation to two persons." "The secrets of the Torah must not be disclosed except to the chief of the Judicial Court." These sentiments sanctioned the antiphilosophic propaganda spread by the Barcelonian Talmudist Solomon ibn Adret and his abettor Abba Mari, leaders who repeatedly cited the fact that Maimonides himself, though saturated with secular knowledge, felt the perils of too much philosophic study. The well-known Talmudic account of the four scholars who entered "Paradise", three of whom did not survive the experience, warned of the hazards of speculation. The Talmud, interestingly enough, stated that Ben Azai and Ben Zoma were immature youths when they ventured forth upon their unsuccessful metaphysical quest.

The uniqueness of Maimonides' position resided in this, that he first satiated himself with the substantial food of the written and oral Law, and completed a commentary on the Mishna at the age of twenty-eight, before he turned his mind to metaphysics. His background rendered him impervious to the errors of metaphysics. Abba Mari cited also David Kimhi to the effect that the Torah must have priority over philosophy. From this Abba Mari concluded that only persons of mature age and adequate Hebrew learning might safely gratify their intellectual yearnings; all others must avoid philosophy. Particularly was it the solemn duty of the rabbi who was a preacher and an authority to maintain an exclusive interest in the Torah.

Abba Mari voiced the current view that Israel anciently possessed metaphysical lore, most of which had disappeared as a result of the dispersion under the Romans, when the writings perished. An extremely meagre part of universal Hebrew wisdom had seeped through into the speculative literature of the Greeks; we see it in their proofs for the existence, unity and incorporeality of God. But the greater part of the original universalistic lore of Israel could not be recovered until the Messianic Era.

Beginning of the Struggle; Solomon ibn Adret

With the aid of Ibn Adret and other notables of Spain and France, Abba Mari started a lively agitation to issue a ban against Greek writings and to excommunicate those who read such works. The propaganda covered a period of about three years. Few of the letters gathered

by Abba Mari were dated, but fortuntely we have two
definite dates, Ellul, 1304, and 1306.[4] A good deal of the
controversy must have taken place before Ellul, 1304;
but we are at a loss to place its beginning accurately.
Bearing in mind that the correspondence collected by
Abba Mari is only a part of the polemical literature, and
remembering also that the ban proposal brought to Montpellier in Ellul, 1304, was preceded by considerable propaganda, we need not doubt that several years of intense
struggle led up to the final Barcelona ban of 1305.

Abba Mari had enlisted one of the foremost authorities
of his time, Solomon Ibn Adret (1235-1310) in his cause.
At an early age he became the chief rabbi of Barcelona,
his birthplace, and the capital of the kingdom of Aragon.
His Responsa, numbering thousands, were addressed to
France, Germany, Italy, Palestine, Asia and Africa. His
teachers were the two conspicuous Talmudists and theologians, Jonah Gerondi and Nahmanides,[5] both of whom
had been active in the anti-Maimonidean conflict of 1232.

Although he fought against putting the sciences and
metaphysics into the course of studies for young people,
Ibn Adret was not an ignorant reactionary. He was familiar with Jewish rational theology, and had a more
open mind than Asher ben Jehiel who soon joined him.
It is interesting to find that he expounded the Talmudic
legends in a way that banished their literalism. Ibn

---

[4] The second of the three bans proclaimed in Barcelona on July 31,
1305, states that the anti-philosophic propaganda had extended over a
period of about three years. This would place the beginning in the fall
of 1302. There are no letters in the *Minhat Kenaot* of that year; the
first two dated letters are for Ellul, 1304, one by Moses ben Samuel
of Perpignan to Abba Mari ben Moses, describing the effect of Ibn
Adret's proposal upon the Perpignan congregation; the other reports the
failure of the ban in Montpellier due to the Tibbonide opposition.

[5] Perles, p. 59, note 4.

Adret had a deep affection for Maimonides and cherished his writings which demonstrated so clearly that the great sage always stood on *terra firma* and was immune against the disintegrating influence of alien learning. He adroitly used philosophy and science as ingredients to preserve Judaism. Ibn Adret showed great respect for the sage's memory. He aided in the translation of the Arabic Commentary to the Mishna into Hebrew, and was considerate of Maimonides' grandson, David Maimoni, leader (nagid) of Egyptian Jewry (1223-1300). David had sought financial aid from Ibn Adret, probably in order to bribe the Sultan, when his relations with the latter had become strained. Magnanimously, Ibn Adret sent Simon ben Meir of Toledo with letters to all Spanish congregations, and as a result, the sum of five thousand novenes was collected.[6] Ibn Adret himself took part in the anti-Maimonidean controversy of 1290, by backing the Exilarch Hezekiah of Damascus against Solomon Petit, the anti-Maimonist.[7]

Our documents begin with a debate on the permissibility of using the talisman in the shape of a stone with a lion engraved on it to effect a cure. Ibn Adret had approved its use, in reply to a query from the Perpignan physician, Isaac ben Judah de Lattes. Abba Mari took issue with Ibn Adret on the ground that the use of the talisman bordered on idolatry and should be prohibited.[8] It came under the law prohibiting the practice of magic (Lev. 19:26). The scholars of Provence do not allow it.

---

[6] *Min. Ken.*, p. 138; *Sefer Yuhasin*, p. 219.

[7] *Israelitische Letterbode*, Amsterdam, IV, (1878-1879), p. 130; the documents referred to by Ibn Adret are unfortunately not extant.

[8] *Min. Ken.*, pp. 21 seq., cf. Ibn Adret, *Responsa*, Vienna ed., no. 168. See on this subject, Preuss, *Biblish-talmudische Medizin*, 1911, pp. 159-171.

Ibn Adret cited as his precedent Nahmanides; and also evidence from the Talmud that countenanced certain forms of magical activity. His theory was that God endowed nature with multifarious healing properties. The forces of nature must restore that which has deteriorated. Even language may possess this power. He therefore permits the use of incantations and amulets. Hence, in healing one who is sick, all scruples concerning the "ways of the Amorite" might be disregarded. The adjuration: "thou shalt be perfect with the Lord thy God," was not directed against magic arts of healing, but against demoralization through degenerate heathen habits.

Ibn Adret displayed some tolerance by refusing to condemn categorically all that was contained in books of magic. "We cannot put them all in one class and either permit or forbid all, for even in books of witchcraft and magic there are things that are permissible." Even philosophic writings that were permeated by the vicious principle that the laws of nature were immutable, consequently ruling out all the miracles of Scripture, might nevertheless contain some good views.

Along with this question of magic Abba Mari broached the further matter to Ibn Adret of taking action against the heresies. At first, Ibn Adret, although admitting the existence of the abuses, declined to join his colleague, and the latter had to use his most persuasive powers to win him over. He argued plausibly that the problem was not a local one, for the French Jews only. As a matter of fact, Montpellier, his native town, was distinguished by great piety and rabbinic scholarship. He was confident that the Jews of this community would approve any anti-philosophic proposal. The conflict between religion and philosophy is of general concern. The flood tide of secularism and irreligion must be checked wherever and whenever it broke through the dam of the people's self-sufficient life based on the Torah. Abba Mari dwelt upon the seriousness of the rationalist heresies. The rationalists did not resort to secrecy, but publicly taught their views in synagogues, lecture-halls and at wedding gatherings. In this manner, they corrupted the faith of many. The fervent Psalms of David and the prayers were displaced by lectures on Aristotle and Plato. As mentioned before, Abba Mari displayed a certain tolerance toward original Greek writings because they were professedly non-Hebraic. Whatever good they contained might be used. The real peril came from books written by Jews indoctrinated with foreign philosophy, while falsely purporting to expound Judaism. In this duplicity lurked treachery to Israel. He proposed the enactment of a ban, such as was used in Talmudic times, or as those issued by the authority, Rabbenu Gershom, in the 10th century, as the most effective way to stamp out Jewish heresies.

Abba Mari could not have chosen a more sympathetic defender of tradition than Solomon Ibn Adret, one more ready to halt the trespass of the maid servant philosophy upon the domain of Jewish cultural life. Sarcastically, he ordered the people to renounce their loyalty to Akiba and Judah the Prince for their failure to bequeath them secular and philosophic knowledge. Yet with all his eagerness to serve the cause of Judaism, the Spaniard doubted the success of his leadership. He felt that the Provence, a hot-bed of rationalism, would resent the intrusion of an outsider. "If I should announce myself and place the trumpet to my mouth, who will listen to me?....I know that they will say to me, 'Who is he that dares to command us in our own household and give us understanding?' " He gracefully suggested that Abba Mari seek a champion of the ban in his own country.

He advanced even a step further than Abba Mari in condemning original Greek writings as the source of heresy. These books patently made secular learning the sole quest of man and the acme of his achievement. The Greek mind pondered upon nature and reality, subjects possessing a great fascination for man. Life being in a great measure physical, it was only natural that we should be curious about the natural sciences. One must therefore exert all the more caution against the tyranny of the scientific habit.

Regrettably, Jews had cast their lot in with Hellenistic philosophy. The very names of the Greek speculators charmed them. Even the uninformed who had not read the works in question accepted their statements, out of sheer hero-worship for the authors. In such hands, philosophy became a devastating fire licking around the base of faith; marring, if not completely wiping out, the observance of Judaism.

"He who teaches that Abraham and Sarah are only form and matter," remarked Ibn Adret, "proves more than a hundred witnesses could that he is not of the seed of Abraham, not even of the seed of Esau and Ishmael, but descended of the nocturnal demons." Scientific knowledge, he went on to say, might be in the same questionable position as the book of Ben Sira, which, although it was cited in the Talmud, and was good in parts, was proscribed because of its dangerous tendency.

Science and religion opposed each other irreconcilably. Science demanded evidence of the eyes and of reason; religion was built on faith. Naturalists, for example, did not believe in answers to prayers for rain; whereas religion taught that God in His goodness and wisdom could answer all entreaties, even when they ran counter to nature. Ibn Adret alluded to the book *Malmad* by Jacob Anatoli, as a type of heretical work and reported that it had been banned in his city, as being destructive of Judaism. Elsewhere, however, it was studied as a text book. "If the breach is made by such great scholars, what can I say or do?" he asked.

Chapter XIX

FAILURE TO ENLIST THE PERPIGNAN CONGREGATION

Although at first Ibn Adret had declined to be the defender of the faith, he soon took up the cudgels against the rationalists. He moved to enlist the aid of an influential scholar of Provence, communicating his fears to Don Crescal Vidal of Perpignan, at this time in the Spanish kingdom of Aragon and the home of prominent scholars. Here lived the heretic Levi of Villefranche, the storm center of the conflict, and his defender, Samuel Sulami.[1]

Crescas Vidal, writing from Marseilles, agreed with Ibn Adret that a grave situation existed, but he would not put himself forward as a leader or initiate any proposal. Due to his short stay in Perpignan, he could not align himself with either party, but would hold himself in reserve. He placed upon Ibn Adret the burden of issuing a ban which would prohibit the study of philosophy and science, with the exception of medicine, to persons under thirty years of age. Such restrictions would send the people to the Talmud to appease their proverbial hunger for learning. Very characteristically, Crescas averred, "The inhabitants of this country are not idlers, neither do they stroll in the parks and gardens. They all study; some alien books, others the Talmud. If the former be withheld from them, the Talmud will be their only

[1] *Min. Ken.*, pp. 46, 52, 56, 176, 180 and no. 97. Geiger, W Z J T, V, (1844), pp. 82 ff., surmises that Sulami belonged to the Ibn Tibbon family.

choice." Even philosophers saw something awry in mere youths mouthing unintelligible or platitudinous metaphysical ideas. Crescas hints that if the civil authorities find out how far the rationalists had gone in discarding revealed religion, they might be brought within the toils of the law.

While passing through Montpellier Crescas Vidal was informed by Todros de Beaucaire of a certain rationalist whose commentary on the Torah was thoroughly rationalistic, and consistently avoided literal exposition. This book had been withheld from publication by the author, but was circulated by his son. He stated also that two or three times he had listened to "the philosophers" preach in the synagogue and found nothing objectionable in their lectures. He really did not know whether his presence put the speakers on their guard and caused them to refrain from heretical utterances, or whether they spoke sincerely.

Crescas Vidal found the attitude of Levi ben Abraham puzzling and he would not pass summary judgment upon him. Levi was very secretive and he did not know whether his public silence was due to chassidic piety or to the fear of being exposed. Levi had regularly evaded Crescas' request for his writings. He cast only one stigma on Levi's character, that owing to extreme poverty he taught Greek and Latin to old and young people. Crescas Vidal also defended Samuel Sulami, renowned for learning, piety and charity, who had roused the suspicions of the rabbis by his friendship for the tree-thinker.[2] Crescas had investigated and had found that Sulami did not concur with Levi's views, but welcomed the latter to his home either to aid him in his poverty or possibly to learn

---

[2] *Min. Ken.*, p. 47; Otzar Nehmad, II, (1857), p. 97.

at first hand the arguments of free-thinkers so as to be able to refute them.

When his daughter died, Sulami took his affliction as a penalty from God for sheltering the reputed heretic, and sent him away. Levi went to Beziers, where he lived with his relative, Samuel ben Reuben, an eloquent defender of Levi to Ibn Adret, and at the same time an advocate of the restriction of the study of philosophy.[3] "If it please the king, and if I, the servant am pleasing to him, let his life be granted him on his request, let him not lift up his voice to quarrel with him. For he has many qualities, pious, clad in Urim and Thummim, innocent without sin, pure of all guilt." Samuel ben Reuben declared that Levi was within his rights in his so-called heretical methods, that his expositions remained within the bounds of Judaism, that he was following precedent. For the early scholars had permitted great latitude in the interpretation of Scripture.

Ibn Adret informed his Beziers correspondent that he had cautioned Levi of Villefranche about his unorthodoxy. It is not a question of Levi's right to his individual opinion but of the spiritual welfare of the greater number. There are times when personal freedom must yield to the good of the majority. If Levi had done him some personal wrong he could have forgiven him, but he was guilty of disloyalty in repudiating his religion and casting dishonor upon God. For this, as for jeopardizing the faith of young people by his unorthodox instruction, he must be held to account. Public opinion was so hostile toward him that no intercession by friends, nothing but the abandonment of his liberal teachings, could restore him to the Jewish congregation. Ibn Adret did not hesi-

[3] *Min. Ken.*, pp. 93-96.

tate to praise Levi's writings for whatever merit they had, but he could not give up the conviction that absorption in philosophy leads to stripping the Bible of all Jewish value. He also discounted the imputed usefulness of philosophy to furnish counter-arguments in answer to disbelievers. Whatever benefit might accrue to religion through philosophy was more than offset by the harm it inflicted.

Ibn Adret bewailed the fact that the tables had been turned; that Judaeo-Greek writings were accorded prophetic reverence, while the Torah was converted into a book of myths.[4]

At the same time Crescas Vidal was asked by his brother, Bonifas of Barcelona, at Ibn Adret's instance, to head the anti-rational movement. Bonifas wrote to him about his deep anxiety over the irreligiousness of the age. The miracles of Scripture were openly flouted and doubt was even cast upon the Sinaitic revelation. It was imperative, therefore, said Bonifas, for the Provencal rabbis to align their forces under the eminent standard-bearer Solomon Ibn Adret. He urged that every community enact drastic measures against the pursuit of philosophic study by young men.[5]

However, the leading scholars of Perpignan, Crescas Vidal, Samuel Sulami, Solomon ben Abraham, a pupil of Ibn Adret, Moses ben Samuel ben Asher, relative of Abba Mari, Isaac de Lattes,[6] and the greatest of them all, Menahem ha Meiri reacted unfavorably to Ibn Adret's suggestion. The failure of his effort aroused the ire of Ibn Adret and he excoriated his antagonists there in

[4] Ibid., p. 45.
[5] Ibid., p. 13.
[6] Ibid., p. 96.

wrathful language. He could not understand the wavering and non-committal attitude of Crescas, and bitingly decried his false modesty in not coming out militantly to uphold ancient traditions. He had no choice now but to put himself forward as divinely destined to lead the war against the rationalists. The specter of heresy that once had appeared in Spain, and had been laid low, again stalked through the centers of Jewish life. Had it been limited to a small circle, it might have been tolerated, but it had spread far and wide, and presented a real hazard to Judaism. The Jewish progressive was a more dangerous offender than the believing Christian; the latter did not deny the inspiration of the Bible, but merely deviated in his interpretation of certain parts. The Scriptures had always commanded universal veneration, and the treason of the Jewish free-thinker was that he cast aspersion on the divine origin and teaching of the entire Bible. Even a Mohammedan believer would be preferable to such a traitor.

As for Sulami, his boyhood friend, Ibn Adret thought he should not expose himself to severe criticism by providing a home for an outspoken heretic. Whatever protestations Sulami might make about the religiousness of Levi ben Abraham, the fact remained that he belied the Torah. That was common talk and Sulami should have considered the effect of his association with a man of that kind. Everybody whom he met frowned on their intimacy. "If he wishes to strangle himself let him do it in another house, not in yours."[7] His action could not be excused on the ground that he sought first-hand information from the heretics, so that he might the better controvert their views.

[7] Ibid., p. 53.

Ibn Adret appealed strongly to the wealthy Sulami to discard his new-fangled ideas and to be content with Talmudic lore. Why court danger "by walking among beasts?" His intentions might be right, but his actions certainly were not. It was very easy to be trapped by the seductive wiles of the intellectualist. He should emulate the example of the great rabbinic authorities of Provence, particularly the scholars of Narbonne, who spurned metaphysics and paid full homage to the Torah.

A disappointing report on the Perpignan situation came from Moses ben Solomon to Abba Mari, a relative of his.[8] The letter was received September, 1304. Abba Mari thought he had a useful ally in him and Ibn Adret had asked his townsman, Don Profiat Gracian, to induce Moses ben Samuel to favor the ban proposal.[9] But Moses did not share the bigoted mind of Abba Mari, and did not conceal the fact that Ibn Adret's letter had evoked considerable bitterness. The community split into three factions on the question of accepting Ibn Adret's proposal of restriction. One party resented the audacity of a foreigner in setting himself up as a judge over large and renowned congregations. The second favored some measures against the guilty, but asked that it be determined first what was and what was not permitted. The third submitted to the proposal of the restrictionists.

Moses accused Abba Mari of spreading false rumors

[8] Ibid., p. 59. The date is the 29th of Elul; Meshullam, the son of Abba Mari, had married the daughter of Moses, *Min. Ken.*, p. 83. Moses was a pupil of the celebrated Perpignan Talmudist, ha Meiri, and a friend of Isaac ben Avigdor (En Duran) of Lunel. Moses ben Samuel and his father had obtained permission from the king of Majorca to establish the Jewish refugees in Perpignan after the French expulsion in 1306.

[9] Ibid., p. 83.

concerning Provencal Jewry, and cautioned him to be as
sincere in his dealings with people as he was with God.

Abba Mari cleverly defended himself and lauded the
Perpignan community for its scholarship and piety. He
would not brand it nor any part of it with the stigma of
heresy. Furthermore, no ulterior motives had prompted
him to agitate against rationalism. It was in a casual
way, while interested in Ibn Adret's reply to a local scholar, Isaac de Lattes, on the question of the use of the
talisman,[10] that "he apprized him of certain radical
teachings." He has acted in good faith in not making
public the names of these heretics nor their places of
residence, for that would be the despicable work of an
informer. But his failure to single out the offenders
should not be construed as a wholesale condemnation
of Jewry.

We hear nothing more of the agitation in Perpignan
until the counter-ban was issued. Abba Mari at that time
asked Menahem ha Meiri, its leading rabbi, for his opinion on the legality of that measure. His answer will be
discussed a little later.

[10] Hoshen Mishpat refers to this query as the beginning of the controversy.

Chapter XX

DISCORD IN MONTPELLIER OVER THE
BAN PROPOSAL

A second attempt to legislate philosophic study out of existence was made in the city of Montpellier.[1] The ban-proposal was delivered by a messenger (Rabbi Mordecai) of Barcelona and called for the excommunication of any one who should study philosophic writings before his thirtieth year. Montpellier, the capital city of lower Languedoc, rivalled Lunel as a stronghold of Jewish learning. Although the Jews inhabited a special quarter, their situation otherwise was privileged, and they engaged actively in commerce. The congregation won renown for its eminence in Talmudic study and for its scientific and philanthropic achievements.[2]

In 1180, Guillen III of Montpellier had granted the Jews the right to practice medicine, a profession that flourished among them. Their most distinguished physician, Jacob ben Machir, was appointed in 1300 regent of the Faculty of Medicine at the Montpellier University. It was Jacob who stubbornly opposed the introduction of the Barcelona ban into the Provence.

The petition for the ban, signed by Ibn Adret, his son Isaac, and thirteen other scholars, flayed the intellectualists for withdrawing religion from the sucklings of the Law, for turning inspired books into a collection of metaphors, and for assailing every command. The new

[1] *Min. Ken.*, pp. 60-61.
[2] *Temim Deim*, no. 7; Ibn Adret, *Responsa*, I, p. 418; *Itinerary of Benjamin of Tudela*, p. 3; and Jedaiah Bedersi in His Letter of Vindication.

intellectualism was pronounced as detestable as the idolatry of Biblical days. Even non-Jews would not tolerate such sacrilege against Scripture, as the statement that Abraham and Sarah were philosophic types; because they, too, accepted Scripture literally, and traced their descent from the patriarchs. The authors of the proposal suggested that, because of the prestige of the Montpellier congregation, it should be the first to enact the ban.

Realizing the need of strategy the Barcelona rabbis instructed the messenger to hand the document to Abba Mari and to a small committee of his confidants. They were to see which way the wind was blowing. If public sentiment favored the proposal, it should be read, adopted and the ban should be proclaimed; otherwise it should be suppressed. These preliminary arrangements attended to, the traditionalists decided to read it before the congregation on a certain Sabbath in September (Ellul), 1304.[3]

Opposition of Jacob ben Machir

The project created greater alarm in Montpellier than in Perpignan. In fact, it disrupted the congregation. On the Friday preceding the reading of the ban, Jacob ben Machir, noted no less as astronomer and translator than as physician, and a formidable antagonist of the traditionalists, visited Abba Mari to protest against reading the letter.[4] The Nasi of Montpellier, Solomon de Lunel, and the Tibbonide Judah ben Moses, stood with Jacob ben Machir. As a patron of the free spirit fostered by his father-in-law, Samuel ibn Tibbon, Jacob informed Abba Mari that he rejected every term of the proposal

[3] *Min. Ken.*, p. 62. In this month Abba Mari received the unpleasant news that Perpignan rejected his ban proposal.

[4] Ibn Adret had halakik correspondence with Jacob ben Machir, *Responsa*, I. Levow, 1811, p. 395; Kaufmann, *Die Sinne*, p. 4, note 3.

against secular learning. He was ruffled by the meddling of the Spanish authorities in Provencal affairs, and sought vainly to postpone the public reading in the hope that the anti-philosophic propaganda would die.

Abba Mari insisted that the letter had a three-fold claim upon their attention, and that it was his right and duty to place it before the congregation for action. The alleged claims were its high purpose to safeguard the Torah, the respect due to the sender, involving the distinguished rabbinical court of the Barcelona community, and the honor of the recipient, the city of Montpellier. He charged Judah ibn Tibbon with being revengeful, because the anti-Maimonists were inveterate foes of his grandfather, Samuel ibn Tibbon, and of the latter's son-in-law, Jacob Anatoli.

The reading of the proposal could not be staved off, and it produced the desired effect upon almost the entire assemblage of notable men. Jacob ben Machir, however, organized an opposition party of such size and power that the traditionalists thought it best to defer their answer to Ibn Adret until after the High Holy Days, when the spiritual leaders would have more time to deliberate on the proposal. As a matter of courtesy, Abba Mari and Todros of Beaucaire penned a rhetorical letter to Barcelona, omitting all reference to the Montpellier situation.

Meanwhile the intellectualist party strengthened its forces. Abba Mari learned that this group was secretly gathering signatures for a letter to Barcelona.[5] Not to be outwitted, in September, 1305, he hurriedly despatched a message with twenty-five signatures, informing the Spanish leaders that the ban proposal was unsatisfactory to

[5] *Min. Ken.*, p. 64.

several individuals and hence must wait for some later disposition.

It is significant that Abba Mari characterized Maimonides in glowing terms and sought to exclude his books from the scope of the ban. He pointed out that the great sage "fought with Aristotle and his colleagues who believed in eternity, denied miracles, belittled the form of God, and rejected providence. He plumbed their books to their depths to clarify their abominations in the alembic of his intellect and he overcame every opponent of the principles of Judaism."

Abba Mari obviously felt that he had to explain the failure of his efforts in his own community. He denounced Jacob ben Machir's entire course as smacking of duplicity and intrigue. Jacob ben Machir had accused Abba Mari of venting his spleen against the philosophers, Jacob Anatoli and his father-in-law, Samuel ibn Tibbon. Abba Mari counter-charged that Jacob ben Machir's letter to Barcelona had been signed by non-residents of Montpellier; and that, furthermore, by misrepresenting the contents of the letter he had obtained the signatures of supporters of the measure.

A week later a letter from the liberal party of Montpellier followed,[6] rebuking Ibn Adret and his associates for relying on the hearsay reports of Abba Mari and for acting in a manner that cast the slur of heresy upon the entire community. The more dignified and fairer course would have been to carefully investigate the charges and take sworn testimony. Under no circumstance was the evidence of one man, like Abba Mari, sufficient to subject an entire community to a ban.

Although the liberals affirmed their unswerving fidelity

[6] Ibid., pp. 66-67.

to the Torah, "their beloved, their only one," they defended philosophy. Numerous passages of the Talmud show that the sages utilized many branches of science and metaphysics. Their proficiency in these fields even surpassed that of non-Jewish scholars. During the dispersion, the nations developed new fields of learning and it was Israel's task to discriminate between the wasteful and the useful, and to support the latter.

They advised their opponents that the seriousness of the anti-religious situation was overestimated. Philosophy was studied by very few, and only in an irregular or clandestine way for whatever mental refreshment it might bring. When, as rarely happened, someone attacked the contents of Scripture, it became an individual problem and should be treated as such.

Jacob ben Machir criticized Ibn Adret's decree as a virtual attack on Maimonides and his philosophic spirit.[7] He pointedly asked why the study of philosophy should be allowed after thirty years of age, if, as argued, it was pernicious. Anything so antithetic to revelation would endanger the religion of the mature and the aged as well as of the young. Might one advanced in life risk his firm faith by indulging in philosophy?

Jacob ben Machir scored Ibn Adret also for belittling Samuel ibn Tibbon, a man of noble ancestry, of prominence and of unquestionable fidelity to Judaism. He reminded Ibn Adret that both he and Abba Mari were descended from the patron and scholar, Meshullam of Lunel, who encouraged secular learning. His own grandfather, Judah ben Moses ibn Tibbon, had made notable contributions to Hebraic culture. Maimonides recognized the value of this literary activity. If at that time philoso-

7 Ibid., pp. 84-86.

phic pursuits were sanctioned by the outstanding authorities who should dare to interdict them now?

Jacob ben Machir did not wipe out the line of demarcation between Holy Writ and philosophic books. They were by no means on a par. But since Jews purported to be a wise and understanding people, they must uphold their reputation by being familiar with worldly wisdom. Of the latter they should be critical and distinguish between its good and bad elements.

On the burning question of Scriptural interpretation, Jacob ben Machir pleaded for wide latitude. One must grope for the thought as best one could. At the same time, he declared, he knew of no one who expounded the Torah as mere metaphor. He certainly was not one who did. In closing, he implored the Spanish leader to restore peace. Since he practically began the movement, he should endeavor to bring it to a satisfactory conclusion.

Opposition of the Nasi of Montpellier

As will often happen, controversies lead to personal animosity and mud-slinging. Solomon de Lunel, physician and popular figure, was a determined foe of Abba Mari. He charged him before Ibn Adret with deceit. Solomon led a demonstration against Abba Mari in the synagogue on a Saturday in July, (Parshah Korah) 1305. Spitefully the *Malmad ha Talmidim* by Jacob Anatoli was read to the congregation on the next Sabbath, (Parshah Hukat) 1305, in the afternoon.[8] Abba Mari admitted to Solomon ibn Adret that he was taunted regarding his hostility to Samuel ibn Tibbon and to Jacob Anatoli; but he denied ever having said a word against them.

Ibn Adret himself was asked by Solomon de Lunel to withdraw from his anti-philosophic position and cease

[8] Ibid., p. 139.

his disguised attacks on Jacob Anatoli, "the old king." Ibn Adret had exceeded his prerogative in circulating his letters and proposals. "This country was like Paradise, tranquil, fraternal; the people were bound together by one language and common interest; diligent scholars hastened daily to the study-halls of the Torah, like angels, ascending and descending the ladder. But now strife is rampant throughout our gates. . . . in truth, as you probably do not know, the country is very faithful and rich in scholarship and piety." His advice was, "Keep aloof. Let them gather sprouts of wisdom in love and moderation, walking as did our forebears. So will we, our progeny and all generations. We beseech you, our teacher, bestow upon us thy blessing, leave us not in perplexity. Place balm upon our wound, and the healing of love and brotherhood amongst us."

To sum up, many of the Provencals were vigorously antagonistic toward the ban because they considered it an affront that Ibn Adret, an outsider, should set himself up as censor of the religious evils in their country; and because the heretical situation complained of was not widely prevalent nor as virulent as charged, but was aggravated largely by the chicanery of one man, Abba Mari. The ban they argued, was aimed at Maimonides and Jacob Anatoli. But granted that philosophic study flourished, there was nothing inherently wrong in it; indeed, many precedents existed for its cultivation; it was useful for the thorough mastery of the Talmud, confirmed many Jewish beliefs, and enabled the intelligent mind to appreciate the wondrous beauty of the cosmos. If there were heresy, it should be treated as an individual case, and not by a general ban. The conflict disturbed the solidarity and fraternity of Jewry. The restrictionists had sent their propaganda to France, and incited Jew against Jew. The rationalists recalled that the issues had been fought out in 1232-1235 to the advantage of philosophy, and there was no good reason to revive them. And the chief reason was that the ban would not be enforceable, if enacted.

The Predicament of Ibn Adret

These communications from friend and foe alike, drew a respectful reply from Ibn Adret to the Montpellier liberals. He justified his hostility to them on the familiar ground that Judaism must be safeguarded in every way. As to his right as an outsider to meddle in the domestic affairs of Provencal Jewry, he declared that he had declined the offer when it was first tendered him. He had waited three years before taking action. The movement had sprung from Provence itself; pressure had been brought to bear upon him not by Abba Mari alone but by as many as one hundred scholars.[9] He did not mean to slight their self-respect nor interfere with their autonomy. He argues the point that the petition had been approved in Barcelona for Spain and applied only to the Spanish congregations. On the initiative of the Provencal scholars it had been brought to Montpellier where he understood it would be accepted. Furthermore, the bearer of the proposal had been instructed to deliver it to a certain person who should determine the advisability of publishing it. If it was found to be objectionable, it was to have been withheld altogether. This was no inquisition; neither the names of the heretics nor their homes had been reported. He justified his part in proposing the reform for Provence because the Jews were everywhere

[9] Ibid., pp. 125-131.

a united, cohesive people, and it was his right to seek the welfare of Jewry everywhere. He would like to see the sciences and philosophy checked in Provence as they had been in Spain "which once was full of worldly wisdom, but has now become like fine flour."

In the present deadlock, he had nothing further to do. "Since as I see, you do not wish to adopt our proposal and we being fully convinced that we have performed our duty to the best of our knowledge, you, great in knowledge and counsel, may do as your reason dictates. We are through with it."

He answered the liberalist contention that Maimonides absorbed himself with philosophic study with the statement that he disfavored its promiscuous use. The sage cautioned one who could not swim (speculate) not to venture into deep water. He had also warned that the abstruse character of philosophy, was like heavy food stuffs, unfit for the young or weak. Personally Ibn Adret said he was an earnest admirer of Maimonides, and cited his present friendship with his grandson, David.

As was general with the restrictionists, Ibn Adret excluded astronomy and medicine from the contemplated ban; the former on account of its usefulness in determining the festivals and other religious events, the latter because it was necessary to cure sickness.

He deplored the undeserved attacks made upon him, because he was an innocent party. Instead of becoming an agent for doing good, he was condemned as the trouble-maker. Stubbornness on both sides would widen the schism and the results might be calamitous unless the upheaval subsided at once. His advice was that the Montpellier congregations act independently of Spanish influence and remedy the vexing situation in their own way.

Ibn Adret appealed personally to their leading liberal, the Nasi Solomon de Lunel, to protect the youth against the dangers lurking in the insidious teachings of philosophy. To keep silent in the face of the rationalist blasphemies was tantamount to acquiescence and to complicity in their impious doings. Youth must not be impregnated from infancy with the seeds of alien knowledge, lest every avenue for the conveyance of Judaism should be closed.

Ibn Adret also warned Abba Mari not to fight his opponents by foul methods. "A man like you who covenanted with God to bring back many from sin should have the proper motives and do the proper deeds." The solution of their present problems could not result from strife, but from a peaceful understanding between him and the Nasi Solomon de Lunel.

He added the further suggestion that the Montpellierians select some influential fellow countryman who had their confidence and respect and whom the traditionalists would follow blindly. Ibn Adret would negotiate with him concerning the ban.

But knowing the stubborn resistance that faced him at home, Abba Mari pleaded with his Spanish supporters to enact a ban in their country to prohibit the study of philosophy and the rationalization of Scripture by anyone under thirty years of age. The same ban should be forwarded to him, and on the strength of the Barcelona action he would seek to put it through in Montpellier over the protests of the minority. His failure to accomplish this purpose the first time was unexpected. He had grounds to believe that influential opinion favored him, and did not think that the opposition would be so obstreperous again.

He related a case in point to illustrate the benefit that might be expected from a ban. A relative of his had repudiated the literalism of the Bible and his family had interceded for him. They feared that he might come under the ban. Thereupon the heretic retracted his interpretations and had been absolved of guilt by Ibn Adret.

Chapter XXI

FAVORABLE REACTION OF OTHER PROVENCAL CONGREGATIONS

In the meantime, the Barcelona proposal was given impetus by a noted Provencal scholar, Jacob de Beaucaire, who lived in Trinquitailles, near Arles, at this time the capital of Provence.[1] He was a brother of the better-known Todros de Beaucaire, partisan of Abba Mari.[2] Upon the death of Todros who had corresponded with Ibn Adret, Jacob in a letter written January 31 (23d of Shebat), 1305, volunteered to travel through Provence with the ban to obtain its ratification by the various communities. His offer was made just five months after the Barcelona ban-proposal had been turned down in Montpellier. He contemplated visiting Aix first, there to enlist the cooperation of his teacher, Abraham ben Joseph, and then to make a five day tour of Provence stopping at Avignon, Venaissin, Argentierre, Montelimar and Tarascon. Montpellier was to be his ultimate destination.

The Jewry of Argentierre, Languedoc, which had produced the famous Maimonist, Joseph ibn Caspi, unqualifiedly committed themselves to the proposal of Ibn Adret. In a letter signed by eight scholars,[3] they extolled

---

[1] Its history went back to the fifth century. The scholars of Arles, like the *Princes* of Narbonne traced their ancestry to King David. In Arles, Samuel ibn Tibbon completed his Hebrew translation of the Guide for the Perplexed on November 30, 1204. Here, too, the Maimonist, Joseph ibn Gaspi lived and wrote his philosophic book *Sefer ha Sod* in 1317; See Geiger, W Z J T, V, p. 121; Benjamin of Tudela in 1165 counted there 200 families and at this time it probably had many more.

[2] *Min. Ken.*, p. 115.

[3] Ibid., pp. 101-103.

the initiative of Abba Mari, whom they ardently admired as the father of wisdom, their glory and pride, the distinguished sage and exalted prince, "whose reputation is known far and wide, and who sustained the work of his sainted forebears in the land."

The Jews of Aix and of Avignon through their respective rabbis, Abraham ben Joseph and his son, Joseph ben Abraham, assured Ibn Adret of their loyalty and of their endorsement of the ban.[4] Abraham ben Joseph reported that in his town sentiment was decidedly anti-philosophic, but that near-by communities were plagued with heresies. The heretics chirped and hopped about as young chicks whose eyes are not opened. He made the extreme suggestion that philosophy should be absolutely forbidden, without setting an age limit. He gave his pledge that as soon as the ban reached him it would be adopted by the community. The rabbi of Avignon, a papal domain, described his people as being immersed in Talmud and Halaka, engaged in writing books that would be cherished by posterity. However, he was anxious to introduce the ban so that "we be not like an invaded city without a wall."

Beziers, too, bound itself to the restrictionist policy of Ibn Adret at the same time that its representative Samuel ben Reuben defended Levi of Villefranche.

In acknowledging the endorsements of these Provencal congregations, ibn Adret confessed that he had no first hand information of the conditions in Provence.[5] He posed the rhetorical question, "Will the world come to an end if children are not nurtured on philosophy?" It was a

---

[4] Ibid., pp. 97-101. Ibn Adret corresponded with them on halakik matters; See *Responsa*, III, Livorno, (1778), pp. 221, 286.

[5] *Min. Ken.*, Letter to Samuel ben Reuben of Beziers, pp. 93-96.

foregone conclusion that children trained philosophically
would inevitably discard the dogmas of Judaism, would
deny the creation of the world and miracles, and ridicule
such customs as Mezuzah, fringes and phylacteries. According to the contentions of the rationalists, the Talmudists of old had been, forsooth, enemies of Judaism, because they did not prate about Aristotle. Actually, they
were ambassadors of the Most High, the finest exem-
plars of humanity. It was they who erected for Israel an
invulnerable bulwark of defense about Judaism. Moreover, Israel was wedded to the Torah since Sinai, and
she could have no other consort, either philosophy or science, be he ever so fair and lovely.

He vowed that he would not retreat from his anti-
rationalist position. Should he lose the power of speech,
his hand would almost instinctively write the dictates of
his heart. "But what shall I do, if I battle and they keep
silent; how can I raise up alone the falling tabernacle?
Truly, you are the people of the God of Abraham, and
with you is wisdom to establish the house and build the
wall. Your words are like towers to save Mt. Zion from
desolation so that foxes should not walk in it?" His was
a cumbersome task. "How much ink have I poured
out," he mourned; "how many pens have I broken; I
have contended and fought with the great to put up a
fence at the border, but without success." He exhorted
his correspondents to agitate among their co-religionists
so that the controversy might come to a fruitful conclusion.

Interposition of Asher ben Jehiel

Abba Mari informed Ibn Adret that the enforcement
of the anathema must be approved by the civil author-

ities, and that any individual might obstruct his plans. He hit upon a new way out of the impasse, namely, to over-awe the opposition, and suggested the renowned Talmudist Asher ben Jehiel of Toledo (chief rabbi there from 1305 until 1328) as a strong ally. Toledo had been the home of two other great figures in this controversy, Meir ben Todros, who attacked the Book of Knowledge just one hundred years back, and the repentant anti-Maimonist Jonah Gerondi. Abba Mari recognized a favorable omen in the appearance of this new star, Asheri, in the same constellation (Spain) with Ibn Adret. They should combine their efforts in persuading their rabbinical courts to enact the ban and send it to Provence where it certainly would be heeded.

Somewhat reluctant to be dragged into politics because Spain was his new home and also because he had shortly before passed through the Provence and had enjoyed the hospitality of the people, Asher ben Jehiel and his rabbinical court were won over by the efforts of Ibn Adret's active propagandist and pupil, Samson ben Meir of Toledo.[6] The latter had toured Spain and obtained the ratification of many notables. Samson promised to get fifty congregations to sign the ban and even offered to carry the letters with their signatures to Montpellier.

Asher ben Jehiel, a disciple of Meir of Rothenberg, had emigrated from Germany, his native country to the duchy of Savoy.[7] His residence there was short-lived because the ruler of Savoy, Giovanni Savoya, friend of the German emperor, refused to let him remain. He removed to Provence, where he was struck by the high intellectual level of the Jews, but discouraged at the

[6] Ibid., p. 138.
[7] Ibid., p. 111.

weakening of Torah-true Judaism. Montpellier alone impressed him as a most flourishing center of the Torah. Asheri possessed little secular learning. To him all philosophers were comparable to infidels.[8] The Torah and metaphysics could not be squared. The former was revealed and traditional knowledge; its exposition followed certain accepted hermeneutic rules. Philosophy grew out of speculation and research. One who began the study of philosophy before that of the Torah was lost to Judaism.

He chastised the religious leaders for their neutral attitude toward heretics. Upon them rested the blame for the let-down in Judaism, for no one of them was willing to assume authority. They could, if they would, interfere and "uproot these abominations."

He was exasperated that heresy should be so deep-seated. Its harm was aggravated because it festered in secret. Relatives, fearing the consequences of an indignant public opinion, shielded their liberal-minded kin. Thus a remedy for the evil became doubly difficult. Mere threats would not extirpate it. Only the pressure of a common decision by recognized authorities would avail. Procrastination was harmful. As these "disciples of Aristotle," become more audacious, who would dare to judge them? Asher ben Jehiel counselled that a synod of liberals and conservatives of France and Spain be called to deliberate on the question. Ibn Adret should be present to defend the proposition of rigid adherence to the Torah. Thus would a schism be averted.

[8] Ibn Adret, *Responsa*, Vilna, Ch. 55, no. 9, p. 53a.

Chapter XXII

THE PROCLAMATION OF BANS AND COUNTER-BANS

Bans Enacted in Barcelona

In the winter of 1305, occurred a lull in the movement. Serious illness for eight months enforced silence upon Ibn Adret; and the Montpellier leader grew uneasy fearing that he had lost interest.[1] The agitation resumed, reached its climax in the summer of 1305, when Ibn Adret's insistence that the Provencal scholars take the initiative in formulating the restrictionist measure triumphed. He made an overture to Todros ben Kalonymus, the Nasi of Narbonne, to whom he conceded a position of seniority, to draw up the ban. Being on the spot, the leader of Narbonne and others could agree on a perfect measure. Whatever he might do would be captiously criticized and resented by the Provencals. "How," he demanded, "can I go forth at the head of the thousands of Israel to end trangression, to exterminate sin, to purify the land from all these abominations? Let them make the start and I am certain that I will enlist twenty congregations to accomplish their purpose."[2]

Kalonymus received Ibn Adret's letter on Passover Eve, 1305, and aroused by its firm request, forwarded it to Abba Mari on April 19 (24th of Nisan).[3] He had encouraged Abba Mari in his propaganda, but had per-

---

[1] *Min. Ken.*, pp. 132-133.
[2] Ibid., p. 135.
[3] Ibid., p. 136.

sonally held aloof from direct action. Now the persuasive powers of Abba Mari won him over completely.

Remembering the unexpected clash that obstructed the
plans in Montpellier in October, 1304, Abba Mari advised
Kalonymus to keep the utmost secrecy. Two stipulations
were to be inserted in the ban; first, the unconditional
prohibition of the study of the natural sciences and metaphysics from Greek books by persons under twenty-five
years of age; and second, the sanction of such study after
that age, but not its public dissemination in synagogues
or at public festive gatherings. This decree written on
parchment, should be passed upon by the Jews of Narbonne and the names of the dignitaries affixed.

They accordingly drafted this statement, which they sent
to Ibn Adret:[4] "We, therefore, agree not to allow anyone
to engage in the study of natural science or metaphysics
in books written by Greek philosophers or other Gentiles
until the youths grow up and reach maturity, so that they
fill their belly with the dainties of the Torah and the
Faith and receive their required food. To this purpose
we hasten to set a time, the twenty-fifth year, at which
time the virtues and powers are fully developed in people
and they have already grown up in the wisdom of the
Talmud. After this period they are permitted to engage
in the study of secular books, the writings of the Gentiles and the Greeks. They will take the food and cast
away the shell and seeds. This is the desirable way; for
the Torah will then protect and aid them. We have excluded from the prohibition all the books of Jewish philosophers, although they may contain some elements taken
from the philosophers of other faiths. If the great Rabbi
with his holy congregation will decree this with a curse

[4] Ibid., p. 141.

and an oath, every man among us who blesses the faithful God will answer 'Amen' to his blessing." No Provencal congregation or rabbinic court had participated in drawing up this draft. It was the work of Kalonymus and Abba Mari and bore their signatures alone.

But a ban embodying these features was proclaimed on Saturday, July 26, 1305, in the synagogue of Barcelona.[5] It was signed by all the Jewish dignitaries of the city without exception. Ibn Adret made public three proclamations of the ban signed respectively by thirty-seven, thirty-eight and thirty-five rabbis, including himself. It is significant that these bans were proclaimed at the time the Council of Vienne interdicted the writings of Averroes.[6]

The first one applied to the Jews of Barcelona and read, "We decreed and obligated ourselves, our progeny and all who join us, by the power of the ban, that no one of our congregation should study the Greek books which were composed on natural science and metaphysics, both such as are composed in Greek or that are translated into another language, for fifty years from this day, until the person is twenty-five years of age. No one of our congregation should teach any Israelite any of these philosophies until they shall be twenty-five years old, lest these philosophies be continued and make the learner depart from the Torah of Israel, supreme over all these philosophies. . . . We exclude from this decree medical science. Although it is derived from natural science, yet Judaism recognizes the right of a physician to heal. This we have banned with the Scroll of the Law in the

[5] Ibid.
[6] Steinschneider, *Jewish Literature* (Hebrew trans.), p. 136.

presence of the congregation on Saturday, July 26, 1305."[7]

The second proclamation sent to all congregations summarized the heretical deviations of the rationalists, among them the reduction to a mere metaphor of the contents of Scripture from the creation to the revelation at Sinai. The intellectualists upheld the views that Abraham and Sarah were matter and form; the twelve tribes, twelve constellations; Urim and Thummim the astrolabe; that the four kings against the five symbolized the four elements and five senses. This renunciation of the literal meaning of the Bible discredited the ordinances of Holy Writ. The rationalists were more to be condemned than Gentiles who venerated the Scripture and observed some of its laws. The document attacked the teaching of philosophy to the youth as certain to lead to heresy. Philosophy rejected miracles and the creation of the world. The conditions of the ban were repeated.

The third ban proscribed all books in which were found any of the subversive views mentioned in the former ban. It applied to Jews in every land. Strangely enough, it cited a passage from Maimonides to the effect that one who deliberately violated a Biblical law because he rejected the authenticity of the Torah was a blasphemer deserving death.

The Rationalists Issue the Counter-Ban

A second time the Barcelona ban met with a cold reception in Montpellier. The liberals strenuously demurred against its enforcement and thwarted it by issuing a counter-ban. As the civil authorities generally interfered with the operation of such measures so that none could

[7] Ibn Adret, *Responsa*, Vienna, 1812, p. 52; Halper, *Post Biblical Hebrew Literature*, 1921, p. 176.

be valid without this consent, the counter-ban received their sanction. It was directed against any one who, heeding the Barcelona ban, would not study or teach the seven sciences and metaphysics to youth, or against those who spoke derogatorily of the writings of Maimonides, or any other Jewish philosophic writer.[8] The governor of Montpellier gladly approved of the first aim, because he saw in secularism an entering wedge to apostasy.

The conservatives appointed twelve men to halt the introduction of the counter-ban; but to no avail. It was published with the evident support of a majority of the congregation. Again, Abba Mari was on the defensive, this time seeking to convince his followers that the counter-ban had no binding power, primarily because it had not been projected with the object of protecting Judaism. He therefore drew up an Appeal (adrabah) signed by more than one hundred people, serving notice that his party takes exception to the terms of the counter-ban. He sent the Appeal to the rabbinical court in Barcelona, to elicit opinions on the legality of the counter-ban.

The Montpellier liberals hastened to apprize the Barcelonians of the grounds of their opposition. The principal signer was "the father of wisdom, our aged patriarch, the light of Israel, the great Rabbi Solomon (de Lunel,"[9] whose name headed those of Isaac ben Abraham of Avignon, Solomon ben Joseph of Marseilles, and Saul ben Solomon. Once more they took the Spanish

[8] *Min. Ken.*, p. 142. The hokmat 'Gamaliel' referred to may be medicine. Acc. to legend, Gamaliel was a great physician. Some scholars hold that Gamaliel was confused with the Greek medical authority, Galen of the second century; See S. Sachs, Kokebe Vizhak, XXI, p. 62; Kaufmann, *Die Sinne*, p. 7.

[9] Israelitische Letterbode, IV, (1878-1879), p. 173. Geiger, (W Z J T, V, p. 100), takes Solomon de Lunel as related to the Tibbon family.

leaders to task for overstepping the bounds in legislating over the affairs of another country, and attacked the imprudence of relying on the uncorroborated charges of one man.

Although they granted that here and there secular study was cultivated, they insisted that it rarely led to the uprooting of faith. It was unfair, too, they thought, to withdraw the traditional tolerance and indulgence of the Jew toward non-rabbinic studies because of some unpleasant results. Instead of being frowned upon, philosophic and scientific knowledge should be welcomed as a tribute to the creator of the universe. "Why should not a man be permitted to fill his soul with a full measure of delight in his creator, to gaze at His work, and to behold His deeds for the good of man?" Everything God created served a purpose. Although philosophic study might be harmful to a few, it certainly was a blessing to most people. Like wine it invigorated some and enervated others. The injustice of the ban was intensified because it prohibited those in the prime of life and best able to grapple with the sciences and metaphysics, from studying them.

But the severest criticism was launched against the Barcelona anathema because it virtually interdicted the writings of Maimonides. For how could one master his books unless he possessed alien learning? "If ye shut the doors of wisdom, then ye shut the doors of this book (the Guide)." They enacted the counter-ban to exonerate the books of Maimonides as well as to allow the study of the seven sciences. Their action emulated that of the Exilarch Jesse of Damascus in excommunicating the anti-Maimonist Solomon Petit and his partisans in 1291 for banning the Guide and the Book of Knowledge. They sent a copy of the Exilarch's ban to Ibn Adret. They requested the Barcelonians not to send an emissary throughout the country to campaign for the adoption of their ban on the ground that it would engender further animosity. Religious conflicts had been waged in all ages, and philosophy always retained her ground, undefeated.

Abba Mari's lieutenant in Montpellier, Simon ben Joseph, known as En Duran, reported to Ibn Adret that the liberals felt that the writings of Jacob Anatoli and of Maimonides were the target of the bans.[10] For three months now the liberals had been preaching their objectionable ideas to huge crowds every Sabbath afternoon. The issue, he declared, was not Maimonides, but Aristotle and Averroes, who certainly were not fit for study by children. He assured Ibn Adret that they would carry their point, because they were in the majority.

Spanish Authorities Attack Counter-Ban

No news is good news, Abba Mari reflected, when the congregational and six personal letters giving the approval of the Spanish authorities reached Montpellier thirty-six days late, on December 1, 1306. The congregational letter rehearsed the reluctance of the Barcelona scholars to take the initiative and their final consent following two years of urging by the Montpellier rabbis.[11] They delivered a verdict that only books by Gentile authors were to be proscribed. The writings of Maimonides, whether Hebrew or Arabic, "are excluded from the measure, because they restore the soul of an intelligent people." This fact should remove all objections to it on the part of the liberals. At the same time the tra-

---

[10] Letterbode, ibid.
[11] *Min. Ken.*, pp. 154-155; Letterbode, V, (1879-1880), pp. 53-57.

ditionalists were urged to use peaceful means to adjust their troubles with the opposition.

A second letter recorded Ibn Adret's decision, seconded by twenty-five colleagues, that the counter-ban was not binding.[12] In order to be legal a public ban must have an unimpeachable objective, either mounting guard over Judaism or removing from it an intolerable burden. In this instance, the ban of the liberals imperilled the integrity of Judaism by compelling the study of alien subjects. The illogic of the counter-ban, condemning one for his conscientious scruples against philosophic study, was like banning one who shunned wine because of its deleterious effect on him. Yet another reason invalidated the counter-ban. Where a congregation was divided, the proponents of a ban must obtain the weight of an outstanding scholar's endorsement; otherwise a mere majority would not avail. The further point was made that in this case there was a majority only with respect to the opponents of the ban, but not a majority of the entire community. As a token of good-will the Barcelonians acceded to the wishes of their partisans in not sending an agitator to tour France and Spain.

A number of scholars of Barcelona wrote personally to Abba Mari expressing their accord with the conservative party.[13] Moses ben Isaac ha Levi stated that out of deference to the notable men on both sides he held himself aloof from the agitation. For his part, he perceived unmitigated good in the restriction of secular study. Aristotle and his coterie were not needed by Jews. The patriarch Abraham pointed the way against philosophy when he charged his progeny to observe the virtue of justice

[12] *Min. Ken.*, pp. 156-157.
[13] Ibid., pp. 158-160.

and righteousness only. It was advisable to exempt Maimonides, the pilot of philosophers, who, obviously, appreciated the priority of the Torah; for he said that the student should first satiate himself with the substantial foods of Judaism before strolling through the fragrant paths of the Garden. His writings radiated strength and quiet; they satisfied man's higher speculative cravings. The counter-action of the liberal party would not dampen the ardor of the faithful. The Barcelona ban would stand. He concluded with a plea to the Montpellier leaders for fraternity and mutual understanding. The present disputation should be like that of Hillel and Shammai, and the interposition of the civil authorities in their quarrel should be avoided.

In the same spirit of fraternal effort the author wrote to his brother-in-law, the Nasi Don Mumit of Narbonne, imploring him not to take sides in the conflict, but to strive for a reconciliation which would permit every person to act as he thought fit in the choice of his studies.[14] The appeal evidently found Don Mumit a ready listener, for we do not hear that he championed either side, despite Ibn Adret's attempt to gain his favor.[15]

Solomon Gracian, a prominent scholar and signer of the congregational letters, who died in 1307, also wrote separately to En Duran de Lunel proposing a treaty of peace.[16]

A more militant note was sounded by the brothers Sheshet and Jacob ben Shealtiel ben Isaac of Barcelona, staunch supporters of Ibn Adret.[17] They summoned the Provencal rabbis to enforce the ban, to quell all opposi-

[14] Letterbode, IV, p. 160.
[15] *Min. Ken.*, p. 152.
[16] Graetz, *Geschichte*, VII, p. 241.
[17] *Min. Ken.*, pp. 161-162.

tion. They disclaimed any intention of proscribing the Maimonidean writings, the much criticized Guide and Book of Knowledge; these dissertations were sacred, thoroughly Jewish, and no one might impugn their importance to Judaism.

The noted Bonifas Vidal who had figured in the early stages of the controversy deplored the appearance of a schism and its dire consequences.[18] Abba Mari's contentious conduct called forth his censure. The spark of friction must be watched, lest it blaze forth in a disastrous conflagration. According to him the Barcelona ban was imposed only on the local community and such others as agreed to submit to it. Furthermore, no intention to proscribe Maimonides was present in the minds of the signatories, and he permitted the use of other philosophic books in connection with the study of Maimonides when necessary.

A trenchant reply to Abba Mari was penned by the renowned Talmudist, Asher ben Jehiel of Toledo.[19] First apologizing for not aggressively espousing Ibn Adret's cause, due to a feeling of obligation to French Jewry for their hospitality toward him, he pronounced the counter-ban void forasmuch as it interdicted the study of the Torah. The latter must monopolize all of our time, and alien works detracted from contemplation of it.

To avoid being misunderstood Abba Mari joined with Ibn Adret and four colleagues of Montpellier in a manifesto to all communities that the Barcelona ban restricted only the study of physical and metaphysical writings by Gentile authors.[20] The opposition was certainly unfair

18 Ibid., pp. 164-165.
19 Ibid., p. 178.
20 Ibid., pp. 144, 149-151.

in charging that Maimonides was proscribed, as the opening sentence of the counter-ban imputed. Maimonides' name could not be mentioned in the same breath with those of other rationalists, so far above them did he rank by acknowledging the doctrines of creation *ex nihilo,* Providence, and other Jewish concepts, whereas the rest traduced the Scriptures and rejected the indispensable dogmas.

The turn of affairs must have greatly embarrassed the conservatives, for we find Ibn Adret inquiring about the exact situation in Montpellier and the reason for Abba Mari's protracted silence. He asked for the return of the bans with the signatures of the local congregations, and promised to obtain the signatures of at least twenty more. He was surprised at the silence of the distinguished Don Mumit of Narbonne.

Provencal Communities Oppose the Counter-ban

Fearing that his opponents might ignore as prejudiced the decision of Ibn Adret and his college on the counter-ban, Abba Mari solicited opinions from several Provencal authorities. One answer which reached him on March 30th (14th of Nisan), 1306, came from Mordecai ben Isaac of Carpentras, grandson of David Kimhi, in the county of Venaissin, a Papal domain.[21] Mordecai held that the Barcelona ban followed the line drawn by Talmudic precedent which cautioned against public instruction in the vision of the chariot and the story of creation. Youth should be deterred from the study of logic. The ban was not unduly severe, because it permitted instruction in astronomy and other academic

---

[21] Ibid., pp. 167-170; Gross, *Gallia Judaica,* pp. 386, 607, does not identify this writer with the poet, Mordecai ben Isaac Ezobi; Cf. R E J, XII, p. 34.

knowledge. The prohibited subjects were advisedly banned because they became a burden and a vexation to the
learner. They raised the difficult problem of harmony
between faith and reason, which required more than
ordinary skill in sifting the principles of both philosophy
and revelation. Especially undesirable were the writings of non-Jews, because they were permeated with a
definite non-Jewish spirit and their object was to preserve the peculiar teachings and ideas of their various
national cultures. It was patently absurd and suicidal,
therefore, to proclaim a decree like the counter-ban
which would virtually force the youth into un-Jewish intellectual spheres to the detriment of his own spiritual
heritage. Judaism required constant vigilance.

Attacks on the counter-ban reached Montpellier also
from scholars in Beziers, Arles, Capestang, Narbonne,
and Perpignan. The renowned Talmudist, Menahem ben
Solomon, of the last named city, declared the counter-
ban ineffective, although he did not favor the restriction of philosophic study.

From Narbonne came a message from Samuel ben
Judah de Lunel, known as Don Samuel Bongodas, in
which the usual objections to the counter-ban were repeated;[22] the rationalists were attacked for disseminat-
ing their heresies in theatres and synagogues, and philosophers were rated lower than Karaites, who at least
recognized the binding power and the truth of everything in the Bible.

The representative Jewish congregation of Beziers, in
a letter sent by Solomon ben Nathan, endorsed the prohibition.[23] If Scrolls of the Law, written by a heretic

[22] *Min. Ken.*, pp. 174-176.
[23] Ibid., pp. 173-174.

were interdicted, how much more should this be the case with out-and out heretical writings? All philosophy was heretical because it assumed the eternity of the universe, and Aristotle was the arch-heretic. The cautious action of King Hezekiah in concealing certain medical books was prompted by the fact that people relinquished faith in God after resorting to the cures prescribed therein. The traditionalists had a perfect right to forswear philosophy and physics if only as a matter of self-abnegation and self-discipline.

Judah ben Solomon ben Meiri of Arles advised Abba Mari to stand firm by his policy and for its extension by Ibn Adret over all Europe.[24]

Fifteen scholars of Capestang, a town near Beziers, supported Abba Mari and assailed the counter-ban as a reproach on the character and authority of Ibn Adret and the Barcelona community.[25] They held that a Jewish court might exercise arbitrary power in the defense of Judaism. The historic Jewish attitude placed religion above philosophy in such views as "the fear of sin must precede wisdom," (Pirke Aboth, III, 11) and that "it is forbidden to any person to teach his son Greek wisdom" (Sota, 49b). Exception was made in the case of the Nasi Gamaliel, whose relations with the government were strengthened by a knowledge of philosophy. In Berakot, 28b we read the terse prohibition: "Withdraw your children from the study of logic." To the question "I have studied Scripture, Mishna, Talmud, Halaka and Agada—can I learn Greek wisdom?" he replied, "Seek a time that is neither day nor night, as it is said, 'Thou shalt

24 Ibid., p. 176.
25 Ibid., p. 172. The most noted signer of this letter was Isaac ben Moses hakohen, an important cabalist who is mentioned by the liberal Isaac Albalag in his translation in 1307 of the *Mukassid* by Algazzali.

meditate in it (the Torah) day and night.' " Hence, there
was no time for philosophy.

To sum up, the counter-ban was declared illegal for the
following reasons: It was not in keeping with Jewish
policy. It made alien studies mandatory upon the Jews
and thus set up a competing interest involving the nullification of Jewish study and precepts (bittul mizwah).
It was not approved by a majority of the Montpellier congregation. Lastly, its ostensible motive to spare the good
name of Maimonides could not be justified, since the
Barcelona ban was not aimed at Maimonides.

Meiri and En Duran

The city of Perpignan, which played a significant part
in this conflict, dissented from the restrictionist proposals of Ibn Adret and Abba Mari. Its most prominent
rabbi, Menahem Meiri (1249-1306) although sympathetic
toward the philosophic party, kept silent for a long time
possibly because of his great respect for Solomon ibn
Adret. But after the bans had been issued and he had
been pressed hard to commit himself, he vehemently
condemned the Barcelona ban and voiced his disfavor
of the Montpellier counter-ban in a letter to Abba Mari.[26]
Abba Mari delegated his lieutenant, En Duran, known
also as Simon ben Joseph, to refute Meiri. Meiri's letter
is lost, but the grounds of his opposition are known from
extracts cited in En Duran's reply.[27] From this evidence
it appears that Meiri's statement was a logical, practical
and powerful challenge to the traditionalist party.

[26] Meiri and Ibn Adret had an active legal correspondence. It is worth
noticing that Meiri strongly objects to the interference of Spanish
scholars in Provencal laws and customs, *Magen Abot*, p. 11.

[27] Hoshen Mishpat, *Zunz Jubelschrift*, pp. 155-174 (Hebrew) and pp.
143-151 (German). Abba Mari's esteem for Meiri appears from eulogy
on Meiri which he addressed to congregation of Perpignan. Letterbode,
V, p. 76; *Shalshelet hakabbala*, Warsaw, 1877, p. 59a.

Meiri's support was eagerly sought by both parties. We hear frequently of his meetings with the physician and scholar, Isaac de Lattes, who would report to him as a direct witness on the situation in Montpellier. Meiri regarded the traditionalists as acting the part of inquisitors and trouble-makers. It was the height of temerity to impute heresy to the people of the Provence country, known for aristocracy, wealth and learning. Abba Mari's action was too hasty and drastic. The ban had been put over without the unanimous approval of all the Provencals. In fact, it had been actively opposed; and it had been an error to invite Ibn Adret, an outsider, to adjust a Provencal difficulty. Perhaps Meiri had this conflict in mind when he declared the four causes of a religious quarrel to be the desire for authority, the intrinsic difficulty of the problem, the ignorance of the parties concerned and loyalty to early association and ideas.

Meiri Defends Philosophy

Meiri advocated the free study of philosophy, and could find nothing in it of a diabolical or destructive quality.[28] It was not inherently incompatible with the Torah; in fact, the two commonly went hand in hand. He referred to several outstanding living scholars of his region,[28a] who combined rabbinic and universalistic cultures without sacrificing an iota of their religious fidelity. Other instances occurred where scholars were more familiar with philosophy than with the Talmud, yet their faith remained firm. The Perpignan leader cited the case of a young pious Talmudist whose knowledge of mathematics made him his (Meiri's) indispensable companion

[28] Besides the Hoshen Mishpat his theological views are expressed in his Commentary on Abot, *Bet ha Behira*, and in other works.

[28a] Samuel (ben Abraham) Shakali, Gerson of Beziers, Reuben ben Hayyim, his teacher.

to elucidate some technical discussions in the Talmud. This demonstrated beyond the shadow of a doubt that scientific training was urgently demanded to understand the Talmud. In fact, a liberal education would increase the admiration of the world for the Jews. Not intellectualism alone, but both faith and reason were essential to enable man to reach his highest development.

Meiri unqualifiedly defended the Jewish philosophers and laid the blame for misunderstanding them on the uncomprehending reader. Even Greek books translated by Jews were welcome; they corroborated the dogmas of God's existence, unity and immateriality. These books held treasures of wisdom and must not be condemned because of some objectionable parts. A case in point was, he thought, the objection raised against the book of Ecclesiastes on the ground of heresy which was overridden by the rabbis, and the inclusion of the book in the canon for the good that it possessed. If a certain individual succumbed to the pernicious teachings of philosophy, he alone should suffer. But it was unreasonable to abolish all philosophy. The conditions laid down by the ban were too general and too extreme. Warning and reproof should be sufficient.

The Mistake of Enacting the Ban

Because of its many deficiencies the ban was a mistake. People were actuated by different inborn likes and dislikes and would follow them, ban or no ban. Ordinarily, a person has opportunities to acquire academic knowledge in youth, but if a prohibited time, up to 25 years, was set, the chances favorable to the attainment of knowledge after that age, became less and less. Other objections were that it aroused bad feeling; it practically sealed the Guide, for without a knowledge of physics and metaphysics, one could not comprehend the twenty-five propositions and many other sections. Then again, there were many Hebrew books that incorporated facts and theories of natural science, so that the ban against Gentile books was useless.

He predicted correctly that the ban would fall into desuetude in the near future, and that the children of the present, forgetting the compact, would engage in philosophic study. In the same way the anti-Maimonidean struggle in 1230-1232, resulting in the bans against Maimonides' writings, frittered out into nothing. His books were openly read. To Meiri's knowledge, the ban had never been formally revoked. He therefore foretold the same fate for the anti-philosophic ban of 1305. He recalled, also, to the Montpellier leader, the ill-feeling and disruption engendered by the controversy over the sage's writings.

Meiri attacked the ban from still another angle. The evils which provoked the traditionalists' wrath, the metaphorical interpretation of Scripture and rationalistic preaching, would not be checked by its terms, because the preachers really knew very little of natural science or metaphysics. Some were completely ignorant of the primary sources of those studies, having gleaned their information from the Guide, the *Malmad ha-Talmidim* by Jacob Anatoli, the commentary on Ecclesiastes and the book *Yikawu Hamayim* by Samuel ibn Tibbon and other writings.[29] The ban, therefore, might better be directed against the extravagant preaching of the rationalists rather than against scientific and philosophic writings.

29 The *Yikawu ba-Mayim* is mentioned in *Shaare Ziyyon*, p. 42, as a most wonderful book and is cited also in Hoshen Mishpat.

In his opinion, the rationalists should be allowed to deal metaphorically with certain Holy Writings — Job, Proverbs, Canticles, Ecclesiastes, certain Psalms, and Midrashim, but not with theology and cosmology.

Meiri adopted the progressive method in his interpretation of the Bible and the legends.[30] Certain passages where the language was hyperbolic could only be taken metaphorically. The same applied to all corporealistic expressions and also to the legends that related unreasonable and impossible things. However, the literal method must be used, in connection with the moral precepts and simple stories and facts narrated in Holy Writ. Divinely ordained precepts must be observed, although their purpose could not be fulfilled by mere observance, but by an understanding of their objectives. In these instances it was not enough to cling to the correct belief and purpose: one must also observe the precept.

We note also a compromising tendency when he divides the principles of Judaism into two classes, a method that is found among the Christian scholastics.[31] These were the philosophic beliefs, such as the existence, unity and incorporeality of God, established by reason and the purely theological ones, like creation, divine retribution, providence and miracles which must be taken on faith. This division attained popularity among the Jewish rationalists because it made room for metaphysical study. Since a conflict of opinion over the philosophic doctrines was inevitable, because they were not factual like sense data, the Torah had proclaimed the one and final truth concerning them.

[30] *Commentary on Abot,* pp. 18, 19.
[31] *Magen Abot,* p. 1.

Meiri's carefully thought out defense of secularism was answered by En Duran. He, too, hailed from Perpignan, but evidently was living in Montpellier. After the French expulsion in 1306, he went to Aix where he wrote to his parents in Perpignan to intercede with the officials to allow him to reside there. En Duran informed Meiri he concealed his letter because of its open hostility to the traditionalists, but, to his surprise, he found that the contents were already common knowledge.

Philosophy had, to be sure, a certain saving grace. When properly groomed it could accompany Judaism as in the case of Maimonides.[32] It would be folly, therefore, on their part, to abolish philosophy completely. They only want to restrict its study to certain persons. Their object was to silence the heretics and stop the youth from perusing Greek writings. The latter are not a garden *Pardes* but a parched field. Whatever gems were scattered therein could not redeem their obnoxious teachings. The fact that the Talmudic sages did not respect the royal author of Ecclesiastes but subjected his book to scrutiny showed their dread of heresy. How much more vigilantly should ordinary books of questionable content be probed!

Again, it was more advisable to take up the study of the Torah in the prime of life rather than delay it, because opportunities for such study might not present themselves in later life. In that case the individual would have exposed himself to the undesirable effects of scientific education without possessing the counteracting stimulation of religion.[33]

He asked Meiri to be tolerant toward the champions of

[32] *Hoshen Mishpat*, p. 137.
[33] *Aboda Zara*, p. 7b.

traditionalism. It was not Abba Mari, but the erring rationalists who kindled the conflict. The fact remained that no one appeared to curb the heretics. In such a case, intervention from whatever region was welcome.

En Duran granted that secular learning was a distinction to Israel, but not when it clashed with Judaism. The argument that some scholars combined rabbinical and metaphysical study without detriment to the former was not sound. Those scholars concentrated in their youth on the Torah and acquired secular knowledge as they grew older, and then very cautiously. Instances where philosophy was pursued in youth without intruding upon faith were exceptions. Furthermore, the traditionalists only excluded studies that impinged upon the Jewish doctrines, as natural science and metaphysics, and these only when studied by young people. The seven sciences were not prohibited.

En Duran attacked the concept of the soul as intellect with the argument that according to that view the unlearned but pious man was ranked in the same class as a brute and could not expect reward or immortality. Forsooth, the sages who devoted their lives to rabbinic study and to the practice of virtue toiled in vain.

The writer described an experience he had had at a wedding in Montpellier, when a renowned rationalist told his audience that Abraham and Sarah symbolized form and matter. In this way he expounded Genesis 12: 4-16 and connected with this the legend of R. Benai in Baba Batra 58a.[34] If he had not been there on the platform and heard it, he would not have believed it possible. He argued with the preacher, taking exception not so

[34] *Hoshen Mishpat*, p. 147.

much at his explanation of the Talmudic story, but at his daring treatment of the Biblical story of Abraham's life. En Duran inveighed strongly against the allegorization of the Torah and its precepts. Because of practices like this he defended the Barcelona ban as the equal of the historic ancient bans and as the only effective way to curb the religious evils of the day. Protests and exhortations were not adequate. The present ban was not put through by a minority. Although the heretics were few, it was the duty of the community to weed them out in the same way that it would remove a social evil or alleviate distress. He minimized the fear of strife resulting from the measure, and declared besides that heresy was worse than communal dissension. It was true that the ban did not overtly strike at the heretical preachers, but at natural science and metaphysics, because the latter were the source of contamination and gave rise to the vagaries and errors of the preachers.

The failure of the ban imposed many years before by the French rabbis on the Guide and the Book of Knowledge was no criterion of the fate of the present ban. The earlier ban was unjustified in the extreme and could not morally be enforced. The present ban neither interdicted nor cast any discredit upon the Guide. This book belonged to a different category from that of the Greek philosophic works. Whatever Greek portions it contained did not stamp it as alien. If that were the case, certain Talmudic tractates would be forbidden because they embodied scattered elements of foreign lore. There was no harm even for a youth in reading the Guide. The difficult parts that he might encounter were tinged with religious spirit and would become understandable as his intelligence ripened. At any rate, the only subjects banned were natural science, or the study of minerals, plants and animals and the study of time, space, motion, and other abstract problems.

En Duran gladly welcomed the opinion of Meiri that the counter-ban was ineffective, but he twitted him for not furnishing more weighty proofs for its illegality so that the rationalists might be induced to give up their attacks.

Chapter XXIII

JEDAIAH BEDERSI'S DEFENSE OF PHILOSOPHY

Another powerful voice lifted against the Barcelona ban was that of Jedaiah Bedersi, the greatest Jewish poet of Provence and a fervent admirer of Maimonides. He inherited his scholarship from his father and grandfather. His interest in rationalism expressed itself in commentaries on the Midrashim, Aboth and Talmudic treatises.[1] The esteem showered upon Maimonides by this scholar in the closing lines of his poem, *Behinat Olam*, has been frequently re-echoed: "In fine, incline thy heart to whatever the great Moses ben Maimon, last of the Geonim in time but first in importance, has believed, who is without parallel among all the sages since the close of the Talmud."

Before the expulsion of the Jews from France in 1306, Jedaiah wrote to Ibn Adret a memorable defense of philosophy in which he summed up all the pros and cons of the conflict.[2] The band of rationalists, argued Jedaiah, was too small to give any cause for alarm. He failed to see any destructive element in the faith taught by the progressive rabbis of Narbonne, Beziers, Lunel, Montpellier, and in other cities of Provence and Venaissin. The charge that young children imbibed philosophy he dismissed as not exactly true. The practice had been not to impart any mystic or secular information unless the

---

[1] Renan, *Les Ecrivains Juifs Francais*, pp. 359, seq.
[2] Iggeret Hitznatlut, in Solomon ibn Adret, *Responsa*, Vienna, 1812, pp. 53 seq. Kokebe Yizhak, V, (1864), pp. 12-17. It is supposed that Jedaiah settled in Barcelona at the invitation of Ibn Adret, who wished him to translate certain philosophic writings into Hebrew.

pupil was gifted enough to judge it properly. It had happened some time before that an impoverished scholar was forced to teach logic for a living; his pupils, however, were none the worse off for it. On the whole, nobody there taught the sciences or metaphysics. These subjects were acquired by self-education, and then only in a fragmentary way, as they were needed in the course of one's Hebrew studies.

He was shocked at the loss of the laudable fraternal spirit that had formerly existed among Provencal Jewry and the solidarity of local and Spanish Jewry before the conflict broke out. He was deeply perturbed over the condemnation of his countrymen, especially by the curse that his native land should be uprooted as the seed of Amalek.[3] In his opinion, the progressives were guilty not of heresy, but of indiscretion in spreading publicly ideas that should be reserved for the discriminating few. To save the honor of Maimonides, esteemed even by philosophers of other religions, for his own honor, and for the honor of the distinguished Jewry of Provence, Bedersi pressed Ibn Adret to repeal the ban. It was wasted on the Provencals, who excelled in Torah and worldly wisdom, in religious piety, charity and aristocratic genealogy; who fought the Greeks more courageously than did the Hasmoneans by their strict allegiance to the Torah.

The hatred stirred up by this controversy only increased the misery of Provencal Jewry, already overflowing to the brim because of their political troubles.[4] The posi-

---

[3] Ibid., p. 54b.

[4] On July 22, 1306, all the Jews in France were ordered to be imprisoned; in September of that year they were expelled. The distress affected Beziers and Montpellier and other cities of the Provence as well as North France.

tion of the orthodox toward the sciences was inconsistent. He could not see why they excluded medicine and astronomy from the ban, holding that, scientific and experimental by nature, they lured one to stray from the Torah and tended to destroy trust in divine help as surely as the prohibited sciences.[5] If it were argued that the danger of medicine to religion was small when compared to its great value in curing the body, well, what about the good done by philosophy to the soul? Should one pay more attention to the body than to the soul?

Bedersi assured Ibn Adret that the effects of philosophic study had been grossly exaggerated. The charge against the allegorists that they identified Abraham and Sarah as form and substance, the twelve tribes as the twelve signs of the zodiac, the war of the kings as the battle of the four elements against the five senses, and the Urim and Thummim as the astrolabe was really not serious. It must be borne in mind that while the figurative interpretation of Scripture and legends might not be desirable, it was not identical with heresy[6] and should not be condemned. Because the use of the literal method has its abuses. It would result in one of two evils, either acceptance of the texts with all their improbabilities, against which common sense rebelled, or complete rejection, imputing error or deficiency to the scribes. It was, therefore, imperative to explain the passages in question metaphorically, providing that the resulting harmonization did not harm any basic principles of the faith.

Bedersi gave his own account of the exposition of the legend concerning the Amora R. Benai and the graves of Abraham and Sarah as he had received it from the

[5] Ibid., p. 57d.
[6] Ibid., p. 54d.

preacher and from others who heard him.[7] The legend
was that R. Benai, marking the rabbis' graves, came to
that of the patriarch Abraham, to find his slave Eliezar
standing before the gate. He inquired, "What doth Abraham?"   And the slave replied, "He is sleeping in
Sarah's arms, and she is contemplating (examining) his
head." "Tell him that Benai stands at the gate," he said.
The reply was "Let him enter; it is known that the evil
spirit has no power in this world." So he entered, marked the grave and went out.

The preacher, one of the finest men in the country,
said that the passage could not be taken literally; that
it was impossible that the patriarchs, in their graves, indulged in any sensual practices. The sense of the story
was this: R. Benai was studying the life of the righteous
during their stay on earth, set forth as a cave. This was
the meaning of the marking of the wise men's graves.
He compared them and determined their various grades
of perfection. He found that even the most nearly perfect human intellect (Abraham) never escaped weak-
nesses such as sleep, forgetfulness, error, difficulty of
seeing, and the like. Sleep was the resting of the senses
from perception. Weakness of the intellect was caused
by its association with matter (Sarah), till the association was broken by its rising from the cave (earthly life)
to heaven (perfection). This was "sleeping in the arms
of Sarah." The rest of the story merely embellished the
allegory and tended to obscure the thought. The prophets portrayed form as male and matter as female; the
rabbis followed their example. Abraham and Sarah were
chosen because they were an ideal couple and could best
represent the combination of form and matter. Far be it

[7] Baba Batra, p. 58a.

from the Jews not to believe in the existence of the patriarchs — this belief was one of the pillars of their faith.
Bedersi admits that the preacher went too far in ex-
pounding the story publicly to an undiscriminating audience. What he said would have been better unsaid. Yet
it does not warrant the drastic action of the Barcelona
rabbis.

Bedersi was ignorant of the allegory that the twelve
tribes of Israel represented the signs of the zodiac.[8] He
never heard any one preach it. The nearest thing to it
was a statement that the Jews were ruled by the constellations as were the Gentile nations, for there were
twelve of these just as there were twelve tribes.

He turned a deaf ear to the charge that the Urim and
Thummim were said to be an astrolabe, and that the four
and five kings represented the four elements and the
five senses.[9] This was untrue. The Urim and Thummim
were an instrument of prophecy as indicated by the
query and reply, "Why were they called Urim? Because
they gave perfect pronouncements." As such the oracu-
lar predictions of the Urim and Thummim could not be
compared to the results of magic or astrology. Magic
whispered obscure hints; but the Urim and Thummim
foretold things as clearly as did prophetic dreams in
which the parables were easily interpreted. Astrology
was a little nearer the truth than magic, yet it could not
be trusted, because of the great number of conditions
it needed but did not always have at command.

Bedersi's rationalism appeared clearly in his attitude
toward the Bible and the legendary elements in the Talmud. Concerning the first he made a distinction be-

---

[8] Iggeret Hitznatlut, p. 55a.
[9] Ibid., Jedaiah denies he ever heard these allegories preached.

tween things physically impossible and things logically impossible. Thus certain events and stories in the Bible which contradict the laws of nature may very well be taken literally, for with God, everything is possible. He created and controls all cosmic and natural forces. The stories of the flood, the miracles in Egypt, etc., are therefore true.[10] The only statements that must be taken figuratively are the references to the corporeality, finiteness and form of God, because these are logically impossible and contrary to Judaism.

Legends of the Talmud were divided into four classes: (1) Possible but only remotely probable; these were taken literally on the testimony of the narrator. (2) Impossible except by way of miracle. If belief in these strengthened faith, they might be taken literally. Such were the miracles related about the pious, the Messiah's coming, the greatness of the Temple, or resurrection. If particular anecdotes or sayings contradicted other general sayings, the general were accepted. For example, the opinion that Palestine would grow cakes and silk garments in the time to come was negated by the broader one that there was no difference between life in this world and at the time of the Messiah except that Israel will not be subject to the nations. (3) Impossible, but useful, such as stories about Rabba bar bar Hana told to refresh and stimulate the students' minds. (4) Absolutely impossible views concerning God, such as that He lays phylacteries or that He said, "Woe, that I have destroyed my temple."[11]

Jedaiah Bedersi kindly solicited an opinion from Ibn

---

[10] Other events are the wonders in the Desert, those connected with the conquest of Palestine, the wonders of Elijah, Elisha, and of Daniel.
[11] Ibid., p. 58d.

Adret on this expository method, and posed the question, "Can anyone believing in the creation, the miracles of the Bible and the rabbis, be called an unbeliever just because he says certain things are impossible?"

He laid down the proposition that logic, natural science and metaphysics are beneficial, even essential for religion.

Bedersi held to the rationalist view that the chapter on creation and the chariot vision represented the sciences and metaphysics. They formed the Paradise which the wise men entered and left in peace. Entering in peace meant the grasping of philosophic truth and its reconciliation with the Torah. Leaving in peace meant the improvement of the ethical life, when the thinker leaves his seclusion for practical, worldly life.

Philosophy demonstrated the principles of the existence, unity and incorporeality of God.[12] The truth of God's unity excluded His possession of any attributes. It was an almost unavoidable error to think and to speak of the Supreme Being in terms of human personification. When one described God, he should do so negatively. Characterizing him in positive terms could do no more than convey the thought of what He is not. For example, by saying that God is first, one implied that He is not created, and not merely that He is chronologically first, which applied only to things limited by time and motion. Wise meant not failing to understand all. Incorporeality meant that He does not occupy space; for everything in place was limited by surrounding space. It implies that He is not a power within a body, as is the human soul. Scriptural language referring to the divine abode and throne must be taken in the same way as any

[12] Ibid., p. 56b.

other expressions of corporeality and finiteness. Philosophy also proved the existence of angels and their immateriality. Due to the influence of Arabic-Greco philosophy the once wide-spread notion of a corporeal God gave way to the more agreeable one of incorporeality.[13] Maimonides must be credited with having brought about this change. This fact alone was sufficient to favor the study of philosophy without which Maimonides would not have reached his conclusions. Philosophy did not harm his piety.

There was nothing to fear from philosophy's effect upon the theory of the world's creation. It could not prove that it was impossible, and according to natural law, creation was not only possible, but quite probable.[14] The eternity of the world has been demonstrated by very questionable propositions. It was prophecy that affirmed the creation.

Philosophy cleared up the problem of miracles. Bedersi admitted that there were certain things God could not change. There were two categories of the impossible. The first, apparent impossibility, the bringing about of results without their causes, such as striking fire without heat, could be overruled by the divine will; for the Creator of the world could change its operation or destroy it at will. But another kind of impossibility existed, where the nature of a thing was part of its existence, so

[13] Ibid., p. 57c. From Jedaiah's language it appears that the corporeality of God was not a figure of speech with the rabbis and the people, but literally believed in. Jedaiah's enumeration and characterization of the following Jewish thinkers and their writings is significant: Saadia, Isaac ben Giat, Moses ibn Ezra, Solomon ibn Gabirol, Judah Halevi, Abraham bar Hiyya, David Almakmetz, Joseph (ibn Zaddik), Isaac Israeli, Isaac ben Mukatel, Jonah ibn Ganah, Abraham ibn Ezra, the greatest of these and finally Maimonides, who had no second.

[14] Ibid., p. 57a.

that when its nature was altered, it ceased to exist; or, for example, the existence in one thing of two opposites at the same time, such as likeness and unlikeness or past and future. This was impossible. Was there heresy in believing that there were impossibilities for God? Galen the Greek physician and philosopher (c. 131-200) ridiculed the Torah for putting everything up to the will of God, thus rejecting the law of cause and effect.[15] To this Maimonides retorted that the Torah did not deny the law of causality, but merely stated that when God willed, He might change the cause and the effect, since He brought them about; but normally such changes did not occur.

Philosophy lent its support to the possibility of prophecy which early unbelievers denied, as did certain Jews at one time. It allowed for a gradation of rank among the prophets, with the incomparable Moses heading the ranks.

Again, it proved the existence and value of free will; otherwise how could one be punished for his sins, or rewarded for his good deeds?[16] Besides what sense was there in certain precepts, for example, in building a railing around the roof to prevent one from falling off, or in announcing before the battle that the fearful should return home, if everything were predetermined? Scripture said, "Lest he should die in battle and someone else marry her." The word "lest" showed that there were two possibilities. The people's refusal to heed the prophet could be accounted for in a similar way. They believed that everything was forecast by planetary movements.

[15] Ibid., p. 58b. Jedaiah severely attacks Galen; the scholastics believed in the principle of Impossibilia.
[16] Ibid., p. 56c.

Philosophy dispersed the ideas of magic which crowded the human mind, especially of women, children and
the mentally sick. Delusions that invisible spirits roam-
ed about or that a spirit could enter an image of clay at
a certain propitious season and foretell the unseen were
forms of insanity. The Torah wished to put a stop to
such superstitions and philosophy came to its aid.

Among its other advantages was the affirmation of the
belief in immortality. Some believed that human beings
continued to function after death exactly as they did in
this world; others said they functioned in a more lofty
and sublime way; still others that the body continued but
only as an inert frame for the soul; others that the body
was shed and that the soul alone lived as a separate entity. Opinions vary as to what the soul is, substance or
accident, the name for the totality of impulses, or that it
is the breath, or the blood. Philosophy investigated the
true nature of the soul and proved it was an emanation
from the universal Reason.

A corollary of this belief was the denial of transmigration which some held took place even between different species. Bedersi was satisfied that this preposterous idea had been adequately disproven. The ordinary
person held himself accountable for his distress and suffering, but a believer in transmigration could blame another's sins for his sufferings. This belief also contradicted the idea of resurrection; for if there were but one
soul to two or three bodies, how could they all live again,
since each body needed a soul?

After a painstaking refutation of all the charges made
against the study of philosophy, Jedaiah appealingly asks
ibn Adret to spare the good name of Maimonides and to

save his own face by desisting from his attempt. He tells him that he has tried his utmost to put through the ban and has failed. What more can he do?

Chapter XXIV

END OF THE CONFLICT

The anti-philosophic party in the tense struggle we have described paid no heed to history. They might have remembered the failure of the two attempts made in the previous century to ban the Maimonidean writings, True, they planned to proscribe other philosophic writings and not the Guide, but the motive was the same. As at previous times the traditionalists mustered enough strength to put through their bans, only to be defied by the progressives. It was the progressives who spoke the last word in the controversy. The counter-ban which proved to be the anti-climax to the long drawn-out struggle, put Ibn Adret and his party on the defensive, and they could expect nothing but stubborn resistance from the rationalists. The situation became more and more confusing, and the issue in the end remained unsettled. The conflict had already dragged on for years, and wearied the people. Some of the leaders had passed on; others discreetly kept themselves out of it. The man who gave prestige to the agitation, Ibn Adret, lived far from the center of the activity, and this fact hindered the traditionalist cause. Furthermore, aside from the unpopularity of Abba Mari, many of the Provencal traditionalists were lukewarm in the whole matter. They hesitated to come forward, either because they regarded the effort as futile, feared discord and violence, or preferred temperamentally the seclusion and quiet of the study-hall. The clearest indication of the unpopularity

262

of the anti-philosophic policy was the fact that the bans could not be proclaimed in Provence, but had to be put out in Spain.

The failure may be laid also to the very character of Abba Mari, who apparently had many enemies in his home-town, Montpellier, and throughout the country. A wide gap in culture separated him from such representative liberals as Jacob ben Machir, Judah ibn Tibbon and Solomon de Lunel, men of the highest scientific culture and eminent physicians. They had little respect for the Talmudist and often charged him with dishonesty and unscrupulousness in prosecuting his aims. Only the weakness in Abba Mari's influence, as in his policy, would have made possible the enactment of a counter-ban. At the very start then, the effort to restrict philosophy was doomed to failure. Meiri, the respected Perpignan scholar, had predicted that the conflict would die of itself. Its close was forced abruptly by the expulsion of the Jews from France on July 22, 1306 by Philip the Fair.

Great indeed was the economic distress, the social and spiritual ruin in the Provencal communities of Montpellier, Lunel, Beziers and Narbonne. The Jews of Montpellier were expelled in October, 1306. Some fled to Perpignan, hoping that the King of Majorca would allow them to stay; others settled in Provence. Abba Mari went to Arles and then to Perpignan. The liberal party there, still sore, maneuvered to have his partisans refused admission, but Moses ben Samuel and his father successfully interceded with the king in their behalf. Ibn Adret suffered his misfortunes as a sign of divine disapproval of the irreligious ways of the progressives.

Abba Mari had his own troubles. But keenly aware of the importance of the quarrel and desiring to preserve the viewpoint of the restrictionists for posterity, he collected the letters on the controversy and published them under the name *Minhat Kenaot,* "The offering of Jealousy." It is certain that his collection is not complete. Many letters went astray, and others which strongly reflected against his character or championed the rationalist side were purposely omitted.

Chapter XXV

CONCLUSION

This book is the history of the Jewish attitude toward secularism. It covers the ground, in a narrower scope, of the conflict outside of Judaism between religion and science which has fascinated and vexed mankind. The conflict may be viewed from several standpoints. It may be antagonistic, as when secularism or science sets out with a definite atheistic aim to dethrone religion. Or a sympathetic current may underlie the conflict as when the scientists endeavor to rationalize and show that religion and science interlock. From another angle, religion may find itself in trouble in an internal war between fundamentalists and modernists, over the question of dogmas or of central authority. Here the conflict, bitter and violent as it may be, is nevertheless carried on under the aegis of religion. We find also reconstructive movements within religions that aim to reform ceremonial abuses, improve organization or stress social principles.

The conflict between Judaism and secularism was not of the first kind. The rationalists never offered the challenge of atheism to Judaism. The clash that we observed between religious tradition and physical theories, philosophic hypotheses and comparative religion, was turned into an accord by the Maimonists. They did not allow the secular forces to negate Judaism. Aside from philosophic differences, the Maimonists represented the liberal tendency, that manifested itself in a rational construction of Scripture and in newer interpretations of the dogmas. In so far as they dealt with the sciences,

265

with culture and other philosophies, they dispersed ignorance of such matters among their people. In so far as
they applied common sense to religious experience, they
disapproved of superstition. Although not very pronounced, we find among the Maimonists, as in the case of
Jacob Anatoli and Joseph ibn Caspi, some criticism of
synagogue formalism, of the ritual and of the prayer service; while Moses of Coucy exhorted the people to observe the precepts, these men appeared to oppose con-
ventionalism in the synagogue.

The controversy, therefore, was an internal one and it
forms a link in the series of dogmatic clashes between
the main spiritual trends in Judaism, the orthodox, the
mystic and the rationalist. The Sadducee of Talmudic
days and the reformer of our time are represented by
the rationalist or scholastic of the Middle Ages. These
contending schools represent the dualism of the human type. The revelationist believed. He found in faith,
in the Torah, the be-all and end-all of life. Empiricism
asked questions, weighed arguments in the balances and
wanted to be convinced. From this combat Judaism
emerged, tested and true. The rationalist had only added
more luster to it; he did not intend to impugn its inherent, sacred character.

The story goes back to a time long before the geology,
astronomy and evolution that we are familiar with harassed simple faith. It was the special virtue of the Jewish mind that it dallied early with rationalism as witness
the wisdom books of the Old Testament, the secular
knowledge scattered through the Talmud, the Hellenism
of the Alexandrian school, the Kalaam of the Geonim,
the neo-Platonism of the mystics and the Aristotelianism

of the rationalists. In this study we have confined ourselves to the last phase as it emerged in Maimonides and was extended by his admirers. Maimonides' rationalism resulted in deviations in concept from the norms of Judaism, deviations that did not lead to schism or sectarianism. Even so, they went dangerously far. Hence the serious efforts of the orthodox to check their influence. In the first two conflicts they expected to accomplish this by attacking the germ of the dissension, the *Guide*. Later, action was taken against other philosophic writings.

What were the norms and rules which Maimonides had violated? They were the general, commonly accepted teachings, often only concepts, that had not been clearly defined or classified. For example, there was much obscurity about the personality of God. Equally vague were orthodox concepts of soul, prophecy and the world to come. The paradox is that the orthodox did not dogmatize; the rationalists did. It was Maimonides who wrote the creed of thirteen articles.

Fortunately for Maimonides, he was not himself molested, as has happened only too often with the broad-minded thinkers of other faiths. In Judaism conduct outweighs creed, and Maimonides had balanced his rationalism with conformity to the ritual and with unusual juridical activity, thus making himself immune to condemnation by the synagogue or by any court. He had been criticized by Abraham ben David of Provence in his lifetime, but only as an innovating Talmudist; Meir ben Todros of Toledo tried to instigate violent propaganda toward the end of Maimonides' life, but failed.

The outbreak came a quarter of a century after his death, when the war of the church against Aristotelianism became rife. The conservative party attacked philosophy as anti-religious. It was said to destroy the old traditional concept of God, of soul, of after-life and of the divine inspiration of the Bible. The people's absorption in philosophy interfered with their study of Talmud and Bible. It drove out the "fear of God" and people neglected the precepts and ceremonies. Maimonides' Book of Knowledge and Guide became the new Bible, the philosophy textbooks of thoughtful Jews. From them they were led to Maimonides' sources, to Aristotle and his commentators, to Alfarabi and Avicenna. The conservatives believed that they could check the liberal tendencies by banning the Book of Knowledge and the Guide. Their attempt threw the Jews into further turmoil and aroused the subborn resistance of the philosophic party. The burning of the Guide that followed was not the result of an established Jewish policy toward such works. It was a "mistake." The incident was condemned by the anti-Maimonists. It is possible that the burning of the Guide was advised or inspired by the bishop of Paris as a part of the church's campaign against philosophy. After this act the opposition fell away. Jonah Gerondi deserted the anti-Maimonists, Solomon ben Abraham was deeply apologetic, Nahmanides counselled a compromise.

About half a century after this conflict, an unsuccessful attempt was made by Solomon Petit to abolish the study of the Guide. He loathed the rationalistic interpretation of Judaism, and its spiritualization of Jewish doctrines. After traveling through Germany, France and Italy to agitate against it, he went to Acco, Palestine, a center of cabalists, with endorsements of European rabbis. The grandson of Maimonides, David, who was the head of Egyptian Jewry, went also to Acco and used his prestige with the Oriental authorities to quell the agitation. Their drastic bans destroyed the opposition.

During this century, rationalism grew by leaps and bounds, and the appearance of suspected free-thinkers and a large crop of untraditional ideas precipitated a new conflict in the first decade of the fourteenth century over Jewish educational policy. This struggle was of greater consequence for Jews and for general culture than those that preceded it. It involved the question whether education for the Jew should be restricted to Bible and Talmud, or may it include the profane studies in early youth. The issue then was not the complete abolition of philosophic study, but only its restriction to persons under twenty-five years of age. Furthermore, medicine was excluded from the prohibited studies. The trouble this time started over the *agadot shel dofi,* the false exposition of the Bible and Talmudic legends by the preachers. The practice spread of allegorizing the lives of the patriarchs and other figures and stories in the Pentateuch, to make these illustrate the principles and ideas of Aristotelian philosophy. Along with this, the preachers rationalized the precepts. As in the former conflicts the progressive party was charged with holding un-Jewish views about God, creation, miracles and the revelation of the Torah. The Guide of Maimonides was at stake again, because it had become the classic philosophic text, the inspiration of the rationalists. True, the orthodox protested that they had no objection to the Guide, but the opposition just as vigorously argued that their bans were directed against it and similar writings. Such documents as have survived, like the *Minhat Kenaot,* the *Hoshen Mishpat,* and Jedaiah's *Vindication of Philosophy,* show the seriousness of the situation. The foremost scholars in Spain and Provence led the controversy, which came to an abrupt end by the expulsion of Jews from France in 1306.

The types we have learned to know in the twelfth and thirteenth centuries, Abraham ben David and Maimonides, Meir ben Todros and Jacob Anatoli, Alfakar and David Kimhi, Solomon ibn Adret and Jacob ben Machir, continued to exist in the fourteenth, fifteenth and sixteenth centuries. Maimonides is the gauge by which we estimate the scholars who followed. All of them without exception took a stand toward Maimonides. There was a type like Isaac ben Sheshet who had no philosophic training, and opposed it strenuously. Crescas, with a philosophic mind and education, spurned Aristotelian thought. There was Levi ben Gerson, more extreme than Maimonides in his philosophy, and Joseph Caspi, a critic of orthodoxy.

In the fifteenth century we have a polemic between Shem Tob ben Shem Tob and Moses Alashkar over Maimonides' theology, and in the next century Jehiel of Pisa wrote the *Minhat Kenaot* in the spirit of the *Minhat Kenaot* by Abba Mari ben Moses in which he refuted at great length Jedaiah Bedersi's Defense of Philosophy.

As to the motives of the conflict, there can be no good reason to doubt that it was first of all a question of dogmas. The participants had honest differences of opinion on how to interpret fundamental Jewish beliefs. This matter of dogmas from many points of view was the most important aspect of the controversy for those who participated in it and for us today. Dogmas had to be properly defined and defended. It began even in Maimonides' day over eschatological beliefs, resurrection, retribution, immortality and the world to come. Questions concerning God, His inner nature, His providence and His justice had to be answered. In view of the contacts with Islam and Christendom, the Jewish attitude toward the true prophet and his revelation had to be made clear. The orthodox were inclined to let the principles remain elastic. They had precepts, but they did not care for dogmas. It was the rationalists, who, accustomed to the scientific method, brought it into the study of Judaism and with it classification and definition.

They differed also as to the wisdom of raising a hue and cry over the spread of rationalism, as a divisive force in Jewish life. We need only point to the varieties of Judaism in our day, when fortunately a great deal of tolerance is shown on all sides. But in an age when religion ruled the state, heresy or dissent was a crime, as violation of the law is today. The church gave strength and stability to the medieval state, to the whole order of life. To discredit the church by rejecting its principles meant to strike a blow at the state. Hence the severe punishment exacted of heretics. Orthodox Jews held the beliefs of the rationalists to be destructive of the unity and strength of Israel. Hence the anti-philosophic wars.

But these religious attitudes were aroused by other circumstances. The growth of scholasticism in the church and the appearance of heretical sects had a repercussion

in Judaism. Parallel movements developed in Israel with
the orthodox frequently pointing to Christian zeal in preserving the standard teachings of revelation as against
the doubts raised by the rationalists.

Maimonides himself suggested jealousy as the cause
of hostility toward his books in his day and in the future.
Nahmanides in 1232 and Hillel of Verona in 1290, also
attributed the anti-Maimonist movement to rivalry and
politics. Jealousy is natural enough among scholars. An
older scholar will be envious of a younger one. Heads
of schools in the same city will compete for honors and
income. Another intensifying source of friction was the
independent spirit of different Jewries. These usually
developed their own customs and preferences for studies.
Each Jewry jealously guarded its prestige. So in the conflict of 1232 we find the Spaniards as a whole opposed
to the Provencal bans, and in 1303-1306 the Barcelona
bans are resisted in Provence on the ground of local
hegemony. The philosophic and orthodox parties belonged, with some exceptions, to different social strata, which
corresponded roughly to cultural differences. Maimonides himself was an intellectual aristocrat and set an example to his followers. The anti-Maimonists, as a class,
were often poor and led restricted lives. They could em-
barrass, but not harm the Maimonists. Although they
succeeded in banning and burning the Guide, they suffered cruel torture for it.

The rationalists disliked Abba Mari personally. Jonah
Gerondi is slandered because, aside from his part in the
conflict, they regarded him with disdain. Each group
had its own leaders and when the controversies developed they were often fought on party lines. So that the

question of authority or control over the congregation looms as a contributing cause of the controversy. The conservatives claimed they alone had a right to speak for Jews and Judaism because they had the true, unadulterated Torah from Moses, the progressives just as vigorously protested that they should have the last word on Judaism and its ideals.

It is possible, although not wholly probable, that Maimonides' sharp criticism of the unsophisticated orthodox rabbis, here and there in his writings angered the anti-Maimonists and added fuel to their general dissatisfaction with his rational theology. One recalls in this connection his policy not to accept salary or fees for his rabbinical work and the slur he cast upon those rabbis who did otherwise.

In these exciting clashes between Maimonists and anti-Maimonists neither side could claim a victory. The matter of a choice between Talmudism and secularism was left where it was. The Guide continued to be read and studied. The Jew imbibed all his flair for philosophy from it. But the vast rationalistic writings it engendered and much of the polemical literature was like still-born. Much of it remained unpublished for hundreds of years, and whatever did appear dwindled away before the Guide. As for the Guide, it fascinated the intelligent; it kept the ignorant masses at a safe distance.

After each conflict the bans of the traditionalists remained a dead letter, yet the net result was not an overwhelming victory for rationalism. Excessive interest in Talmudism developed in the course of time. After the Spanish expulsion, Holland, Turkey, Germany, Poland and Russia, whither the Jews fled, were not favorable to rationalism and affiliated studies. The reason for this was the lack of broad culture in those countries and the political and social segregation of the Jew, which kept him from acquiring whatever culture was available. Although philosophy was legally and morally permitted, actually the Jews had little opportunity to cultivate it. In some countries the Torah became their exclusive subject of study.

Hence, with all the popularity of the Guide in the Middle Ages, it did not prove detrimental to Judaism. Quite the contrary, it had been a wholesome if not a welcome contribution to Judaism. It had tided Judaism over a critical period when the hate of the non-Jew and the allurements of universal philosophy threatened to annihilate it. In those dark hours, the intelligent Jew could hug the Guide and draw inspiration and a calm mind from this masterly defense of his religion.

As we survey the dramatic events and brilliant personalities in this history and the vast and learned literature produced by them, the conviction gains upon us that during these centuries, as throughout its troublous history, Israel maintained itself as the people of the book. The great concern of the leaders on both sides was to preserve the literary tradition of the race, embodied in the contents and spirit of Holy Writ. This conflict gives further proof of the intellectual alertness, liberality and idealism of the Jew. Besides being traders, moneylenders, artisans and aristocratic servants of the kings in financial or diplomatic matters, the Jews are here revealed to us again as scholars, thinkers and scientists.

BIBLIOGRAPHY

PRIMARY SOURCES

Abba Mari ben Moses, *Minhat Kenaot*, Pressburg, 1838.

Abraham Abulafia, The Seven Paths of Faith in Jellinek's Philosophie u. Kabbalah, Leipzig, 1854.

Anatoli, Jacob, *Malmad ha Talmidim*, Lyck, 1886.

Azriel, Commentary on Ten Sephirot in Meir ibn Gabbai, *Derek Emuna*, Padua, 1563.

Bedersi, Jedaiah, Ketab Hitznatlut in *Responsa* of Solomon ibn Adret, (no. 418, pp. 53-60), Vienna, 1812.

Benjamin of Tudela, *Itinerary*, Adler ed. 1907.

ibn Caspi, Joseph, *Commentary on the Guide.*

En Duran and Meiri, Simeon ben Josephs Sendschreiben an Menachem ben Salomo. The title of the Hebrew letter is Hoshen Mishpat in *Zunz Jubelschrift*, Berlin, 1884.

Filipowski, H., *Sefer Yuhasin Hashalem*, Frankfort a/m, 1924.

Gedaliah ibn Yahia, *Shalshelet Hakkabala*, Warsaw, 1887.

Gikatilla Joseph, Hasagot in *Sheelot Saul hakohen*, Venice, 1574.

Ginze Nistarot, ed. Kobak, III and IV.

Hillel of Verona, *Tagmule ha Nefesh*, Lyck, 1874.

Isaac ibn Latif, in Klatzkin's *Anthology of Hebrew Philosophy*, Berlin, 1926; Hashahar II, pp. 81 seq.

Israelitische Letterbode, Amsterdam, IV, 1878-1879.

Maimonides, *More Nebukim*, with commentaries, Wilna, 1904.

   Mishneh Torah, with commentaries, Wilna, 1924.

   Kobetz Teshubot ha Rambam, Leipzig, 1859.

   Commentary on Mishna in various editions of Talmud.

   Sefer ha Mizwot, Warsaw, 1891.

   Millot ha hi gayon, Warsaw, 1826.

   Teshubot Harambam, ed. A. Freimann, Jerusalem, 1935.

Maimoni Abraham, *Highways to Perfection*, ed. S. Rosenblatt, N. Y., 1927.
Maase Nissim, Paris, 1867.
Birkat Abraham, Lyck, 1859.

Marx, A., Texts by and about Maimonides, J. Q. R. XXV (1935), pp. 371-428.

Meir Ben Todros Halevi, *Kitab Alrasail*, Paris, 1871.

Moses ben Hasdai Taku, *Kitab Tamim*, Otzar Nehmad III, (1860), pp. 54-99.

Nahmanides, *Commentary on the Pentateuch*.

Narboni Moses, *Commentary on the Guide*, Wien, 1852.

Menahem ha-Meiri, *Bet ha Behira*, Vienna, 1854.
Magen Abot, London, 1909.

Recanati, Menahem, *Perush al ha Torah*, Venice, 1523.
Taame ha Mizwot, Basle, 1581.

Samuel ibn Tibbon, *Yikawwu ha Mayim*, Pressburg, 1857.

Simon Kahira, *Sefer halakot Gedalot*, Warsaw, 1874.

Shem Tob Palakera, *Moreh ha Moreh*, Pressburg, 1837.
Iggeret ha Vikuah, Wien, 1875.

Solomon ibn Adret, Responsa, Vienna, 1812.

Steinschneider, M., *Moreh Mekom ha-Moreh*, Kobetz al Yad, I (1885).

Zerahiah Halevi, Correspondence with Hillel of Verona, Otzar Nehmad II, (1857), pp. 118-143.

Secondary Sources

Abrahams, Israel, *Hebrew Ethical Wills*, Philadelphia, 1926, (also a primary source).

Alharizi Judah, *Tahkemoni*, Warsaw, 1899.

Beer B., *Philosophie und philosophische Schrifsteller der Juden*, Leipzig, 1852.

Bernfeld S., *Daat Elohim*, Warsaw, 1897.

Brull, Jahrbucher fuer judische Geschichte, IV, (1879), pp. 1-33; Die Polemik fur und gegen Maimuni in dreizehnten Jahrhunderte.

De Boers, *History of Philosophy in Islam*, London, 1933.

Efros, I., *Philosophical Terms in More Nebukim*, N. Y., 1924.

Finkelscherer, I., *Moses Maimonis Stellung zum Aberglauben und Mystik*, 1896.

Gandz, S., The Astrolabe in Jewish Literature, H. U. C. Annual, IV (1927), pp. 469-486.

Geiger, Abr., Nachgelassene Schriften, III, (1876), pp. 34-96.

Wissenschaftliche zeitschrift fuer Judische Theologie V, (1844), pp. 82-123.

Judische Zeitschrift fur Wissenschaft und Leben, IX, pp. 282-298.

Graetz, H., *Geschichte der Juden* (German), VII; (Hebrew), V.

Gross, H., *Gallia Judaica*, Paris, 1897.

Letters de Simson sur Maimonide, REJ, VII, pp. 44-48.

Guedeman, *Ha Torah v' ha-Hayyim*, Warsaw, 1896.

Guttmann, J., *Moses ben Maimon*, Sein Leben, seine Werke und sein Einfluss, ed. J. Guttmann, Leipzig, 1903.

Halper, B., *Post Biblical Hebrew Literature*, Philadelphia, 1921.

Horodetzki, S. A., *Moses Isserles;* ha Goren, I.

Husik, I., *History of Medieval Jewish Philosophy*, 2nd ed., N. Y., 1930.

Jellinek, A., *Beitraege zur Geschichte der Kabbala*, Leipzig, 1853.

Jost, I. M., *Geschichte des Judenthums und seine Sekten*, Leipzig, 1857-1859.

Kaufmann, D., *Die Sinne*, Leipzig, 1884.

Krauss, Nahmanides and Maimonides, ha Goren V.

Isaac ben Jacob de Lattes, *Shaare Zion*, 1885.

Malter, H., *Die Abhandlung des Abu Hamid al Gazzali, Antworten auf Fragen*, Breslau, 1894.

Mann, J., *The Jews in Egypt and in Palestine under the Fatimid Caliphs*, 1922.

Texts and Studies in Jewish History and Literature, Cincinnati, 1931.

Marx, Alexander, The Correspondence between the Rabbis of Southern France and Maimonides about Astrology, H. U. C. Annual, Vol. III, 1926.

Michael, J., *Or ha Hayyim*, Frankfort a/m, 1891.

Munk, S., *Melanges de Philosophie Juive et Arabe*, Paris, 1850.

Notice sur Joseph Ben-Iehouda, Paris, 1842.

Munz, J., *Moses ben Maimon*, Sein Leben und sein Werke, Frankfort a/m, 1812.

Obermann, J., *Der philosophische und religiose Subjektivismus Ghazalis*, Vienna, 1921.

Poznanski, S., *Die babylonischen Geonim im nach gaonischen Zeitalter*, Berlin, 1914.

Perles, J., *R. Salomo ben Abraham ben Adreth*, Breslau, 1863.

Renan, E. (Neubauer), *Les Rabbins Francais du commencement du 14 siècle*, Paris, 1877.

Les Ecrivains Juifs Francais, Paris, 1892.

Sarachek, J., *The Doctrine of the Messiah in Jewish Literature*, N. Y., 1932.

Schechter, S., *Studies in Judaism*, First Series, N. .Y., 1911.

Schreyer, S. B., *Das psychologische System des Maimonides*, Frankfort, 1845.

Steinschneider, M., *Jewish Literature*, London, 1857.

Die hebraischen Uebersetzungen des Mittelalters, Berlin, 1893.

Die arabische Literatur der Juden, Frankfort a/m, 1902.

Tchernowitz, C., *Toledot ha-Halakah*, N. Y., 1934.

Weiss, I. H., *Dor Dor v'Dorshav*, Vol. V, Wilna, 1904.

Zunz, L., *Zur Geschichte und Literatur*, Berlin, 1845.

INDEX OF SUBJECTS

Index

INDEX OF PERSONS, PLACES AND BOOKS*

* Comments have only been given under Maimonides because of his central importance and the frequent mention of his name.

Index

Index